The Healing Power of the Drum

BOOK TWO

The Healing Power of the Drum

BOOK TWO

A Journey of Rhythm and Stories

Robert Lawrence Friedman

White Cliffs Media
Gilsum, NH

The Healing Power of the Drum, Book Two
A Psychotherapist Continues to Explore the Healing Power of Rhythm and Drums
1ST EDITION

White Cliffs Media
Imprint of Avocus Publishing
4 White Brook Road
P.O. Box 89
Gilsum, NH 03448
Phone: 800-345-6665
Fax: 603-357-2073

Disclaimer:
The contents of this book do not constitute medical advice. The techniques discussed in this book may impose stressors on the body that involve certain health risks. The reader is advised to consult with his or her physician before attempting any of the techniques discussed in this book and should attempt the techniques only with the advice and approval of his/her physician. In addition, though various techniques using drums and rhythmic devices may have provided benefits for those mentioned in this text, this book does not purport that the methods used will provide the same psychological and/or physiological benefits for others.

Printed in the United States of America

ISBN: 978-1-890765-20-0 $17.96 Softcover

An Iconic Drummer's Personal Story

"I was very insecure and frightened at first when I drummed, and I believe that drumming was a defense mechanism for me. As I continued playing I found that the drum provided me with a cocoon of safety, where I could function and feel very free and not inhibited. Over the years, as my drumming evolved, it became a communication tool, like a two-way mirror, for myself and the audience.

I had to become mature to understand what drumming really meant, and the responsibilities that came with it. If I played well, had a clear idea of what I wanted to say and how strongly I wanted to say it, the drum would reflect my feelings perfectly. The drum became my voice. It was as if I was speaking passionately, except it was the drum that was doing the speaking. Drumming will reflect your emotions perfectly. You cannot lie. It tells everyone who you are, how you got that way, and what you want to do down the road. Everything comes out in your playing. It's all based on your past experiences.

In some ways, life is a drum — you can express your feelings through the drums. If I feel sad, I play sad. I want to convey my emotions through the drum. I watched the positive effects of drumming with autistic patients. I watched as miraculously they went from being completely unconnected to the world to watching them speak when a certain sound frequency was played. If I do something that is correct and right, everything else falls into place. I know when I know.

When I play the hand drums, I feel mesmerized. Sometimes when I play I feel like I am floating out of my body. The only other time I felt this is when I do Tai Chi. If I get very relaxed when I'm drumming, and the band and I are in harmony, it's transcendant.

The first instrument is the voice. The second is the drum. The drums never lie. They will tell you first, who you are and where you come from, and if you don't believe that, the drums will tell you it is false, it's without support. As soon as you play with meaning, the drums go out to everyone.

The drums have to play themselves. If you are in conflict, the drums will let you know. Every element of playing will have a comment on it — that is what playing the drums is all about."

–Billy Cobham

Billy C. Cobham is a Panamanian American Jazz Drummer, composer and band-leader. He is generally acclaimed as one of the greatest drummers of this or any era. Billy Cobham has played with trumpeter Miles Davis, Stanley Turrentine, the Mahavishnu Orchestra, and has recorded with Carlos Santana, Chaka Khan, John Mclaughlin, among many others. Since he began his career in drumming in the early 1960's, he has played on hundreds of albums and has released 9 albums of his own to date.

"Playing the drum connects us to our ancestral past and the prehistoric ages, as far back as our pre-human and animal ancestors. The oldest musical instruments found are over 40,000 years old and the scientists who found them are astonished by their sophistication leaving many to believe that humans might have been playing music for as long as twice as many years ago as that. Scientists who study the melodies and rhythms sung by animals such as birds, wolves and whales have come to recognize that the melodies and rhythms that these animals sing for different purposes, such as mating and hunting are similar to the ones that we sing for the same purposes. Throw in the fact that music has been played by all peoples, no matter how separated from each other, being disconnected in continents separated by great bodies of water from Africa to Alaska, from South America to Australia, and from Hawaii to Indonesia — all play music. This proves to me that music and playing the drum helps connect us to something deep within us – deep within our bodies, deep within our minds, deep within our unconscious as well as deep within our soul and spirit."

– Tony Scarpa, MA, Music Therapist,
Licensed Creative Arts Therapist

*I would like to dedicate this book to my wife,
Marissa E. Friedman, for her devotion, dedication and love
throughout the writing of this book. Time and time again
she has demonstrated to me an innocence and trust that
we sometimes lose as adults, and one that we all need to retain.
After searching for over five decades, I found someone
who reflects back to me, the essence of the
spirit of the drum... joy, play and love.*

Acknowledgements

I would first like to acknowledge some of the elders of the community of drummers who have laid the groundwork for this book, Babatunde Olatunji, Arthur Hull, Mickey Hart and Jim Greiner.

My thanks goes out to those who came before me who began this journey of drumming and health in its early stages, including the 'Rhythm for Life' organization, Alicia Ann Claire, Ph.D., MT-BC and many others who have devoted years of their lives to the pursuit of uncovering the health benefits of rhythm.

Arthur Hull has been extremely generous to me and created stellar training programs that have sent thousands of facilitators to do their incredible work. Over three-quarters of the drummers and drum circle facilitators who have shared their stories in this book have attended one or more of his training programs. I'd also like to thank famed drummer Billy Cobham for offering his personal insights into drumming and Saturday Night Live percussionist Valerie Naranjo for offering her wisdom and thoughts.

Thanks to the contributors who shared their heart, mind and soul with the readers of this book through their heartfelt stories: Jim Anderson, Nupur Arora, Jane Bentley, Bob Bloom, Nathan Brenowitz, Jana Broder, Randy Brody, Otha Day, Michelle Drieberg, Natalie Driver, Steve Durbin, Jane Featherstone, Jim Greiner, Beverly Griffin, Bonnie Harr, Patricia Hatfield, Nellie Hill, Simon Faulkner, Dave Holland, Arthur Hull, Alyssa Janney, Moe Jerant, Lulu Leathley, Jonathan Murray, Valerie Naranjo, Augie "Doggie" Peltonen, Shannon Ratigan, Kaoru Sasaki, John Scalici, Frank Schaeffer, Tony Scarpa, Margaret Sowry, Scott Swimmer, Christine Stevens and Cameron Tummel. I would also like to acknowledge Shannon Ratigan for offering to the readers his extensive compilation of the drum circles currently found around the globe. Shannon has spent the last ten years compiling this data at drumcircles.net and I am very grateful for his generosity in offering this to our readers.

I would like to acknowledge the Percussive Arts Society, the Health and Wellness Committee, and the Interactive Drumming Committee for creating a meeting arena for drummers to connect and share their insights; the Yahoo group Drumcircles (drumcircles@yahoogroups.com); the Drum Circle Facilitators Guild (dcfg.net) for providing a support network for drum circle facilitators who are venturing out to help create a better world, and for both the current President Nellie Hill, and the founder and past president Jonathan Murray for their continuous support; Dr. Connie Tomaino, Dr. Barry Bittman, and the many researchers, music therapists, and drumming facilitators who have helped change the landscape of this work; Remo Belli and his vision to support the world of drumming and health through the creation of HealthRHYTHMS; Alyssa Janney and John Fitzgerald for their continued support at Remo, and for giving me permission to republish the very poignant and moving HealthRHYTHMS stories; and all those who affect positive change in others through their work in the area of drumming and wellness.

My gratitude goes out to pioneers of the drumming movement who are no longer with us: Happy Shel, who created the Drums, Not Guns organization; Barry Bernstein, MT- BC, for his playful spirit and for his innovations in rhythm, including his "Take One, Pass One" shaker game; and Babatunde Olatunji, who brought African drumming to America.

I would like to acknowledge my family: my mom, Sylvia Friedman, who always supported my drumming; my sister Elyse Glenn and her husband Mel Glenn, for supporting my two nephews and first two drumming students, Jonathan and Andrew; my brother Dr. Jeffrey Friedman, his wife, Lisa, and their beautiful children and my first drumming students in California — Sage, Sequoia and Uriah; and my father, Phillip Friedman, who will forever remain in my heart.

Table of Contents

An Iconic Drummer's Personal Story   3

Acknowledgements   9

Foreword: Forever the Pioneer by Arthur Hull   15

Preface   17

CHAPTER ONE
Drumming and Indigenous Tribes   **19**

The Senoi Tribe – Drumming and Dreaming   19

The Tempo of Life by Jim Greiner   21

Cherokee Wellbriety by Beverly Griffin   22

The Power of Orenda by Valerie Naranjo   23

CHAPTER TWO
Universal Rhythms   **27**

Cultural Spinning and Drumming   27

Nagoya Japan Peace Drum Circle by Christine Stevens   28

Coming Full Circle by Jim Greiner   28

Drumming with Orthodox Women   29

Drumming in Taipei, Taiwan by Arthur Hull   30

Rhythm: The Universal Culture by Jim Greiner   31

CHAPTER THREE
Blocks And Releases   **33**

Release by Arthur Hull   33

Helping Me to Remember by Nupur Arura   36

Drumming Out Loss   36

Transcendance through Drumming by Nellie Hill   38

CHAPTER FOUR

Drumming with a Purpose   **40**

My First Facilitated Drum Circle by Arthur Hull   40

Asthi Drum – Drum Salam by Christine Stevens   42

DrumSTRONG: The Good that comes from the Bad
    by Scott Swimmer   46

CHAPTER FIVE

Drum Lessons   **50**

Cataclysms and Compensation by Cameron Tummel   50

Drumming at the Edge of Consciousness—Qualities
    of Drumming by Jim Anderson   52

Renewing Intentional Rhythms by Jim Greiner   54

Bashoowee!   56

Drumming to Reinforce Positive Life Rhythms by Jim Greiner   58

Tuning In – The Social Power of the Drum by Jane Bentley   59

Create Some Rhythm, Share Some Magic by Dave Holland   63

CHAPTER SIX

Training Programs   **66**

Drumming with Dad: End of Life Rhythmical Journey
    by Moe Jerant   68

Intergenerational Rhythms by Bonnie D. Harr, MSN, MS, RN   69

Lionel, "A Changed Young Man" by Margaret Sowry   71

Harmonizing Discord: Lessons from Hardened Hearts
    by Margaret Sowry   72

My Experience with Drum Circles by Frank Schaffer   76

CHAPTER SEVEN

Drumming with Specific Populations   **87**

Dancing Hands and Smiles by Lulu Leathley   87

Drumming Without Sound by Bob Bloom   87

The Value of Technology: Drumming Via Webcam
    by Shannon Ratigan   88

Drum Circles at Children's Hospital by John Scalici   91

Benefits of Drumming for the Blind and Visually
   Impaired by Patricia Hatfield   93

Senior Citizens with Disabilities Not Seeing is Believing   95

Connected through Rhythm by Steve Durbin   95

Drumming with Alzheimer's Patients   96

A Story of Remembering by Jana Broder   95

Dementia and Alzheimer "LuluJam" by Lulu Leathley   97

Life, Eyes and Miracles by Randy Brody   98

Standing Up for Rhythm by Kaoru Sasaki   99

A Small Movement – A Great Delight by Nathan Brenowitz   100

Impactive Drumming by Jonathan Murray   101

Drumming and Parkinsons Disease by Jonathan Murray   103

Story, My Left Foot by Arthur Hull   103

Drumming at the World Burn Congress   105

Drumming at the Burn Retreat   106

Chemo Patient by Augie "Doggie" Peltonen   107

Rehabilitation Hospital Drum Circles
   by Augie "Doggie" Peltonen   108

Drumming with Psychological and Psychiatric Populations   110

Pathways to Possibility by Patricia Hatfield   110

Drumming and Schizophrenia   113

Rhythm Establishes Connections by John Scalici   126

Drumming and Family Practice   128

Drumming and Relationships in Therapeutic Practice
   by Jim Anderson   128

CHAPTER EIGHT
Drumming and Societal Challenges   **129**

Drumming and Conversations   129

"Join Us" (Drumming and the Community) by Otha Day   129

Drumming Out Drugs – Research from
   Dr. Michael Winkelman   130

CHAPTER NINE

Where Have We Come, Where Are We Going?   **132**

Drum Circles Then and Now   132

APPENDIX I

Music Therapy Vs. Drum Circle Facilitation   **135**

Appendix I Resources   138

Music Therapists   138

Drum Circle Facilitators   138

Drum Teachers   145

Organizations   146

Products   146

Books   146

CDs and DVDs   148

Related Products   150

Resources   150

Drum Centers   150

Websites of Interest   150

Drumming Mailing Lists   150

Drumcircles in the United States   151

International Drum Circles   173

References   183

Index   187

ABOUT THE AUTHOR

Robert Lawrence Friedman, M.A.   189

Forever the Pioneer by Arthur Hull

Robert Lawrence Friedman did not have a choice. Like all of the early pioneers of the recreational drumming movement, he was called by the spirit of rhythm at an early age. By following his rhythmic bliss into adulthood, he realized that he was on a mission to uncover, discover and recover the use of drumming as a way to create community as well as a way to improve anyone's life and lifestyle.

When Robert's first book, *The Healing Power of the Drum*, was published, the words "healing" and "drum" were rarely used in the same sentence. Through that book, Robert has bettered not only our growing recreational drumming community, but those dedicated to health and wellness. He has taught the medical community how to use the drum with a psychodynamic focus and shown how to bring drumming into everyday life for psychological and physiological well-being.

Robert has shown how drumming can be both fun and healthy, as well as a unifying social activity. Sharing these lessons with the public through stories and research, he has shown how drumming is a viable tool for wellness. Robert's latest offering, *The Healing Power of the Drum – A Journey of Rhythm and Stories* shows readers how drumming improves our mental and physical well-being. He also introduces us to some of the new players and pioneers in rhythm event facilitation, acknowledging his fellow pioneers and elders in our growing community. As rhythm event facilitation is now developing into a professionally recognized job description in many areas, Robert also provides many resources for those taking their rhythmical path to the next step.

In *The Healing Power of the Drum–A Journey of Rhythm and Stories*, Robert shows us how far we all have come since the publication of his first book, and where we have yet to go in this exploration of the healing-through-rhythm path that he continues to pioneer for us.

As he followed, explored and shared his own rhythmical bliss, Robert recognized that he was on a path that he had created on his own. Now looking back down that path, he can see that many others, including myself, are following him.

Thank you Robert for sharing your spirit through this book.

–Arthur Hull

Preface

Since the *Healing Power of the Drum* was first published in 2000, the world has changed immensely. From the World Trade Center terrorist attacks to the killings at Virginia Tech, events have altered how we view our lives. In those horrific events, drumming brought healing, as facilitators like Arthur Hull and Christine Stevens, MT-BC, developed programs using drumming to ignite hope, build community, and express what words alone can not say.

When I first began this journey into the healing power of the drum, I had no idea where this exploration would take me.

I began writing about drum circles and health in 1999. After reading Arthur Hull's brilliant *Drum Circle Spirit* I was inspired to write *The Healing Power of the Drum*.

Though the *Healing Power of the Drum* began as a journey to explore how drumming relaxes people and releases emotional pain, that focus changed. As I continued to explore the health benefits of drumming, I became immersed in a worldwide community of drummers, drum circle facilitators, researchers, therapists and educators who felt that there was more to drumming than drumming. I knew personally that the drum had the ability to heal, because it healed me. A drum could help release the painful emotions of humiliation, anger, fear and stress.

Initially I thought that the first book would be my own, but I was drawn to an advertisement for a drum retreat called "Unity with a Beat" created by Barry Bernstein, Randy Crafton and Bob Bloom. Despite an impending hurricane, Barry not only insisted that I come, but that I drive up with the drumming master Babatunde Olatunji. That three-hour drive opened the door to my journey into the deeper explorations of the rhythms of spirit. That car ride is where *The Healing Power of the Drum* really began, and it was through "Unity with a Beat" that the book developed its soul.

At "Unity with a Beat", I met the pioneers of the drumming movement and the core members of my first book: Arthur Hull, Barry Bernstein, Bob Bloom, Randy Crafton. What began as a book on stress and drumming blossomed into one about a community of drummers and drum circle facilitators. As the concept of the book deepened, rhythmic links began to emerge.

Through many connections with other drummers, I met Rip Peterson, a drum circle facilitator in Long Island, New York, who invited me along and introduced me to Ginger Graziano. Through her own experience in dealing with the death of her child, she opened my eyes to the depth of the drum as a vehicle of moving through grief. As I interviewed each individual, it emerged that the simple hand drum was not so simple. Its ability to touch lives, from babies to the elderly, seemed endless. Christine Stevens, MT-BC played an important role in my first book as she introduced me to Dr. Michael Thaut and Dr. John Burt.

Since the book's publication, I've been contacted by hundreds of individuals from all over the world who have shared how the drum improved their own health. Many of them are drum circle facilitators, music therapists, drummers, educators and psychotherapists. Their stories made me realize the need for a follow-up to *The Healing Power of the Drum*.

This second edition brings together more stories exploring how drums have touched individuals' lives. Ten years ago, there was one primary training program for individuals interested in this field, but it has since expanded greatly. Thanks to Shannon Ratigan, who keeps a current list of drum circles, you can find a drum circle whether you live in Missouri or Australia.

In much of the current music therapy research, the drum has figured only peripherally. Except for a few cases, I wanted this book to focus entirely on the hand drum. *The Healing Power of the Drum — A Journey of Rhythm and Stories* will explore the vast range of experiences offered by drumming, from its ability to create euphoria to its deep and sacred power to heal.

CHAPTER ONE

Drumming and Indigenous Tribes

The hand drum is not new, nor is the use of the drum as a vehicle of healing new. Yet the use of the drum as the focal point of healing, at least in our society, is new. What indigenous tribes, shamans and medicine men have known for centuries, we are just now beginning to understand.

The drum has long been viewed as a sacred vehicle. Cultures worldwide have drummed for millenia. There is rhythm inherent in nature that calls to be echoed through instruments. As we drum we remember who we are. As we drum we remember an ancient calling built within our cells. As we drum we remember our inherent right to joy. As we drum we remember that when we slow down we embrace our soul.

Drumming gives us an experience of eternal beauty and wisdom of nature, and our connection to it. In order to connect with nature, indigenous tribes have used the drum to speak the language of spirit.

In this story of the Senoi Tribe, we see how drumming and dance provided a backdrop for the Senoi Tribe to express their joy and share their connection to spirit.

The Senoi Tribe – Drumming and Dreaming

I have studied the Senoi Tribe for over two decades, and visited them in 2008 when I was invited to do a drumming program in Kuala Rompin, Malaysia.

What fascinated me about the Senoi Tribe was that they were described in literature as the most cooperative tribe in the world. They have no neurosis and no psychosis. It is believed that they are the healthiest tribe psychologically because they have worked through their psychological and emotional issues through learning to awaken in their dream state.

By the time they are 13 years old, tribe members have learned how to become lucid in a dream state. The experience of lucidity in the dream state is an extraordinary one; I've experienced it just a few times in my life. It is the experience of having full awareness that you are dreaming, while you are dreaming.

By the time Senois are 13 years old, they no longer have nightmares. When a scary experience occurs in their dream, they are then told by their elders to remember they are dreaming, battle that which they are afraid of, and extract a creative element from whatever it is that they are in battle with.

The creative elements that they extract from their dream take the form of inventions, songs, dances and poems. In the morning, members meet in small groups and discuss their dreams, what they learned, and what they created in their dream state. As a group, they agree which tribe member created the most useful invention for the tribe, and then together recreate it.

As I drove excitedly through the jungles of Malaysia with my dear friend and drum circle facilitator, Bill Lewis, and his companion, Jaz, we stopped as we came to a large hut and a clearing in the middle of the rain forest. It was the Senoi Tribe's village.

It was in this village that we had an opportunity to meet the Shaman, a serious woman with a tiny frame and powerful eyes. What was extraordinary for me as a native New Yorker was that these people had never met us before. We drove into their village and were greeted like family. This would not happen in Forest Hills, Queens.

The Shaman took a stick with a 10-foot-long hook and picked off fruit from the tree effortlessly. As I tasted its freshness and juiciness, I felt like I was being given a gift from the gods. There was a quality of eating this fruit that I never experienced in New York. We don't get to experience eating much fruit that is picked for us in that moment, unless it is from a grocery clerk picking it out from a box.

They took us into the community hut, where they offered us food. As if this were an ancient 'show and tell' in which they showed their dream-created inventions, they shared with us the creations they made through lucid dreaming – sophisticated games, art, music, and dance.

They showed us to a basket of multi-sized bamboo sticks. Each one of the tribe members grabbed two, one large and one smaller, and then sat on the floor as others remained standing preparing to dance. Tribesmen began hitting the floor with their bamboo sticks and a melodic rhythm emerged. The Shaman and the other tribesmen began singing and dancing one of their ceremonial songs as the bamboo rhythms accompanied us. I felt very honored to be able to witness this sacred creative expression that probably was originally witnessed in a dream.

The inviting sounds of the rhythms, song and dance led Bill and me to grab our own bamboo sticks and join the other tribesman on the floor. The intensity of this Shaman was indescribable. Her eyes piercing, juxtaposed by her smile as her body moved to the rhythms. I watched as the Shaman and the others danced with her.

As they danced and drummed I felt as if I was watching them share their joy of life through ancient sounds and motions. Though they didn't utter one word of English, they knew the universal language of drumming, dance and food, one would feed our bodies and the others, our souls.

Jim Greiner, one of the pioneers of the drum circle movement and a very prolific writer, shares his playful story of the merging of the ancient with the contemporary in his unique style.

The Tempo of Life by Jim Greiner

"Grandfather, what has changed about the drumming from the time you were a young man?"

I asked this question many years ago when I had the great privilege to be invited to drum with a Native American elder of the Chumash people, from southern California, named Semu Haute – though everyone just called him Grandfather.

Grandfather was in his 60's or 70's, though it was hard to tell his age. His broad face was sundried and deeply cut with life-lines, and he carried himself with the inner calm of an elder, but he also exuded the vitality of a much younger person.

Galloping Life Rhythms

I joined Grandfather's drummers around their large ceremonial drum near a fire whose glow barely penetrated the dark, moonless night.

As we played, I had the feeling that his drummers, all guys in their early 20's as I was, kept trying to push the tempo faster. They all respectfully supported Grandfather, and the drumming and singing was truly a profoundly moving experience. But it felt like he was constantly reining in a herd of wild mustangs that wanted to gallop faster and faster!

We played for several hours as we journeyed deeper and deeper into the rhythm. On Grandfather's upspoken cue we stopped, sat together in silent contemplation for a few minutes, and finally returned to "normal" reality.

We talked together briefly, then finally we drummers slapped backs in our youthful male exuberance, and said our "Good Nights" to each other.

I stayed behind after the other drummers had left, and asked Semu Haute that question, "Grandfather, what has changed about the drumming from the time you were a young man?".

Grandfather looked deeply into my eyes and said, "That is a very good question young man...one that no one else asks me."

His eyes then seemed to look far back into his memory... into his own youthful past. A momentary thought flashed through my mind that I was about to be privileged to receive a teaching that he would draw deeply from a well of ancient wisdom.

Grandfather then looked at me intently, and stated in his clear, no-nonsense way, "All my young drummers these days want to play the traditional songs much too fast."

Then, pausing, but still fixing me with his powerful gaze, the laugh lines around his mouth and eyes deepening, he exclaimed... "It's that's damned Rock and Roll!"

Powerful belly-laughter exploded from both of us!

Later, I realized that this was indeed profound wisdom, contained in a very simple, down-to earth lesson:

The rhythms of our lives today are much faster, and more complex, than at any other time in human history. And, they get faster and more complex from generation to generation.

Our intricately-woven, fast-paced Life Rhythms can affect us in profoundly negative ways if we allow them to become our masters: stress-related disorders, difficulty focusing, and a general unwellness of mind, body and spirit are often the results of out-of-control Life Rhythms.

We do have the innate ability to create a calm inner tempo, even when physically and mentally active, that allows us to focus on our core principles and intentions more effectively, and to playfully celebrate the blessing that is Life!

In this story, Beverly Griffin, RN shares her experience of drumming with the Cherokee Indians.

Cherokee Wellbriety by Beverly Griffin

About 10 years ago while at a multicultural Theology school I began to have an idea about how it would be uplifting and healing to participate in a "world drum" choir that would unite people in song. The current program manifested from the experience of a drum circle that my friend from Appalachian State University came and led for us in the Spring of 2005 at a Wellbriety community event. It went over very well, and 5 months later she donated a "seed drum" to me. It is an old, worn, REMO djembe, which lived in my office until our new drums arrived. Everyone who came in wanted to touch it — It made people smile and created lots of positive energy. I facilitate a Wellbriety women's group for ACOA's who also wanted passionately to see a drum group form. We prayed that if it was to be it would be.

I was at first very cautious in introducing the drum as "recreation" because of the drum workshop protocols in Indian communities. They can be very strict and it was a baby step venture which required great care always in explaining the concept. I also have a very popular Women's drum choir at church (where the seed djembe now lives) which is starting to be invited to sing worship at other churches and gatherings because we inspire and empower women to express the spirit through "making joyful noise". The Friday night community drum circle is so inspired that they want to have t-shirts made and have a float in the fall Cherokee heritage parade! The elder in our Wellbriety planning group, who attends the community drum faithfully, wants to have a big drumming event soon for Wellbriety celebration time! I am grateful and happily surprised at the way it has been received and can flourish with enough support. In 2008, White Bison gave me the Woman Firestarter of the year award for all my work in Wellbriety.

Valerie Naranjo has been the percussionist for the *Saturday Night Live* band since 1995. She is of Native American (Ute) ancestry, and has performed with Zakir Hussein, Philip Glass, The Paul Winter Consort and was named *Drum!* Magazine reader's poll's "World Percussionist of the Year" in 2005 and 2008. In this essay, Valerie shares her thoughts on the healing power of the drum.

The Power of Orenda by Valerie Naranjo

I went the other night to hear my husband Barry in a Latin Band. What a nice treat, since Latin music in New York is more of a rarity, not common as it was in the early 80s when I first moved to New York City.

After some banter with the audience, Luisito, the lead singer gave the floor to the band leader. The drummers started a smokin' pulsating rhythm and the audience of office workers, teachers, clerks and nurses took their place on the dance floor. What a great time they were having! What joy and what healing movement – what beautiful Orenda everyone and everything had!

Orenda is the Huron peoples' name for the force that exists in all life. Animals, plants, deities, humans, even inanimate objects – all have pulsating Orenda within them. REN, the root of this word is associated with the power of song, which, in Native American culture, is the direct means of communication with the spirit world. Therefore, through music, we touch the enlivening spirit that is within all things.

I am from Colorado's 60 mile wide and 100 mile long San Luis Valley. My family is from the Southern Ute Nation. Reputedly, my musician grandfather, a farmer like most of my elders, enjoyed wintertime because of the opportunity it gave for him to invite all of the musicians to his house to make music.

Drumming – all music – is, for "earth people" all over the planet, treasured for its ability to attain and maintain balance and order, physically, psychologically, socially, and spiritually. Whenever a misfortune or calamity occurs, it is only the symptom that this perfect natural order is out of sync. Since vibration is the essence of life, we try to restore perfect order by reintroducing a bountiful harmonious vibration. The drum can do that so well. The drum then, is not only for entertainment, intellectual stimulation, or social pursuit – it is for changing the life condition of individuals and of the community. It recreates balance and harmony in the mind body and spirit.

In the Native American community the drummers are regarded as sound healers and important teachers. The instrument makers, and even the plants and animals involved, are blessed and initiated, and they hold a special place among the people. Yet it is understood that every person has the privilege to make music and to enjoy the healing, bonding and empowerment that this brings. It is actually the energy of the drum's sound vibration that heals.

It is also believed in Native America, that drumming is a powerful way that people from different nations can communicate heart-to-heart with one another. One of the first aspects of spiritual healing involves accepting and respecting ourselves and those around us, near and far. When our hearts are open, we can use our differences as a source of enrichment, enlightenment and creativity, fueling the development of a better world community, and initiating a healing process that will benefit both us at present, and those yet unborn.

In order to further appreciate drumming in the Native American historical sense, it's good to understand more about how traditional Native Americans orient themselves in the Non-Native American world. Immigrants can often tend to think in terms of linear time; everything from personal success to family progress takes place in a steady linear progression of definable events. For the traditional indigenous American, on the other hand, the place on earth – the environment, the land and those who take care of it, are the point of reference. We live within a wholistic framework that assumed "there is plenty of time, we are part of eternity". Without the pressure to progress through a time line, the traditional American is free to explore and experience notions of self-awareness and spirituality without having to define them immediately.

To us, drumming is less about defining than it is about feeling. What you feel in your life is real, and singing and drumming is one of the primary experiences that you can have to help you to embrace that reality.

It is important, however, to note that drumming like other expressions, has a language; and it is important to know and "speak" the language of the drum, whatever that particular language might be at a particular time and place.

Imagine, if you are an English speaking person and you fall in love with someone who doesn't speak English. Yes, you can probably express some of your feelings with gestures, but at some point you might want to learn how to say: "You are very handsome. I would like to get to know you." In that person's language.

Perhaps your attraction to such a person will spur you on to learn more words to better express yourself and hone your communication. The same can be true with our relationship with the drum. When a person knows something about the drum, he/she has more ability to express her/himself.

I have had the privilege to travel to West Africa annually, and experience traditional culture there. I am always struck by the similarities between traditional earth peoples in North America and Africa.

The particular percussion art that I am most in love with was born South of the Sahara desert in Ghana's upper West. There is practiced long standing tradition of healing artistry on the Lobi/Brifo and Dagara marimba called gyil. Calabash gourds enhanced with spider's egg cases give this instrument its special sound, believed to carry a vibration which creates and maintains health and balance individually and within the community. The gyil maestro can use the instrument to diagnose and cure emotional and psychological imbalance. Almost every rural community has its own style of playing and its own tonality.

The gyil music mastery is cultivated within musician families, by youngsters' private apprenticeships with the elder maestros within the family. In this straightforward and strict environment, if you the child have a keen interest, you may be considered for musical training. If you are intelligent and observant, you will begin to grasp even the more complicated music. If you are dedicated for a long time, you will be able to play, and if you play well enough, often enough, and for a long enough time, your elders will allow you to play publicly. The village gyil maestros are, much like physicians, on call to heal, especially when someone dies, since the sound vibration of the instrument is believed to be essential in the transportation of the soul of the deceased from this life to the next.

Although mastery of the gyil is a coveted art, almost every man is able to play at least a song or two. The gyil has been considered, for the most part,

Valerie Naranjo

to be a man's art. During my participations at Lawra Ghana's famed Kobine Festivals, men of all ages were approaching the instrument to share the joy.

In addition, I have also been so happy to practice Nichiren Buddhism, which was founded in Japan. Its most basic practice is the chanting of "Nam Myoho Renge Kyo", alone, but better collectively, and traditionally with a drum. Like Native American song and drumming, like Lobi/Brifo life practice, Nichiren Buddhism uses sound vibration to produce a change in a person's fundamental life condition, including intellect, emotion, and physical health. It uses sound to open the place of pure beauty that exists in every human being.

Collective rhythm making for health and happiness is universal!

These life practices function according to the belief that we humans are fundamentally excellent. This excellence, not the same as perfection, transforms mistakes, problems, evils, and negativity in a lifelong growing process. Excellent sound vibration is absolute, and can with consistency, strip away our delusions, uncover our fundamental greatness, and actually use life's imbalances to build indestructible happiness and beauty.

CHAPTER TWO

Universal Rhythms

As the drum can bridge the ancient and contemporary, so it bridges cultural and language differences. These essays demonstrate the drum's ability to heal some of these differences.

Cultural Spinning and Drumming

In 2003, I was invited to Florida to facilitate a drum circle for the Mad Dogg Athletics Corporation, better known for their Spinning programs offered at gyms throughout the world. I invited drum circle facilitator and drummer extraordinaire Gus Brown to join me.

I entered a very large conference room and realized that everyone was Japanese. What I was not told was that not one of the participants from their Japanese offices spoke a word of English, my sole language.

As I looked into the room of 200 Japanese all smiling in great expectation of what was to come, I knew that I had to either start repeating the only phrase I knew in Japanese, "Arigato Gozi Mashta" (thank you very much) until they realized that either I had just way too much gratitude or my Japanese language was extremely limited. I knew I had to pull something out of my hat since there were no translators. Knowing the universality of rhythm, and the universality of the language of rhythm, and coming prepared, I began handing out my Scat cards™. These cards have nonsensical rhythms on them, so I thought they would work.

As I handed the Scat cards™ to the Asian Spinning instructors, I began creating the universal heartbeat groove on my djembe drum, while Gus began creating the same groove on his djun djuns. As the Spinning group began repeating their Scat phrases, and Gus and I created a rhythm familiar to everyone, a language beyond all of our native tongues that made our own languages unnecessary.

As this was going on, the owner and founder of Mad Dogg, Johnny G, a capoeira dancer (an Afro-Brazilian art that combines martial arts, music and dance) began somersaulting and moving to the music around the room using the mystical capoeira motions and movements.

I felt as if I was in a new form of Cirque du Soleil. Suddenly, they all began a dance, moving their bodies to the heartbeat rhythm, while chanting scat phrases.

A feeling of oneness emerged from the group, and as they continued scatting and drumming, language felt unnecessary, for there is a language beyond those spoken in our countries, it is the shared language of rhythm.

Christine Stevens is the founder of UpBeat Drum Circles and the author of *The Art and Heart of Drum Circles and The Healing Drum Kit*. Since 2000, Stevens has worked with Remo, the world's largest drum company, to develop products and programs for health and wellness, including launching the HealthRHYTHMS group empowerment drumming facilitation training course, co-taught with Barry Bittman, M.D. She is featured in *Discover the Gift* book and DVD.

In many ways, Christine has been the ambassador of rhythm, bringing drumming programs for health, wellness, and peace-building to places in our planet that are needing healing, including Virginia Tech, the World Trade Center, and Iraq. In this story, Christine shares her experience in Nagoya where she held a Peace Drum Circle on Hiroshima's Anniversary on August 6, 2010. The following event was created by Yamaha Music Trading, Drum Circle Facilitators Association of Japan, Remo Inc., and Ms. Yasuyo of Music Together of West Nagoya and Happy Beat Drum Circles.

Nagoya Japan Peace Drum Circle by Christine Stevens

Children danced while a balloon of the world floated about the rhythms of Japan, Iraq, Native America and India.

At the recent Japanese Peace Drum Circle held in Nagoya, over one hundred Japanese, American, and invited guests from India and Nepal took the sadness and shock of the Hiroshima bombing in 1945 which killed 140,000 Japanese and transformed it into a rhythm of Peace through drumming on the anniversary day!

According to Ms. Yasuyo, "it was beautiful to have families participate for the first time with everyone playing together. In the temples we pray alone, but through the drum circle we got to pray together."

"We feel this is a global trend of cultural peace-building through drum circles. I look forward to seeing more and more in the world as we move towards peace, joy, and creativity!

Jim Greiner

In this essay, Jim Greiner shares an insight as to how traditional cultures used the voice as a way to create rhythm.

Coming Full Circle by Jim Greiner

Midway through an all-night drumming session with a group of musicians in the oasis of Tamanrasset in the deep Sahara, I had one of the most profound rhythmic, and life, "Aha!" moments of my entire two-year drumming journey in Africa. I had realized before, that many drummers vocalized the patterns they played. It occurred to me at that moment, deep in the groove zone with these Tuareg musicians, that by vocalizing our rhythmic parts, we were internalizing them! I realized that the stronger I would speak my own pattern, the more I committed myself to it, the easier it was to play it! I called this method of internalizing rhythms "Say and Play".

I later learned that many rhythmcultures around the world use this method to learn and reinforce rhythms. It is a natural approach for people from cultures with strong oral traditions, such as the peoples who developed many of the percussion instruments we play today. We "westerners", being from a visually- based, written-word culture, tend to look, at a drummer's hands and trying to "figure out" how to play his/her pattern. When we say a pattern, we put it into our body, where our physical voice lives... we internalize it and get it out of our heads... where the other voice lives... the one that often tries to over analyze and judge what we're doing. We drum with our bodies and spirits... not our heads! Playing music is all about what sounds and feels good – not what we think we could be doing! Of course, this works in other parts of life, as well!

Internalizing Positive Intentions

We internalize and reinforce positive intentions in the same way as traditional peoples internalize their rhythms – by declaring our commitment to them to ourselves, and out loud to those whom we trust. This is the say part of "Say & Play". The next step, naturally, is acting upon our Internalized Intentions. This is the play part of "Say & Play". We create powerful Life Rhythms by repeating actions that are based upon these Intentions – just as we create powerful rhythmic music by repeating these rhythms until they become automatic. In the 1970's, I read a book called The Relaxation Response by Dr. Herbert Bensen, a cardiologist at the Harvard Medical School. Dr. Bensen demonstrated that repeating an intentional word or phrase while using meditative breathing techniques can put our minds and bodies into an intentional state of relaxation. Of course, this has been known for thousands of years by peoples worldwide who chant, pray, repeat mantras... and drum! Talk about coming "full circle"!

Drumming with Orthodox Women

On August 19, 2004 I facilitated a community drum circle composed of 50 female Orthodox young adults in a section of New York known as Crown Heights. Crown Heights is a divided neighborhood of African-American and Orthodox communities. When Yankel Rosenbaum was killed in 1991, it led to riots between the African Americans and the Orthodox community, and its effects can still be felt today.

Segregation still exists. Each community was bound within its streets. One block was African-American, the next, Orthodox.

Although I would be drumming with only the Orthodox community, I knew that the drum has reverberating effects. In this circle, I would be drumming with a population I had never worked with before.

I learned that evening of many Orthodox customs I was not familiar with. By accident as I extended my hand to greet my client and was informed quickly that a woman was not permitted to shake any man's hand other than her husband's. I learned that an Orthodox Jewish woman could not sing in front of a man, nor could she dance in front of a man unless it was with her husband.

At first the young adults seemed hesitant. I wasn't sure why, but it was palpable; perhaps because a non-Orthodox drummer was in the room who was a man, I wondered?

I began my program talking about drumming and wellness. Then I had the group close their eyes and focus on the power of the drum to relax. As we went through one of my rhythm exercises, and I began watching the women create their own rhythms, it became clear that the drum was going to be an opportunity to help them express their emotions and become rhythmically freer.

As the djun djuns were placed in the middle of the room, four women jumped out of their chairs to grab the mallets. It was fun for me to see this energy from these young adults who in the beginning were so reserved. As the rhythms began to build, these young adults, bounded by Orthodox laws, began expressing themselves in joy. It was an energy that I felt privileged to witness. Their inner creativity arose as they drummed. They began jumping and drumming. The rhythms seemed to go on endlessly as each Orthodox woman shared their play and creativity.

Despite the differences in customs, despite the rules and guidelines of the Orthodox people, on this evening, we found a common bond that joined us all. As I completed the program, one girl came up to me and said, "we all need this, Crown Heights needs this." The drum could bridge gaps in this community. It provided a free, created space, one that provided all of us an opportunity to play together in joy.

Arthur Hull, the father and pioneer of the drum circle, shares his story of drumming in Taiwan with special children.

Drumming in Taipei, Taiwan by Arthur Hull

I went to Taipei, Taiwan to do a drum circle for children, and was told that the children wouldn't understand. Before the circle began, the women were very apologetic. The children were special children who were 4-6 years old. I put the drums in the middle of the circle and the children were given the drums by the staff. The children began playing them. One girl ran out of the circle, but the others played without a problem. As I was finishing the circle, I taught them call and respond, first with the instruments, then I took the instruments away and did call and respond with their breath to help slow them down. I wanted to make sure that the children were not left wild and crazy after the drum circle. As each child finished their breath call and respond, I looked up and all of the health care workers were crying. They did not expect to see these children, mentally challenged to be able to do this exercise.

Jim Greiner shares a story of his experience working with numerous cultures together in a drum circle:

Rhythm: The Universal Culture by Jim Greiner

The young, dark-haired man from India looked across our circle of drummers at a redheaded man of about the same age from northern Europe, grinned broadly and exclaimed, "I loved the part you were playing, so I copied it. It was so very easy for me to play!" The other fellow looked surprised, laughed and said, "I thought I copied it from you!"

Group Grooves

This exchange happened during my Observations & Comments session that was part of a drumming program I did in the 1980's for a young software company... later to become one of the world's largest. I had been brought in to do an icebreaking and team building program for a group of software engineers from Asia, Europe, India and North America who would be working on a project together. They all spoke fluent English, however the organizers knew that the different work styles and cultural expectations among team members might inhibit their collaborative process. Their goal was for me to help them quickly create a group culture of communication and cooperation that transcended their deeply ingrained cultural differences. In addition to the instruments I always provide for these programs, I also brought in examples of small, single-headed frame drums that were found in the home cultures of all the participants. They clearly recognized, in an immediate, down-to-earth way, the universal, cross-cultural connections that already existed among them. After a brief introduction to some basic skills for playing the percussion instruments, I facilitated the group's creation of their own multilayered group rhythm. As we played together, I helped them to learn how to recognize and support each other's unique talents and personalities. Together, we created interlocking patterns as we went on our a rhythm journey.

By the end of the 90-minute session, broken into several segments, the participants had created their own unique culture, complete with shared values, processes and mutual support system... their own Group Groove. A shy, wiry man from South Korea summed up their experience brilliantly when he enthused, "I could never have drummed like this by myself, but the group's rhythm helped me to stay in my own rhythm!" Community Rhythm Skills Group drumming, when done in a focused, purposeful way, is such a great builder of communication and cooperation skills and community bonds, because these activities all have the same core principles and require the same core skills. These include: – Actively listening to other group members with open ears, open minds and open hearts – Expressing ourselves clearly with positive intentions – Responding to what other people contribute, not to our own inner conversations – Leaving space for other people to contribute – Willingly engaging together to share our unique skills, talents, personalities and Spirits!

CHAPTER THREE

Blocks and Releases

When you were growing up, there was a fair chance that certain circumstances occurred that caused you pain. What did you do with that pain? Did you feel it fully and express it, or push it within?

When an individual's pain is not expressed and it builds within, there are many possibilities as to what may occur. Walls of defense may be created, such as denial of the pain, and then a person may then avoid anything that resembles the original circumstances. Inappropriate emotional responses might be released when something reminds that person of the original pain.

The drum has the unique ability to release internalized emotions. Through drumming with intention, feelings can be released. The general recommendation is that a therapist or music therapist be present to support this type of process. The drum provides a means for expressing emotions without expressing words, which can be enormously beneficial when working with children. One of the qualities that occurs when a person drums is the experience of release.

In this essay, Arthur Hull shares his thoughts and an experience on the drum's ability to release:

Release by Arthur Hull

The vibration that emanates from a connected drum circle event, beit family friendly, corporate or clinical, goes to the places in a person's heart, mind or body and massages stress out of those places. The drum circle massage also circumvents any circuitry that is not working and goes to the places that are functioning. (Ask the blind, deaf or mental challenged) All of this causes "Release" and some times tears flow as a result. If it is one thing that I have learned in my 40+ years of drum circle facilitation, it is that Sensitivity to tears in your circle is important, as the person crying also may or may not want acknowledgment or a hug. There is always a story behind those tears, and the participant may or may not want to share it.

Here is one story of a story shared that happened in Kassel Germany: we were well past drum call and the 300 + person percussion groove was solid and "smokin'". (Yes 300 recreational drummers in the heart of Germany) I has just finished a facilitation sequence and turned around to see standing

Arthur Hull

in the middle of one of the drum circle isles, a little, (as in short), old, (as in around 80 years), gray haired lady. She was hugging a doumbek with both arms, and had an excited yet confused look on her face. I walked up to her and with a smile and offered her a seat near the center of the circle. The drum groove around us was to loud for me to speak, so I took the Dumbek from her and showed her of a couple of different ways she could play it. She nodded her head yes, took the Dumbek back and with a smile began to play with the rest of the circle. She picked up my body language quickly and was soon doing responses to my calls with the rest of the group. Seeing that she was settled in, I put my attention elsewhere as the event progressed. Towards the end of the program I noticed that although other people around her had come and gone, she was still there, bright eyes, excited spirit, and participating 100%. But on second look, I saw that her face was wet with tears. I took a step towards her. She saw the concern in my face, and she smiled at me while making a go away motion with her hands and then continued to play. After the close of the Drum circle, I stood out side the entrance, like a minister saying farewell to his congregation after his service. I noticed her standing off to the side of the thank you line. I correctly deduced that she was waiting until I was alone so she could talk to me privately. The only thing that didn't quite fit was she was clutching a young man's hands. It all became quite apparent as I finished talking to the last person in line. With the little old lady still clutching his hand, the young man came up to me, and explained that she had commandeered him as a translator for her. Her eyes burned into mine as she stared speaking to me in German. She spoke with the same intensity that she played in the circle. The tears were coming out of her eyes as the words were poring out of her mouth. She realized that she had to stop talking so the young man could translate and catch up. When he began to speak, I looked at him and realized he was crying as well. Here is what he translated; Her name was Maria. She was 84 years old. She lived in her apartment 1/2 mile from the park where the community drum circle was being held. She heard us playing and followed the sound of the drums through the city, to the circus tent in the park by the river where we were playing. When she got to the entrance, she was handed a drum and was led inside. She felt overwhelmed by the "sound pressure", and didn't know what to do until I greeted her, sat her down' and showed her how to play. She had never played a drum before, never wanted to and never expected to. All though she enjoyed the experience, something very profound and important happened while she was playing that she had to share with me. Her husband died 45 years ago in the war. It felt to her like the drums were "massaging" the place in herself that couldn't let go of him. As she drummed she got in touch with that place and so she was able to let go of him and say goodbye. She had been a grieving widow most of her life and I could see in her eyes that she was about to start a new life. She couldn't thank me enough the young man said as the little old lady let go of his hand and bear hugged me. She wouldn't let go of me, saying over and over" Vielen-dank, Vielen-dank". I hugged her back. Now all three of us were crying. "Vielen-dank, Vielen-dank" she continued to say while hugging me. I looked over at the young man for a translation. He said "It means thank you, as very much as possible". You will never know all the stories that you help create in your drum circles. But I am sure that you will collect enough of them to remind you of all the good you do for individuals and communities by facilitating rhythm based events. And like me you will never want to stop, even the tears. [Reprinted with Permission from Arthur Hull's Drum Circle Spirit]

I met Nupur Arura at one of my drumming programs I offered at Queens College in New York. She shares her story:

Helping Me to Remember by Nupur Arura

My introduction to drumming was not an accident or a fulfillment of curiosity; it was my destiny to be reconnected to my childhood passion, but in a totally different light. I went to the drumming workshop with an open mind and no drum. As the program progressed, I felt in tune with my own rhythm.

By the end of the session, the alertness of my mind was sent back 20 years when I used to be a percussionist during my early school years. It was a time when I was most connected to my musical self and was doing it passionately.

Just prior to Robert's workshop, I was in a situation when I had just returned from back home overseas after my dad's ordeal, a gradual recovery from mouth cancer. Among the many emotions I felt at that time, I felt anger but did not even know it. Through guided drumming, Robert showed me a side to myself that I was not even aware of. I broke down in the middle of the session and kept drumming oblivious to the presence of anyone else in the room. Since then drumming has become a huge part of my existence and my healing on many levels. Drumming has been a huge instrument in giving me peace, perspective, healing and something to turn to in turmoil or happiness. Through drumming I have been able to reconnect with myself, my creator and with the universe that nurtures us all responding to the vibrations of our drums.

In one of my most intensely emotional drum circles, I was asked by a local hospice society to provide children whose parent or parents had died recently, with a vehicle for releasing some of their internalized emotions.

Drumming Out Loss

There were 50 children and young adults in the room, all in a circle. They came together through a local hospice society. All of them had lost a parent. I had been asked by the hospice to give these children support in releasing some of their pain through drumming. As I stared around the room, I took a deep breath, for although my father passed away fifteen years ago, I was 45 years old when he died and the children in this room ranged in age from nine years old to fifteen years old. For some of them, their parents died in a fire, others in an automobile accident; still others through a health-related issue.

My hope for the day was to help them release some of their anger and sadness, and maybe enjoy some rhythmic play. I knew that one workshop would not create a miracle, but I also knew that drums make anything possible.

I began the program lightly, using Barry Bernstein's 'Take One Pass One' exercise to get things started. It is always a winner. Next, to open them up, I used my Scat Cards, which always create some levity and relaxation. I next used Christine Stevens' Body Beat cards, all fun exercises to create some trust, ease and laughter.

I knew that my next task was to touch the untouchable, to provide a space for these children and young adults to focus on something that they might want to push away—the feelings connected to the death of their parent.

I next asked them to focus on their emotions, to close their eyes and breathe. As they breathed, I told them to relax, and asked them to drop their shoulders, soften their stomach, and focus on an emotion. It was an emotion-directed exercise, as I wanted them to think about a series of emotions in a particular sequence. As Dr. John Burt found in his work[1], the emotions flowed from anger to sadness to joy when working with veterans with post-traumatic stress disorder. This was the sequence I would work with.

The first emotion I asked them to put their attention on was their anger. I asked them to think about the feeling of anger, and provided them with Remo Paddle drums so that they would not hurt their hand in this process. They would hold their mallet preparing to hit the drum. The room was quiet, as the children were a bit hesitant about expressing their feelings. With their eyes closed, I hit my drum, providing an opening to others. Like small kernels of popcorn, each child and young adult began drumming. As more of them expressed, others joined in. Suddenly the room became a cauldron of internalized anger expressed as a small window was provided to give them permission to feel their anger and release it through their drum, their anger of losing one or both of their parents, of being alone, not having one or both parents in their life to guide them.

After fifteen minutes, the beating began slowing down. I asked them to create some space through breathing, as the room felt heavy with emotion. After a few minutes of breath, I asked them to think of their sadness and their pain and to find some way to express it in their drum.

The drum has the capacity to take an emotion and with the luxury of not having to find its exact phrase, be expressed through the fingers and hands. There seems to be a direct link from our minds and emotions to our hands.

Again the room was still. All that was heard was the breath. One child

---

1 Burt, John Ph.D, MCAT, RMT-BC. "Distant Thunder: Drumming with Vietnam Veterans." *Music Therapy Perspectives* 13 (1995): 110-112.

softly hit the drum. Another began using her fingers. Small pitter-patters of sadness could be heard as tears began to flow from some of the children. What I found interesting was that there was no drumming patterns or rhythms heard. Each child was in his or her own sadness. There was no community of rhythm. The sadness was a very personal and singular emotion. After fifteen minutes the drumming stopped. Again I asked them to create some space through their breath.

I then handed out Remo hand drums. I wanted them to feel the drums fully in this next exercise as I asked them to focus on their joy. I wanted them to focus on those people who love them now. I asked them to think about the experiences they had that made them happy. With their eyes closed visualizing their positive emotions, I asked them to play that feeling on the drum. While anger and sadness was an emotion that they seemed to feel and play alone, joy was a feeling that was felt and played as a community. The room was transformed into drum play. As they focused on the feelings of joy, they played as one community. As I watched the faces of these children and young adults, and watched their faces light up with their smiles, small body movements and chair dancing, I saw the natural release and potentials of the drum to provide a small respite of relief for them. I saw the possibilities that a drum could be a supportive tool for releasing some of emotions and pains that these children may take with them into their adulthood.

Following the session, the counselors assured me that they would follow through in continuing this practice with the children, and process the experience with them.

As I went around the room and asked each child to share one word of how they felt, amidst their words like "Happy" and "Fun", one child looked into my eyes, paused for a moment, and simply said "More."

The drums provide a tool for transcendence. Through the constant beating of a drum, the body, mind and spirit entrain to a beat that serves as a tool for forgetting about thoughts, beliefs, and the clutter that gets in the way of living.

Nellie Hill is the president of the Drum Circle Facilitators Guild. Here she shares her moving story of the power of rhythm.

Transcendance through Drumming by Nellie Hill

Drumming in church services is not unusual. I was asked to bring my drums to do a rhythm event for small church in my area. I got to the church early to set the instruments in the pews so as the congregation arrived they would have something to play. I greeted each person as they came to their seats and invited them to play along. One woman came and sat in the back. When asked if she would like to join us she very politely said this was her deceased mother's church, she just wanted to sit and reflect during the service. I left a few instruments near her and said if the spirit moved her they were there for her, but otherwise just enjoy the music. The service was all inclusive, with members from 2 to 89 joining in the music, playing quietly for meditation, listening for the chimes and ocean sounds, being joyful for the children's section, and finally we came to the recessional. Big smiles everywhere, all ages standing and playing in celebration. I looked to the back of the church and the woman in the back had a frog rasp in her hand, joining in the celebration. We made eye contact and she gave me a big smile.

After the service she spoke to me about her experience. She said that she had no intention of playing, she just wanted to be there but as the service evolved she felt like a cloud had been lifted from her and she wanted to celebrate. She had to play! It was the first time in weeks that she had not felt the emptiness.

The healing power of the music!

CHAPTER FOUR

Drumming with a Purpose

Although it could be said that most drum circle facilitators are drumming with purpose, there are three drum circle facilitators I would like to feature in this chapter who stand out in terms of the depth and breadth of their work. They are Arthur Hull, a self-described rhythmical evangelist, whose name alone implies his purpose, Christine Stevens, who has traveled the globe in areas where healing is most needed, including the World Trade Center and Iraq, and Scott Swimmer, whose experience with his son and cancer inspired him to create a worldwide movement known as DRUMSTRONG.

Arthur Hull, touted as the father of the drum circle, has inspired tens of thousands of individuals who have attended his circles or learned drum facilitation through his training programs, including this writer. He created one of the most important books on drumming and drum circle facilitation in *Drum Circle Spirit* and most recently *Drum Circle Facilitation—Building Community Through Rhythm*. Arthur Hull created the language of drum circle facilitation and inspired thousands of facilitators to bring forth rhythm into the world through his training programs. Arthur is one of the primary voices of the drum circle movement and his programs are as inspiring as they are educational. Arthur Hull has traveled the globe teaching people how to facilitate drum circles, as well as providing drum circles to the public. He is the ambassador of rhythm and on the mission that Babatunde Olatunji shared, to put a drum into all homes.

In this essay shared by Arthur to Drum Circle Facilitator and the publisher of *Drum Circle Magazine*, Jana Broder, Arthur shares the origins of his purpose-driven path.

My First Facilitated Drum Circle by Arthur Hull

During the "Summer of Love" in the late 60s in San Francisco, I was 18 and in the military. On and off-duty weekends (I'd go) to go to San Francisco and study Afro-Cuban drumming with "Bongo Bob" and a couple of other street drummers.

My teachers told me to stay away from those "thunder drummers" who played in the Golden State Park near the Haight-Ashbury district, where all the

Arthur Hull

hippies were hanging out. What my teachers did not know was that I had been a free form rhythm expressionist from the time that I could walk.

Of course, I immediately went to "hippy hill" in the park and discovered a drum circle environment that was totally the opposite of the culturally specific drum style that I was studying with my teachers. This free-form anarchist drumming circle encouraged and fostered the free expression of rhythmical spirit. In these circles the rules of engagement were, "There are no rules." That was the opposite of the culturally specific drum circles I was involved in with my drum teachers in the city, where the rules of rhythm engagement were handed down from generation to generation and were a respectable representation of a specific traditional "rhythmaculture."

Culturally specific drummers saw the free-form anarchist drummers as ignorant and disrespectful of what they believed to be the traditional source of all rhythms. On the other hand, free-form drummers saw the culturally specific drummers like a wild horse sees a corral.

What I saw was that the essence of one was in the other; they were two sides of the same coin and what the one lacked, the other one had.

With one foot firmly planted in each, I have since straddled these two seemingly opposite drumming cultures all my life and have done what I could to fill the void in between them.

I enjoyed studying with several San Francisco drum teachers at that time and loved playing preset drum parts that when hooked up properly, could be played for hours on end without falling apart, but I did not enjoy being confined to playing one specific rhythm pattern without the freedom of adding my own spirited interpretation.

Needless to say, I spent most of that Summer of Love on Hippy Hill. But I was beginning to be frustrated by the Hippy Hill drummers' lack of understanding of the simple universal principles that foster good group playing consciousness.

The Hippy Hill drum circle offered me short flashes of free-form grace and beauty, interspaced with lots of rhythm noise and train wrecks.

On one of my last Summer of Love drumming weekends, before I was to be shipped out to a military base overseas, I found myself immersed in a powerfully magical rhythm groove. I and other players were getting frustrated as the rhythm was starting to fall apart because of a few drummers.

I understood that these few unconnected players needed only to lift their heads, look around the circle, and connect with the group pulse to help keep the rhythm magic going. So I did the unthinkable. I broke the most basic anarchist drum circle rule of etiquette: "No leaders allowed." After jumping into the middle of the circle, I marked the pulse by pounding my right fist into my up-raised left hand palm.

The unconnected players became more conscious of the pulse. The shaky rhythm solidified back to a magical rhythm groove and I returned to my seat and played. The rhythm came to a smooth finish. I was being thanked by some of the players for "saving the groove" from a certain train wreck death. Then someone yelled, "Next time use a cow bell!" My facilitation career had started.

[Reprinted with permission from Jana Broder and *Drum Circle Magazine*. www.drumcirclemagazine.com]

Christine Stevens has been a pioneer of the drumming for wellness movement, and has traveled to the farthest reaches of our planet. In this story, Christine shares her experience leading the first drum circle training program in a war zone in northern Iraq as a vehicle to heal the many wounds found in that region of the world.

Asthi Drum – Drum Salam by Christine Stevens

"You cannot imagine. Our lives in Mosul are terrible; this is like a dream for us. We have come together to share and learn".

A contagious rhythm broke out in Northern Iraq in November, 2007 calling for the spirit of hope, community building, and creativity through drumming. The five-day drum circle leadership training program hosted by Kurdistan Save the Children (KSC) (www.ksc-kcf.com) marked the first time an international relief organization used music making for conflict-resolution, therapy, and peace-making in a war-zone. Forty trainees from seven different governances attended the five-day conflict-resolution and leadership training program using drum circles called Ashti Drum (Peace drum in Kurdish) and Drum Salam (drum peace in Arabic)

The American training team was led by myself and accompanied by Constantine Alatzas and Mark Montygierd. The project came from a powerful vision of Melinda Witter, a community economic development director working in Iraq.

According to Witter "we were able to see the group from a diversity of religious and ethnic sects, unite into a bonded community. They discovered and implemented key leadership skills within the drum circle program to address elements of peace-making, youth empowerment, alternative health applications and preservation of drumming which is indigenous in the Iraq culture."

Most sessions were conducted in a local youth center that was converted from a former torture center for Saddam Hussein's Ba'athist party. At the local Children's Rehabilitation Center, children suffering from crippling disabilities were able to participate in a drum circle with medical staff, therapists, and families. My team also held a youth activity day for 45 young teenagers with Kurdistan Save the Children and a local drumming group from Darbandikhan that just recently returned from a tour in Italy.

In the course of the training program, a shared drum circle program was developed that blended Iraqi traditional musical instruments and the drum circle's energy, improvisation, creativity, and facilitation. Beginning with wellness exercises in rhythm such as breathing, body percussion, and stretching

Christine Stevens (Photograph by Constantine Alatzas)

the program then included a short drum lesson, drum circle facilitation, a melodic taxim (solo), cultural sharing of rhythms and dances and a question which was answered on the drum instead of using words. After five days, the trainees were comfortable leading the peace drum program. The final activity was a demonstration of the drum circle by the group for more than one hundred friends, family, and local politicians. The event had a surprise visit by the first lady of Iraq, Mrs. Hero Ibrahim Ahmad, wife of President Jalal Talabani.

A cumulative analysis of post-evaluation surveys showed that the forty trainees rated the training program 92% success rating, an unheard of score when bringing such divergent groups together for peace-building training. Why does drumming help promote conflict resolution and healing in war-torn areas of the world? Seven elements contribute to the success;

Drumming is accessible to all. It is an inclusive activity.

Drumming is trans-linguistic; it is a common language for cross-cultural communication, no translation needed.

Drumming allows self-expression, a key component for healing.

Drumming is hope-generating.

Drumming is an ancient cultural tradition in both Arab and Kurdish history.

Drumming together transforms relationships and builds new bonds between former enemy groups.

Drum circles allow leadership development through facilitation.

The participants shared their comments at the end of the training. "I never realized the power of people making music together. Everyone can make music! This program has been the best five days of my life. "Many were moved by the experience of working with people from many different areas of Iraq. "Travel has become too dangerous, so meeting people from Tikrit, from Kirkuk, from Sulaymaniya is a wonderful thing for us. We can share our lives and cultures". In the words of an officer for Kurdistan Save the Children, "This program is good for conflict resolution and reconstruction for our people. The drums create a new way of talking to each other. Through drum circles, we will bring more people together."

Results of the project include ongoing drum circles at Youth Activity Centers, the establishment of the first therapeutic drumming program for children's rehabilitation in Iraq, and drum circles for women's shelters, training programs, and autism therapists.

This project was generously funded by NAMM, the national association of music merchants, REMO Inc, and The Rex Foundation. More information at www.ashtidrum.com

Upon my return to the United States, I wrote this song, reflecting on the power of drumming to create peace. To watch a video of the song, visit http://www.ubdrumcircles.com/video.php

Beat for Peace

Bead by Bead. One by one
They make their prayer to the One.
Beat by beat. They play their drum
For whirling dervishes around the sun.

Step by step. We made our way
A journey here in an ancient way
The Rhythms flowed; the ancient beat
And healing and grief can now be released, oh

CHORUS:
Dance your dance on this ancient sand.
Play your drum in a foreign land
Here by the waters of Babylon
A beat for peace drums on.
A beat for peace drums on.

They drum for words; they cannot say
Holding hands as they dance and sway
Holding beads. Holding guns.
Holding prayers for everyone.

CHORUS:
La ilaha ill-A-llah
La ilaha ill-A-llah
La ilaha ill-A-llah
La ilaha ill-A-llah

I believe there is a way
That we can drop our pain and pray
Heart to heart and bead to beat
We are here to drum for peace.

Scott Swimmer's purpose-driven mission began with what is probably the most devastating news a father can hear: his son had cancer. As both Arthur and Christine have changed the lives of thousands, and the world in their own unique way, Scott is changing our world and has created a bridge between service, drumming and a cause to create funding for cancer research and survivorship support through his organization, DrumsForCures.

Due to this personally challenging experience Scott has set in motion one of the more cause-focused endeavors in the world of drum circle facilitation, DRUMSTRONG.

DRUMSTRONG
The Good that Comes from the Bad by Scott Swimmer

It's one of the hardest things imaginable to hear that your child has cancer.

Your world stops cold; freeze-framed clarity and confusion collide creating a brackish harbor where Life and Death considerations anchor. There's urgency in grinding slow-motion and irreversible decisions are made in often split second unpreparedness. You 'pray' (a lot).

In 2006, our son Mason was diagnosed with osteosarcoma, a bone cancer.

You know what you would do to give your child every opportunity to regain his health; to the depths of sacrificing your own but have no clue what that entails or how to make it manifest. I'm resourceful but not a wizard.

Arduous hours of research yielded mostly more uncertainty. The abyss of cancer information is riddled with question marks.

Ten months of treatments, seven surgeries and countless nerve-racking hours awaiting results later we're on the other side of diagnosis.

Mason's leg and life were saved through a brilliant surgical and caring staff and amazing support from our integrative health team. Mason is whole again. He now thrives with a notch in his belt and a hitch in his gait. 'Lucky' and grateful; you bet!

During the many phases of this adventure, Mason has met some very impressive people – young and old – many who have boldly walked away from their cancer experience and some who haven't. All have inspired us.

My mother, father, brother, and myself have survived our own personal challenges with cancer as well. My wife, Carola, younger son Tobias and friends are all too familiar with the impact this has on life.

How could we make this ominous environment better or at least easier to deal with for the next family?

Love, supportive understanding, humor and music helped soften some of the more stress-filled periods.

I love music. Rhythm touches everybody: we've all got a heartbeat.

My passion in life to help others has been amplified and fortified by this crazy rollercoaster world of cancer.

Through the ups and downs, I was inspired to create an organization called DRUMSTRONG.

DRUMSTRONG manifest as a natural expression of our family's desire to be a vibrant part of beating cancer. Since rhythm is universal we decided that an event centered around the art and fun of hands-on drumming would be a great way to bring people together.

Our mission is to provide a vehicle for health entities and cancer societies to show communities the resources at hand to assist in directing and easing cancer concerns.

Facilitating the 'introduction' and advancement of important organizations supporting those dealing with cancer, promoting early detection and working towards cures is our goal. My family is convinced that there have to be better methods to assist those affected by cancer including early detection/diagnosis, alternative and/or less brutal treatments, more personalized, problem-specific rehab practices, age-specific social and family support and early cancer education through the school systems.

We also believe that research, education, and support for survivors needs to be fortified through community and government efforts.

And what's easier for communities to express themselves in unison than banging on something together?

Our concept is simple, our non-profit, DrumsForCures, Inc. produces DRUMSTRONG, the multicultural, musical, charity events showcasing available resources that support people with cancer and those who love them.

We promote cancer health, education, research and survivorship support through collaborative efforts and through rhythm, Globally!

Drums are the perfect communicator. Rhythm welcomes and embraces all who participate. Music truly engages all ages, wages and stages of health... We invite celebrity talent and gather folks to rhythm (drumming for crazy long periods of time in some of our Drum Circles), focusing on individual and community health; working for cancer solutions.

With the assistance of the most amazing Drum Circle Facilitators and good-hearted folks around the world, DRUMSTRONG events are coordinated to raise awareness and funds for local cancer initiatives wherever they are. Local rhythm communities organize a time and place to drum, encourage participation from local cancer health initiative(s), businesses, schools, religious institutions, etc., and raise 'per hour' drumming sponsorship (or simply take donations) for the cause. We webcast our events so that we can all drum together in efforts to BEAT cancer.

As individuals or as a 'Team' we are making a sound impact on the health of our communities.

visit www.drumstrong.org

What is DRUMSTRONG?

DRUMSTRONG™ is an annual, multicultural, musical charity event produced by DrumsForCures, Inc. a 501 (c)(3) non-profit charity organization, where medical, integrative and holistic health entities and specific cancer societies display their missions and methods showcasing the resources available to address cancer concerns.

It is a gathering to rhythm.

We are employing the simple principles of rhythm to spark communication and attract attention by inviting local and celebrity artists to play with all assembled; drumming non-stop for 24+ hours. Our events are webcast so that drum circles around the world can play together simultaneously expressing unified support and sharing their cancer resources with all.

We are registered with the Guinness World Records for the planet's longest continuous rhythm drum•a•thon.

The music attracts many people to an event where questions about health (particularly cancer) can be addressed. Cancer education and familiarizing oneself to the available tools and resources to deal with the disease simply puts the odds in ones favor; knowing one's adversary is the classic model for survival. People receive guidance from the exhibitors and acquaint themselves with some of the resources that help address cancer concerns.

DrumsForCures encourages cancer awareness at home, in schools and throughout communities. We promote cancer support, education and research. All funds raised are donated to cancer initiatives globally.

We are also organizing a network of percussionists to bring rhythm into children's hospitals and clinics for the unifying, healing and entertainment values. We know that it works on many levels.

The Mission that is DRUMSTRONG

DRUMSTRONG 'Creed' "Drum to rekindle the fire of survivorship in you. Drum in honor of or in memory of or just out of the goodness of your hearts.

Drum with hopes of opening the eyes and hearts of more people to amplify efforts to find cures.

Drum to respect and represent all the fighters and survivors who share this history."

We've created an all-inclusive, collaborative program that allows people of all ages, wages and stages of health to contribute to and gain a wealth of health knowledge, fortification and satisfaction from.

Our family-friendly events take place globally and we embrace ALL cancer initiatives.

As unique as every DRUMSTRONG event is from city to city and country to country, a common thread prevails. DRUMSTRONG embraces the individual spirit of giving and channels the power of community efforts. Young people share the joy of working (and playing) for the betterment together with seasoned philanthropists.

Rhythm is our delivery system. We're using rhythm to help people find focus and solid support in the unsettling world of wayward cells.

It's personal. It's your rhythm, your cause. We encourage people to drum in honor of or in memory of someone, just for the goodness of it, and/or to fortify themselves. People will raise funds for the cancer initiative of their choice. The DRUMSTRONG experience impacts individuals in an inimitable way and will be interpreted and seasoned by each participant. We invite everyone to express themselves rhythmically, regardless of experience and focus on BEATing cancer.

You don't have to have rhythm to participate, just a heartbeat.

Visit www.drumstrong.org or write to scott@drumstrong.org for information on how you can join in.

CHAPTER FIVE

Drum Lessons

Here are essays from some prominent drum circle facilitators and researchers on lessons learned and shared, as well as an exploration into the deeper levels of drumming and drum circle facilitation.

Cameron Tummel is globally renowned as a masterful facilitator of rhythm and djembe specialist whose career spans more than twenty years and more than a half million participants.

Cataclysms and Compensation by Cameron Tummel

The date is August 12, 2001. I'm sitting here pondering the catastrophic reports from the terrorist destruction of the World Trade Center's Twin Towers, the plane crash into the Pentagon, and the crash of another plane that was also intended to be used as a missile full of civilians and highly combustible fuel, that occurred yesterday – thousands of people dead and injured, physically and spiritually; unfathomable loss, grief, anger, sadness and pain.

I just spent the last three weeks facilitating numerous drum circles at colleges and universities up and down the east coast, with thousands of participants. The difference between the elation of all that music making and the grief of yesterday's terrorist strike is almost beyond comprehension.

Facilitating a successful rhythm circle has nothing to do with fancy clothes, nor high wattage amplification, nor the sequences you've facilitated a thousand times before. It has nothing to do with who knows your name, nor who remembers it. It makes no difference whether you arrive in a pair of sandals, or a limousine. And it certainly has nothing to do with money.

When I do what I am supposedly hired to do, the results go way beyond all of that. The evaluation of the "work" is: did you serve the circle to the very best of your abilities, did you facilitate that group of people to their highest level of rhythmical ability, and most of all, did you facilitate the spirit?

Spirit doesn't come in dollars, it comes in smiles, and it comes in laughs, and in all the other signs of joy and happiness that shine from people when its there. Spirit gives people the confidence to try new things, and to take risks. It can be evidenced by the way people who had hardly met one another can feel connected, and empathetic, and feel supported by one another. Spirit is that wonderful stuff which makes us all feel so good when we drum together.

If I have "done my job," and if the event was "successful," the participants will feel joyful, and supported by each other, and happy, after only two hours together.

Most of all of that has very little to do with me, and much more to do with the experience we all go through together, and the contributions we all make to the music. I am only one of the points, one of the many dots, of which the circle is composed.

Nonetheless, I have to be the dot who takes responsibility for it all. I have to be willing to step into the center of the group, make an evaluation, a decision, and do whatever I can to help it succeed, whenever it needs it, no matter how chaotic it may get, and no matter how many people may be watching me potentially fall flat on my face. I guess that is the responsibility for which I receive my compensation. And when I think of the many forms of compensation I receive, I value money a lot less than some of the other pay. Call it karma, call it luck, call it destiny, or call it whatever you want to, but sometimes I seem to be surrounded by an incredible sequence of fortuitous occurrences. For example, consider the events of the last forty-eight hours.

Two days ago, having just completed my "work" at several different universities, with several thousand young adults, and having served the circles as well as I could, I was pulled over by a highway patrol. Caught red handed going eighty miles per hour, with an out of state rental car, out of state driver's license, dark glasses, long hair, and a highly suspicious explanation for the empty rental van. Of all the, ahem, coincidences, the cop turns out to be a fellow drummer, and I am released without punishment, although having confessed to being completely guilty of my offense, which the officer had personally witnessed.

Later that same evening, while leaving Newark, I inadvertently got into a situation where the only difference between my leaving Newark, or possibly staying the night and catching another flight the following day, came down to the difference between whether it rained for another fifteen minutes or so. I was stuck on a plane for more than two hours, while the Newark airport was temporarily shut down, waiting to see whether or not I would be able to leave. The most logical of all alternative flights the following day would have been the non-stop flight from Newark to San Francisco, United flight number 93, because it would have been the one first thing in the morning, and I really needed to get home. There were plenty of seats available on that flight, so it seems nearly certain that is what would have happened, if the rain had continued. But it stopped raining, so we flew off, so I was not on any of the flights that were used as missiles to destroy the tallest buildings in the world, attack the Pentagon, or disintegrate in a crash landing. So consequently my personal atoms and molecules were not part of the monstrous cataclysms in the heart of New York City, Washington D.C, nor over the plains of Pennsylvania.

Fifteen minutes of rain...

Gee, that was pretty lucky, don't you think?

As I lie awake in bed at night and contemplate just how close I was to being on that plane, I will wonder, and pray, as to the how and why of what it is that I do, and the ways in which I am rewarded for the "job" of making people feel happy, and together, and whole.

What is it I really get paid for, and how is it I really receive my compensation?

Difficult to say for sure, but I do believe one thing: it's not about the money.

In this essay, Jim Anderson shares some of his awareness of drumming from the perspective of a family therapist.

Drumming at the Edge of Consciousness —
Qualities of Drumming by Jim Anderson

Have you ever noticed what a great drumbeat does to people? It sucks them in both physically and emotionally. A great song with a great drumbeat is like anti-anxiety medication. It hits us on multiple levels. The patterned repetition of rhythm creates subtle trance induction and the sound texture serves as a thought disruption from our normal verbal world of worlds. And while listening is powerful, it is the playing of the drums that is most inspirational.

Drumming occurs in the "now of life". The here and now experience of playing drums offers all of us new rivers to journey down, new friends to meet and new alternative channels for growth and healing. We all have our own unique rhythms in life. We are all entrained to universal rhythms well beyond our scope of comprehension. Rhythmic entrainment is about finding how our own unique rhythms can work hand in hand with those around us. It takes less energy to pulse with the universe than it does to fight it and pulse against it. Aspiration to living in the "now of life", ultimately connects us to our deepest rhythms, in which we feel most energized and alive. See the rhythm of life as a river to flow down. Listen to the song of the universe and find your own groove – that is your path!

Linear time is the playground in which rhythms are born. The deeper one journeys into their own unique world of rhythm, the greater chance that actual time perception will be altered. The feeling of playing for 10 minutes, to find out later that it was actually 45 minutes can be absolutely mind bending. Many drummers I have spoken to about this phenomenon describe it both as confusing and as a transformational experience. That is because the time shifting that takes place when one loses contact with normal time based consciousness is like an "ah-ha" experience in nature, mainly because people don't often experience time distortions in the waking state. The trick is to turn off the conscious mind and give the unconscious a voice.

Playing drums is an active experience, a way we can enjoy the benefits of that feeling of timelessness. The unconscious and creative part of the mind is that part that is capable of tapping into past positive resources and reorganizing them into a new context for growth. The true magic of rhythmic release is found in the effortlessness in which our creativity unconsciously solves our problems.

Drumming facilitates a release of conscious control, inhibitions, and self-judgmental attitudes and builds an internal connection one feels as this process of confusion organizes creative forces at different levels. Thoughts and feelings recorded verbally after a deep jam session almost always involve a report of euphoria, joy and happiness. Insights are too numerous to list. Yet we all feel trapped at times by society, situations and our own internal set of limitations. We all need a way out for a moment. We all need a little break from reality sometimes.

Drumming can also be understood as a time machine in which pattern shifting can transform our thoughts, feelings, and perceptions. When thought takes over, our minds can run high with fear and anxiety. We all need a break from our own limited conscious sets of thought. Rhythm is the great equalizer, capable of confusing the conscious mind. The non-verbal experience of drumming is even more powerful, engaging the physiology and clearing the mind of its verbal chaos. Think of rhythm as water, flowing back and forth – seeking its own level.

Each person has their own individual theme rhythms. Tapping your deepest theme rhythms will yield the greatest internal awareness. It is in this world of rhythm that new levels of potential will begin to open up. Groove provides the platform where the unconscious is no longer boxed in by conscious limitations. New ideas are revealed when we least expect them!

A break from reality – it's a feeling and an experience we all long for. Drumming is the great conscious mind stop. Drumming gives us a time out from normal everyday life, and it's this pattern interruption of conscious thought that brings us back to a mental state of simply "being". Playing rhythms from the deepest place possible opens states of altered consciousness. It's at those levels we all become much more receptive to a heightened sense of internal awareness, deep sense of relaxation and the ability to tap into meaningful messages from our unconscious.

As rhythm confuses the logical conscious mind, it also provides the conscious mind a break from reality. It is in these moments of flow state that we are able to feel life at a higher level. The pattern interruption of rhythm and the feeling of timelessness likewise provides respite to the logical mind, and a chance to regroup. In these moments, rhythmic confusion is the clear path to greater conscious certainty.

Drumming is a spiritual healing and cleansing process. This is why it is so natural for people to entrain and "get lost in the groove". Maybe we all need to get lost in our own groove. I know for myself that drumming has become my corner of freedom and a timeless escape, if even just for a moment, into a deeper connection to those things which seem most relevant to me.

I think this is what Carl Jung was referring to when he wrote, "True productivity is a spring that can never be stopped up....Creative power is mightier than its possessor." Get into the groove, and the groove will get into you. The rhythmic confusion it creates is your path. The trace state experience is located in the depth of the patterned repetition. It jams the cognitive feedback mechanism with a feeling that cannot be understood as words on a page. It is that rhythm which will be your guide. In its purest state, drumming connects us back to our own humanity, love and connection to each other and all that is truly good.

In this essay, Jim Greiner shares his experience with the power of drum when there is intention.

Renewing Intentional Rhythms by Jim Greiner

"I wanted to stop drumming several times during the session, but each time I said to myself, "No don't stop yet; I'm not ready to stop. I'll know when I'm ready, then I'll stop. Each time I told myself that, I let go of thinking about drumming and started vocalizing my rhythm like you suggested. Before I knew it, I was completely engrossed in my drumming again."

"Why did you want to stop?", I asked.

Angela thought for a moment, then her eyes opened wide, reflecting what was clearly a huge "Aha!" moment, "Wow!", she exclaimed, "I just realized that I wanted to stop because I was afraid that I would get off the rhythm!" Angela's realization goes right to the core, and the powerful simplicity, of one of my basic Rhythm Life Lessons:

Rhythm Life Lesson: Focus on our Intentional Rhythms, what we want to be doing, not on what we are afraid of doing. When we want to change something in our lives that we do not want to repeat, we replace it with something that we'd rather be doing, and then repeat that new action (or thought) until it becomes a settled.

Life Rhythm. As Angela discovered, fear of failure can prevent us from doing simple, practical things to change our self-inhibiting perceptions. Fear is the anxious agitation caused by the awareness of danger. As such, it is a useful survival mechanism. Fear of failure, however, is far too-often an exaggerated emotion that keeps us from doing things that we are perfectly capable of doing.

Rhythm Life Skill: Internalizing Intentional Life Rhythms One of the most profound realizations I had during my two years of drumming in Africa was that many of the people with whom I played were vocalizing their rhythms as

Jim Greiner

they played. It occurred to me that by vocalizing their rhythms, they were internalizing them. This rhythmic concept is found in many cultures around the world. I just call it "Say & Play". By saying the pattern, we are internalizing it, and not analyzing or judging our playing. In practical drumming terms, when we are afraid of making "mistakes" (doing something that does not serve the Groove), we will tend to make those "mistakes" because we are reinforcing that fear. When we vocalize what we want to play, then we are focusing only on what we want to play. On a personal level, letting go of fear is one of the hardest things we ever do, but it is also one of the most rewarding experiences we can have. In fact, every time we replace a negative self-view with a positive one, we are reinforcing, in a practical, down-to-earth way, our innate power to change other negative areas of our lives. I cannot count the number of times people in my corporate drumming programs have said, "I never thought I had any rhythm, and that I would embarrass myself by even trying to play music! So, what else in life have I been preventing myself from doing simply because I was afraid of trying!" A longtime private drumming student of mine named Stan once summed this up in beautiful simplicity when he declared exuberantly, after an adrenline-pumping 30 minutes of drumming together, "One of the most important things I've learned with you, even more important than how to drum, is that letting go of the fear of making mistakes when drumming, has made me let go of the fear of life!"

Bashoowee!

"BASHOOWEE!"My friend and yoga instructor, Chara Rodriguera, yelled it together. "BASHOOWEE!"

Bashoowee is a word I created one day when I decided that there was no word to describe the effusive feeling of being totally spontaneous and trusting in the moment.

Chara and I came up with an idea. It was a very scary idea. At first it seemed just too ridiculous to think about, but with our courage in our hands we decided to create the first Bashoowee Drumming and Yoga workshop.

Our goal was to create a workshop using drumming and yoga that was not planned at all. The presupposition was that if we were to do this workshop, we would absolutely have to be in the moment, and not have any idea what was going to happen, moment to moment. We would have to be in spirit. I was comfortable running an unplanned workshop on my own, but the idea of co-facilitating a workshop that was totally unplanned scared the bajeezus out of both of us. Therefore, we knew we had to do it.

The first Bashoowee program was one hour. The question was whether tell to the audience that this program was unplanned, and we really had no idea what we would be doing. When we did, everyone looked as dumbfounded as we felt.

As two presenters, we did a sort of facilitation dance in which we would watch the energy and feel when it was our turn to go. We had to trust ourselves and be completely present, and be willing not to be perfect. There was another level to the Bashoowee workshop, in that Chara and I agreed that we needed to practice not allowing our mind to move ahead of itself out of fear. It was another level of being present. Every time my mind began planning the next piece; I would consciously let that go, breathe and come back to the moment.

During the workshop either I or Chara would talk, facilitate, guide or drum and the other facilitator would become a participant of the program in that moment. We had to practice the psychological practice of bifocal vision, in which we were both participating in the program as a participant and watching it from the perspective of facilitator, as well. We had to be comfortable with the silence, and the moments when there was no impulse to do anything, that experience was the hardest. In one moment I was drumming and Chara was drumming with the participants. In the next moment Chara would be guiding them and I would follow her instructions. It was a success, and I realized that there was much to be learned from not planning a workshop. It did feel as if we were guided by spirit. I realized then that I should plan less. The mind gets very secure when everything is planned, and feels just the opposite when there is no road map. With no set course, you can live in the moment.

After our successful one-hour workshop, we decided to jump off the security cliff and create a three-hour Bashoowee workshop. We simply showed up to offer our Bashoowee program. As with the first it went smoothly. I realized after three hours of trusting that there is grace in trusting the moment.

When my nephew, Jonathan, was eight years old, he inspired me one day when without any apparent reason, he began running, flailing his hands in the air, and laughing, for no apparent reason, except his need to express a certain spontaneous joy in that moment. As I watched him, I thought to myself, there is something about this young child that we as adults need to remember. In many ways, Jonathan was expressing "Bashoowee" and I wrote a poem to express that aspect of self that I believe many of us lose, and need to relearn, when we become adults:

Through the Eyes of a Child (c) 1990

As children we all were innocent,
So spontaneous and free.
But we all learned how to grow up,
And forget the child's key.

We forgot the child's wisdom,
And learned to mistrust and feel lost.
Where can we find the love?
Doesn't anyone know the cost?

The freedom, love and the trust,
They all lie within our hearts.
We've forgotten they are within us,
Though we've had them from the start.

We all are born with this trust,
Some wonder and some glee.
We all do enter this world,
So fearless and so free.

But we hide the child within,
Afraid of the love that it has.
How much better this world would be,
If that child within would just last.

We must remember some lessons forgotten,
And forget some that we've learned.
We'd return to the state of the child,
And be granted a key that we've earned.

I believe the best way to play the drum is to allow ourselves to be in the moment. As you drum with others in a drum circle you really can't plan the moment. In many ways it is about letting go of the need to control. It is this state of being in the moment that I believe helps relieve an individual's stress, as has been reported by so many through drumming. It requires being able to listen and be aware of what is happening around you. When I watch drummers drumming in their drum circles I see the trust, I see the spontaneity, I see the play. I see Bashoowee!

In this essay, Jim Greiner continues sharing on how to use drums to reinforce positive states of mind.

Drumming to Reinforce Positive Life Rhythms by Jim Greiner

Playing drums with a focus on integrating positive rhythms relieves stress, increases vitality and puts us in the transcendent state of clarity and heightened awareness that athletes call the Zone. This is true whether we are playing by ourselves or with a group of people, and whether playing soft, tranquil rhythms or fast and vigorous rhythms, In fact, drumming is very much like athletics, Yoga and martial arts in its wellness-enhancing power: In each of these activities, we practice relaxed and focused repetitive movements until they become effortless, powerful and intuitive. In drumming, these movements result in patterns of sounds, that is... rhythmic music. These repetitive movements, reinforced by the pleasure of making music, give us a self-sustaining musical feedback experience. This releases our conscious minds from the habits of analyzing and judging our actions and thoughts – to get out of our heads and into our bodies, and to be fully "in the moment". Drumming with this intention, since it is such a physical activity, is also an enormously powerful vehicle to reinforce very productive physical habits. For example, I realized long ago during the hours-long drumming sessions in which I participated during two years in Africa, that I play music much more effectively when I'm relaxed and breathing efficiently. So, I've created a series of rhythm-based relaxing and breathing patterns that can be effortlessly woven into each stage of playing percussion instruments by anyone – from absolute beginners, to very experienced musicians. In this way, as we play rhythm instruments, these relaxing and breathing patterns are integrated into our muscle and nerve memories, and become an innate part of our daily Life Rhythms. These positive Life Rhythms then carry over into all aspects of our lives... even, and especially, when we are stressed!

Our Bodies Are Our Instruments.

Drumming is also a great way to simply move our bodies. Our bodies love to move! When we use our bodies naturally (relaxing, breathing in effortless patterns, using efficient, organic movements, etc.) we are rewarded with increased stamina, strength, flexibility and the powerful sense of being capable that serves us in every part of our lives. Drumming by ourselves allows us to go deeply into our true natures by eliminating mental distractions, physical inhibitions and societal constraints. Drumming with others is a universally time- honored way to connect and to communicate with other people... to build positive community rhythms! And, drumming is just great fun – we call it "playing music" for a reason – drumming is an enormously playful way to celebrate the pure joy of being alive! Drumming is simply one of life's many great "highs"!

In this poignant essay, Jane Bentley PhD, shares her awareness of the deeper levels of drum circle facilitation.

Tuning In – The Social Power of the Drum by Jane Bentley

I began my study with a vague feeling that there was 'something else' going on in gatherings such as facilitated drum circles. Rather than being a drum lesson or rehearsal, people were encouraged to create their own rhythm patterns, and most notably, you didn't already have to be a drummer to participate. Because people with little musical experience could become involved so quickly, this meant that facilitated drumming was increasingly being incorporated in wider contexts such as health settings. But what was really going on? Facilitators were very clear that they weren't offering a 'drumming lesson' at these events, but if not, then what were people actually learning?

To begin with, I thought that what was unique was that drum circles were explicitly accessible to people who didn't feel musical. At the time, many other recreational music opportunities gave the impression that you already needed to have some mysterious musical 'talent' to participate, such as joining an established choir or band. In addition, there was very little prior research in this area, as drum circles don't fit entirely within the fields of music education, performance, or therapy, but instead have the potential to crossover between all three.

Accordingly, I picked a qualitative research method known as grounded theory, which is particularly suitable for studying areas about which little is already known. The basic premise is that you start gathering data (for example, through interviewing and observation), and then develop a theory based on what you find, rather than the more stereotypical method of formulating a theory, and then conducting experiments to prove or disprove it. Alternatively, if you begin with peoples' experience about a subject, the resulting theory should hopefully bear a close relationship to 'what is really going on', rather than being imposed from above by the researcher. On the other hand, this means, that as a researcher, you have to be prepared to have your own ideas challenged and changed by the things that you find.

And this is what happened. What became rapidly apparent was that the purpose of a drum circle was not solely to include beginners. If you imagine a hospital or workplace setting, for example, there will definitely be people present who have never drummed before, but it's also equally likely that there will be those who have a drum set at home, or who played when they were younger. Rather than being the equivalent of a beginners' workshop, there is always variety of abilities and experiences present, and the more musically experienced play just as full a part as the beginners.

So it wasn't just 'drumming 101' after all – but then there was still something that marked this form of music making as different. There was definitely a developmental process at work – people still got better at playing together even though they weren't explicitly instructed in technique. But what was it?

After much talking to people, head-scratching, and analysis, what finally emerged was that when we improvise in rhythm together (particularly in a facilitated drum circle), we are engaged in a process of learning how to 'tune in' to one another. Rather than learning fancier patterns or faster licks, we are creating better music through learning how to listen better; how to leave space for others; how to create rhythm dialogue, and how to put our rhythms 'out there' whilst allowing others to do the same. Or as Arthur says:

"The quality of the music that is being made is not based on the level of rhythmical expertise of the participants; but, instead, the quality of the music being made is based on the quality of the relationship that is being created."

Ideally, the facilitator works to nudge this process along and enable participants to find a maximum sense of agency, or self-expression, combined with a deep mutual, communal interaction. Rather than seeing these things as polar opposites (independence versus interdependence), both can be experienced at the same time. You are creating your own rhythm, while at the same time relating it to the bigger sound of the group and to the rhythms of those around you. John Fitzgerald, head of recreational music at Remo, remembers an event where this was perfectly demonstrated:

"There was about eight to 12 people – [he names a couple of well-known professional drummers] and then some people that had less experience, and then some people who had very little; and we made some of the best music I've ever made, and sustained that sensibility of pure music for a very long period of time – long sections of very beautiful responsive playing. That was as diverse a group of skills as I've ever seen in one place, and it was the person that just played 'tink... tink... tink' who played the perfect thing in that context and made it that much more beautiful."

In John's example, the musical magic was not created by everyone being a fabulous drummer, but rather by their ability to tune in – to take their own contributions and create something bigger than themselves by working together. And that's what the study was ultimately about: tuning in – how it is nurtured during a process such as a drum circle, and what it means for us as participants.

In a well-facilitated drum circle, participants are guided by a facilitator towards increasing degrees of tuning in, or awareness regarding their own playing, the contributions of other group members, and the sound of the group as a whole. Drummers are encouraged to create rhythmic dialogue with one another, by leaving spaces in their rhythm patterns, and building a musical relationship with the spaces left by other people. Not only does this lead to 'better' sounding music, but it also becomes more satisfying to the players as they begin to hear themselves in dynamic relationship to the whole group sound. In a fully tuned-in group, this dialogue can become extended even further. When players are listening to and responding to everyone else in the group, a change in one person's rhythm can have a cascade effect on the whole group, who suddenly and spontaneously find the music taking on a whole new direction. The music making then becomes the human equivalent of a flock of birds or a shoal of fish – appearing to be a unified yet changing whole that dips and swoops as one, yet composed of many individuals with no apparent leader, and no pre-defined plan.

What this all means is that as well as the beneficial physical, emotional, and spiritual effects that drumming can offer (and which are no doubt covered by the rest of this book), there are also profound social implications which may occur as we drum together. So far, this is something that has been given very little attention in research literature. At the end of the recently published Oxford Handbook of Music Psychology, Professors Susan Hallam, Ian Cross, and Michael Thaut [1] note that the concept of music as communication and interaction is as yet a nascent one. They acknowledge that "exploration of capacities that are likely to be central to interactive musicality, such as that for entrainment [...] is in its infancy, and questions of how such capacities relate to broader human capacities for complex social communicative interaction have barely been addressed".

However, pointers towards this social and communicative potential can be found – if you cast the net wide enough. For example, John Blacking [2, 3], in his studies of the music of the Venda people of South Africa, noted the relational aspects embodied within the music, and proposed that the meaning of dialoguing drum patterns did not reside in their existence as sound objects, but lay instead in the interrelationship between the players. In his observations of the Venda national dance, Tshikona, he noted that it "generates the highest degree of individuality in the largest possible community of individuals" [2]. Sound familiar?

If you travel back even further in time – to the first music that we ever made, there may be more than a few clues to the potential of music in the social sphere. The field of evolutionary musicology has taken great leaps since the cognitive scientist Stephen Pinker famously dismissed the role of music in evolution as 'auditory cheescake" – pleasant, but ultimately useless. This provoked a robust "Oh no it's not!" response from musicologists, along with a raft of theories regarding the potential adaptive functions of music. Among these, the theories of Ian Cross [4-6] stand out as particularly relevant to the form of musical interaction found in drum circles today. He suggests that group-affirming activities such as entrainment (playing together in time), cooperation, and social bonding occur when we make music. These are complemented by a property of music he terms floating intentionality, meaning that each participant can simultaneously hold a different interpretation of a musical act. For example, while drumming, individuals might feel elated, relaxed, or work out their frustrations in the same moment. Together, these make music an ideal medium for communicative interaction in situations of social uncertainty. Making music thus offers a setting which is likely to encourage social bonding and allows for a group to explore cooperative interaction: while minimising the risk that these explorations might provoke conflict [5].

A clear example of this today would be the corporate drumming icebreaker, designed to relax, integrate, and focus participants for the day's activities. From my thesis, drumming together appeared to act as a kind of 'behavioural rehearsal', in which participants could engage in or practice cooperative, communicative, and interactive behaviours without feeling the potential pressures of having a negotiation or conversation. In my practical work as a drum circle facilitator in mental health settings, I have been able to witness these effects repeatedly – and two examples in particular stand out. One is a regular weekly community mental health drumming group, run in collaboration with occupational therapy services, which over the past three years has enabled members to overcome shyness and anxiety to form meaningful, lasting relationships with one another, and yet remain open and welcoming to new members at different stages in their mental health journey. At its simplest, drumming together is simpler than having to talk to one another, but also makes it easier to do so once the drumming stops.

At the other end of the scale, I have been working regularly in forensic psychiatry with men classed as the most violent and dangerous in the country, many of whom have profound difficulties in communication and relating to others.

Yet over the weeks we have been drumming together, it has rarely been chaotic, or simply about getting rid of aggression – instead the group seems to have relished the cooperative nature of drumming together, the chance to succeed at something, and even the more interactive aspect. I'll never forget the expression of one man who I found extremely scary when I would meet him outside the drumming room – the first time we did a simple 'me, you' exercise on the drums, his face beamed as radiantly as a toddler's, and he requested it every single week after that. Perhaps it reached the child in him that never experienced that kind of interaction because of neglectful parenting – yet such activities form the most basic building blocks of communication and understanding of others [7].

So it's activities like these which I'd like to propose as the social healing power of the drum – drumming that releases our potential to act and interact productively with others, whether that's in the boardroom, the school, or the maximum-security hospital. Drumming that nurtures our capacity to 'tune in' – to increase our awareness from our own actions, to those of others, and to relate these to one another. The bottom line? Drumming together helps us relate to each other. We live in a world of increasing individualism, loneliness and isolation, where we worry about the influence of screen-mediated activity on ourselves and our children. Societies such as ours boast alarming rates of mental ill health, particularly depression. Perhaps one day, in the way that we engage in sports to exercise our physical bodies, drumming may yet be recognised as a form of 'social exercise', where we can nurture our capacities towards reconnecting with each other again.

Dave Holland is a nationally recognized drum circle facilitator and teaching artist who brings a spirit of creativity, interaction and fun to every rhythm event he leads. He has presented at the International Percussive Arts Society Convention, the International Orff Schulwerk conference and numerous music education conferences across the country. Dave is the author of *Drumagination, A Rhythmic Playbook for Music Teachers, Music Therapists and Drum Circle Facilitators.*

Create Some Rhythm, Share Some Magic by Dave Holland

For me, the most fascinating aspect of interactive drumming is in the hidden possibilities that lie within simple acts of sharing. When we capture a moment of inspiration and then share it with others, we never know where it will lead or whose life might be changed along the way! This story is one such example of how a simple act of sharing lead to rhythmic transformation...

It was a summer night in Hawaii during a Village Music Circles Playshop run by Arthur Hull. Drum circle facilitators, music teachers and rhythm enthusiasts from around the world were all gathered in a late night drum circle. One by one, we all took turns facilitating the circle. What anyone, including myself, did inside the circle that night is a long faded memory, except for one fellow facilitator, John Hayden. John stood in the center of the circle holding an ordinary drum stick high in the air and announcing that it was magic; that any where he pointed, you could hear a magical sound. With the poise of a magician, John began to wave the stick in different directions as we all delighted in

Dave Holland

helping to create magical combinations of improvised sound! Within seconds John had created instant interaction, and a new opportunity for anyone, anywhere to make magic from the center of the circle.

Months later, when I started compiling activities for a book I was writing, I decided to include John's activity in it and title it "Magic Wand". A year or so after the book was published, Judy Guthrie, a music teacher on the Caribbean island of Anguilla posted a note on the drum circle list (drumcircles@yahoo-groups.com) about an experience she had with the "Magic Wand" activity and a particular kindergartener who often had a difficult time with many activities in class. Here's a portion of Judy's post:

"When I gave my student the wand, it was as though some kind of magic passed onto him too. He took his place in the middle of the circle, straightened up very seriously, and with great concentration and a flourish, pointed the wand at various children to create sound. His teacher was amazed and called to other teachers to come and see his heartwarming involvement. The children applauded him afterwards. He was beaming!"

Those young music students in Anguilla will unlikely never meet my friend John, but his creativity sparked a chain of sharing that reached across the miles and helped to bring interaction to their class – and a new sense of confidence to one of their classmates!

As we continue to drum, sing and dance in circles around the world, let's keep our eyes open for those moments of inspiration that we can then pass onto others. After all, as a young kindergartener in Anguilla has reminded us, we all have the capacity to create magic through the power of the drum, rhythm instrument, or even a simple stick!

CHAPTER SIX

Training Programs

Since the first *Healing Power of the Drum* was published in 2000, a number of training programs have emerged focusing on teaching a skillset for facilitating drum circles using various methodologies. Some of these programs include HealthRHYTHMS, a protocol created by Dr. Barry Bittman and Remo based on Dr. Bittman's research, and used for stress reduction, adolescents, and boosting the immune system and DRUMBEAT a program specifically for indigenous people created by Simon Faulkner in Australia. Other training programs include "Therapeutic Drumming Foundation" founded by Barry Wakefield, "Village Music Playshops" developed by Arthur Hull, "Rhythm Planet Workshop", "Drumagination", "The Healing Power of the Drum Training Program", "Music Therapy Drumming" created by Bill Matney, MT-BC and "Developmental Community Music" developed by Kalani, MT-BC.

Village Music Playshops

Having offered his training programs to over 23 countries worldwide, Arthur Hull's Village Music Circles rhythm event facilitation approach has been in existence since 1991, and, therefore, was the first drum circle facilitation training program available. Arthur's playshops are the gold standard of training programs. It offers impactful beginning and advanced facilitation skills training for individuals interested in working with many different varieties of groups. Their basic three-day facilitation skills programs provide participants with the confidence, tools and inspiration to facilitate a rhythm-based event. Their intensive programs held annually in Hawaii are a weeklong trainings which provide extensive practical experience in a safe environment to facilitators of all levels. The Village Music Circles 10 day Mentorship / Leadership training in Hawaii overlaps the basic Hawaii training, providing the beginning students with some of the most experienced facilitators in the world as models. The VMC advanced trainings provide an opportunity for intermediate and advanced facilitators to receive special attention and instruction at their own level of development.

The VMC Rhythmical Alchemy Playshops provides 20 hours of rhythm games in 3 days. (www.drumcircle.com/playshops).

HealthRHYTHMS

One of the first programs to focus on health and wellness was Health-RHYTHMS. The Health Rhythms Division of Remo Inc. is their music therapy and wellness division. They develop instruments, programs, and training and support research into the use of drumming as an effective tool for promoting and maintaining health and well-being. At the forefront of this division's activities is their HealthRHYTHMS® Group Empowerment Drumming program.

The Protocols developed through the research of Barry Bittman, MD and his team (HealthRHYTHMS Protocol and HealthRHYTHMS Adolescent Protocol) were able to strengthen the immune system, reduce stress (in fact reversing the effects of stress on 19 of 46 genes that were studied), improve mood states, and decrease instrumental anger in at-risk adolescents, among other benefits.

At the conclusion of the study of the immune system effects, Christine K. Stevens, Karl Bruhn and Dr. Barry Bittman, worked together to develop the training program to teach professionals how to facilitate the Health-RHYTHMS Protocol (or HealthRHYTHMS Group Empowerment Drumming). This training is taught by the principal researchers on the studies which support the program, Christine Bittman and Dr. Stevens (www. remo.com/health). In 2009, following the publication of the outcome-based research project conducted with at-risk youth in a residential setting, a new training program was launched to teach facilitation of the resulting Health-RHYTHMS Adolescent Protocol. This training is taught by members of the Adolescent Protocol research team, HealthRHYTHMS Endorsed Facilitators Margaret Sowry and Larry Dickson.

Here are brief summaries of Bittman's research using the Health-RHYTHMS protocol:

In 2001, Bittman did his first research study demonstrating that using the HealthRHYTHMS Protocol, there was a statistically significant increase in participants' Natural Killer (NK) cell activity and Lymphokine cells, all which relate to the body's immune system. These NK cells seek out and destroy cancer and virally infected cells.

In 2003, Bittman's second study involved the use of drumming with long-term health care workers. In a six-session study of 112 long-term workers, 46% showed significant mood improvement using the HealthRHYTHMS Protocol.

In 2005, Bittman demonstrated that group drumming reversed 19 genetic switches of 46 that turn on the stress response using the HealthRHYTHMS Protocol.

In 2009, using the HealthRHYTHMS Adolescent Protocol, Bittman's research demonstrated significant improvement in adolescents including areas such as behavior towards others, instrumental anger and interpersonal issues.

Here are a few stories highlighting experiences that HealthRHYTHMS-trained facilitators have had both personally and professionally:

Moe Jerant is a Remo HealthRHYTHMS Endorsed Facilitator. In this very poignant and moving piece, she shares a very personal story about her father.

Drumming with Dad: End of Life Rhythmical Journey
by Moe Jerant

I am very fortunate to be a professional drummer. Since my beginnings on kit many years ago, my rhythm journey has introduced me to several wonderful and powerful healing drums, some incredible teachers and endless numbers of warm, loving people. As a Remo HealthRHYTHMS Endorsed Facilitator I have had the opportunity to bring drums and drumming into many peoples lives on a regular basis. I've drummed in lock down in an adolescent detention center, drummed with kids diagnosed with everything from autisim and ADHD to kids at risk, "well elders", seniors in nursing facilities, families at festivals...You name it and I've probably done it. Every experience taught me something and each one had moments to be cherished. But none of these things prepared me for drumming for my Dad.

My Dad had been diagnosed with dementia about 10 or so years ago. It meant that slowly but surely he was going to lose his ability to intake and process information and his body functions would regress as well. As a retired social worker he knew and fully understood what that meant but he was a fighter and determined to rise to the occasion.

February 2009 he entered a nursing home when it got obvious that we couldn't care for him at home any more. He adjusted well, always looked at the bright side and couldn't wait to "get the gang together"...his family.

Christmas 2009 was a celebration of mixed feelings. We were glad to still have Christmas together but concerned that my Dad's condition was growing worse. One morning in mid-January I went to see my Dad who was still in bed. The nursing staff said he was having one his sleepy mornings and they thought it best to let him in bed for the day. When I returned the next afternoon he didn't look well at all and I had him admitted to the hospital. He was suffering from internal bleeding caused by one of the medications that helped him live. During the next few days he was not conscious much but I know he heard every word that was spoken about tests, results and diagnosis.

To honor my Dad's Living Will and respect his wishes for his last days we moved him from the hospital to a local hospice facility. As Providence would have it the medical director is one of my African drumming students. She suggested that we have our regularly scheduled class at hospice rather than our usual meeting place. So we did. About 10 or so of us brought frame drums, shakers, a Native American flute and lots of Reiki, surrounded his bed for almost 2 hours and just played. This experience was almost beyond words. Everyone drumming knew why we were there. They came to be there and be "all in". The energy we created came from everyone's heart and was filled with more love than you can imagine. You could see my Dad's face relax when he understood what was happening. He knew we were there and why we were there and he joined us. He contributed the rhythm of his breathing to our circle of drums and we supported each other..just like he taught me about life. I stayed with him through the night holding his hand much like he did for me when I was a scared little kid.

By mid afternoon the next day I got a call that I should come to hospice because he was getting close to crossing over. I gathered my brother-in-law and partner and the three of us drummed again. Very gentle rhythms with a soothing shaker and again my Dad joined us with his breath cycle.

After dinner my Mom and the rest of the family said their goodbyes and left for home. A friend and I stayed behind and we began drumming again. My Dad's breathing had become labored and almost painful to watch, but he responded to our drumming as before. He relaxed and we matched the pulse of our frame drums to his breath. We worked together and as his breathing slowed down we slowed to a shaker rhythm. We followed him and his last breath came on the pulse of a shaker.

I took his hand, promised him we would take good care of my Mom and thanked him for everything he taught me in life. It was an honor to be with him at his crossing and an equal honor carry his spirit in me. I won't forget. Thanks Dad.

[This article can be found at the HealthRhythms link at Remo.com]

Bonnie Harr is a HealthRHYTHMS facilitator and shares her unique story about multigenerations in one drum circle.

Intergenerational Rhythms by Bonnie D. Harr, MSN, MS, RN

HealthRHYTHMS drum circles breathe life into any gathered group. As a clinical nurse specialist and counseling psychotherapist, I have had the privilege to facilitate well over one hundred such circles in the last few years. From business and industry groups interested in conflict resolution and empowerment training to cancer support groups; from lovely worship experiences to women's programs and community diversity initiatives — each drum circle has had its own character! The poignant point is simply this – the rhythms of our lives have the power to heal us and to bring us together. Join me in remembering one of the special gatherings.

Mothers' Day was just around the corner. Our lovely local Inn approached me about hosting a Mothers' Day HealthRHYTHMS® Drumming Circle to celebrate themes of motherhood. I thought this to be a very fine idea. They promised to embellish this programmatic offering with tea and crumpets served up on Old English china and in a collection of extraordinary Victorian teapots. Lavender and baby's breath would be woven amidst the finery upon white linen tablecloths. The drum circle would be set up in the center of the large room with the tables on the periphery. The setting was sure to be magnificent! Of course, I said yes! Who wouldn't?

That day, when the 60 or so individuals gathered, I was struck with the eager uncertainty of the group. When I asked, not one of them had EVER participated in a drum circle prior to the engaging moment they were actually in! There were four women who were well beyond their seventies, the oldest being 87! And there were seven young lasses, the youngest being 8 years old. I realized as I progressively met each group member that something incredible was in place – there were three and four generations represented within singular families! The spiritual richness and depth of such a gathering was not lost on me.

And so we drummed. I navigated the gathered group through the basic building blocks of the HealthRHYTHMS Protocol. While everyone seemed to love the apple shakers, they were antsy to get to the drums – tapping out little rhythms and noises here and there! The air was pregnant with anticipation and readiness. I taught. They learned. We drummed. Entrainment happened! Faces and hearts fully opened each to the other and all to some greater something that urged us on in the nameless common bonds that drum circles create.

One Grandmother, who accepted mallets "because I have arthritis in my hands", put her mallets down midway through the event and picked up a tambourine to dance a bit in the middle of the circle. It was so natural and so fine. Another, four-generation family began a rhythm of eye contact with each other that was mystical and captivated us all. Still another mother-daughter dyad stopped drumming for a while, just to embrace each other. It occurred to me that a great many things were happening in this intergenerational drum circle that Mothers' Day.

It's quite easy to allow the rhythms of healing to thrum through a group. One simply has to move out of the way and let it happen! This is not an uninformed or haphazard "moving out of the way", but rather, a well-planned, well thought out protocol of promise. This unspoken promise can be realized when the hearts, souls and minds of gathered individuals are invitationally opened to it, and the facilitator can be the stimulus of all good things, without being or stealing the show!

At the end of this day, one young mother walked up to me with two older women in tow and the eight year old nipping at the skirts of and embracing the one she called "Nana". With tears in her eyes, the young mother reached for me and said, "You will never know what you have allowed to happen here today. My Mother has Alzheimer's disease, and I brought her here thinking it would mean nothing to her at all. But she looked at my daughter during one of those power- drumming moments and called her by her name for the first time ever! My daughter spontaneously jumped up and hugged her – did you see it? – and Nana just rocked her there in her arms!"

By now, my tears were in the mix. I could sense the depths of intergenerational rhythms – ancient rhythms – pulsating through us all. She continued. "My Mother will never remember this day, but my daughter will never forget it! Look at them."I did and felt anew the gratitude I have felt every moment in a drum circle since I first became a HealthRhythms facilitator. [This article can be found at the HealthRhythms link at Remo.com]

Margaret Sowry is the executive assistant to Dr. Barry Bittman as well as the Manager and Recreational Music-making Research Coordinator for the Mind-Body Wellness Center and a *Health*RHYTHMS Endorsed Facilitator. She has been an integral member of Dr. Bittman's research team since 2000 and was directly involved in the development of the Adolescent Protocol. Margaret believes that the fundamental essence of HealthRHYTHMS is to honor every individual, recognizing their value, beauty and uniqueness. Everyone has a story and all the stories are invaluable lessons. The act of sharing them is the foundational step of healing. Following are two of her stories:

Lionel, "A Changed Young Man" by Margaret Sowry

Lionel (not his real name) joined the 12 Heartbeats (the self chosen name of the drumming participants) the second week of the protocol. He walked with a swagger and reeked of attitude born in the "Hood", as he so aptly referred to it. He slumped in his seat, and interjected sarcastic humor into nearly everything.

Lionel deferred any serious thought, reaction or comment to his "jokester" mode effortlessly. "Being funny" he readily acknowledged as his best quality. He offered no apology.

His first drumming contribution was a violent slam on the gathering drum that sent everyone to their feet. The group's awareness drifted to a gunshot in the hood... a sound that was all too familiar.

Over the course of the following weeks, he remained stoic while clinging to the gathering drum. If one of the other members arrived first and took the drum, he immediately reclaimed it. Somehow Grandma Drum was a security symbol for him. The group shared an understanding not to challenge his need. Even when the group rotated instruments, Lionel never allowed Grandma to move from his side.

During the first four HealthRHYTHMS sessions, Grandma reflected his anger, frustration and sense of being lost. Everyone recognized that unspoken eerie connection between Lionel, Grandma and his legendary "gunshot sound."

The first time Lionel put away the mallet for a brief period and placed his hands on Grandma, it was to drum his expression of "running away." The others in the group immediately commented and gave credit to his breakthrough. He had not shared anything "real" previously, and had never tolerated any acknowledgement of an emotional response. He merely nodded sheepishly and appeared pleased.

During the next session, "Inspirational Beats" challenged the group to complete the phrase: "The hardest thing for me to do is?" Lionel immediately blurted: "be more tolerant of others, and not come on so strong." He moved Grandma aside and reached for a djembe. He drummed with freedom and enthusiasm. His hands flew with incredible rhythm and expression.

"WOW, Lionel that was incredible, did you know you could do that?" yelled several members of the group.

He shrugged his shoulders and responded, "I was just ready."

Who could ever imagine what happened within this young man that incredible day? One had only to look into his eyes to witness immense pain, anger and fear. There was no way to measure the significance of that rare moment. The celebratory response from the group echoed the look of new-found strength on his face. He never echoed another gunshot.

Soon thereafter, Lionel was discharged.

Mid-fall, the facility received a telephone call from the principal of the school that Lionel attends. "I don't know what happened there at your facility, but Lionel is a changed young man. He attends school every day, he studies hard, plays basketball and is planning a future. Whatever took place there transformed him and gave him hope." [This article can be found at the Health-Rhythms link at Remo.com]

Margaret Sowry shares another moving story:

Harmonizing Discord: Lessons from Hardened Hearts
by Margaret Sowry

Arriving at the Bethesda chapel I was unprepared for the responses from the twelve angry, disengaged teens who were gathered. Attempts to orchestrate recreational music making via the previously tried and proven Health-RHYTHMS drumming protocol went no where to say the least.

It was obvious that no attempt should be made to do the "wellness exercise" with guided imagery. One would have been more inclined to tether wild horses for a pre-school trail ride. Even rhythmic naming was a challenge. It seemed they spoke another language. Some mumbled, some changed their name mid-sentence, as if revealing their true identity would cause an electric shock. Others refused to look up – their presence seemed to disappear into the floor.

Though the expression of their rhythms on the drums was a cacophony of total frustration laced with obvious anger; even more concerning was the display of apathy and withdrawal by several participants. As we left that first session, I was overcome with a sense of hopelessness – I knew what was not working but had no real sense of what would ultimately impact their lives.

Thus it all begins – if one can only "see" beyond their hopeless expression with a "heart sight" that is genuine, the process of recreational music making (RMM) begins to work its magic.

What were the life stories that had produced these individuals who were unable to trust, to reach out, or even to allow themselves to relax and laugh? Life's battles create scars that mutate without warning or explanation. Yet the intrinsic essence of that which lies beneath their battered surface remains unchanged. The language that penetrates and peels the layers of resistance can only be an expressed caring. The ever present need to be recognized as valuable, and the desire to re-discover one's inner beauty and worth are the innate truths that ultimately afford "re-creation."

RMM bridges barriers and births introspection which ultimately builds connection. However, if the facilitator expects to witness immediately measurable outcomes, it may be disappointing at best. It is the offering and the intent that ultimately matter. It may be as simple as "showing up." Yet even "showing up" can be complicated.

The facilitator does "show up" after spending many moments of concentrated reflection focused on the caveats, characteristics, dynamics and personalities that characterize the challenging group. This investment of genuine commitment is the most essential component of the offering.

Empathy, described by Webster as "identification with and understanding of another's feelings, situation and motives" opens the door to an experience that affords the potential to make a difference. When empathy is present, it reveals itself through one who chooses to care. True caring coupled with the understanding that each journey is unique, and each journeyman is not only precious but has within their being a special gift is the foundation for enabling positive changes to evolve. RMM is a tool that creates opportunities for genuine self-disclosure that lead to transcendence.

Application of these principles is not always easy. The changes that occurred with the court-placed teens were very subtle at first. Leaving the group on more than one occasion, I re-played scenarios and retrospectively imagined handling some situations differently. I made it top priority to actually apologize at a subsequent session if warranted. At least twice, I began the session by stating, " I owe XXX an apology. He made an excellent point last week, and I really wasn't tuned in at the time. I now understand what he was saying. It is impossible to ask the group to be forthright and honest without demonstrating that you will honestly acknowledge an oversight or a mistake.

Several times when responses to Inspirational Beats were lacking, I reiterated that I'd not ask them to do something I wouldn't do myself. Then I shared a personal trial. I've found this to be an extraordinarily effective way not only to demonstrate intention, but to "level the field." Under no uncertain terms could I ever allow myself to forget that each person in this group has been deserted, neglected, labeled and abused.

The first noticeable breakthrough was making eye contact, and when that happened my heart embraced it as a treasure. The first of the barriers was finally breeched. When one captures even the briefest eye exchange, an opportunity surfaces to see beyond the façade. Following eye contact, sensing when an appropriate gentle touch of the hand or shoulder would be fitting is a next significant step. When they are ready to accept it, a touch speaks volumes.

Frankly I was never fully cognizant of the changes in the moment. They were so subtle that an observer would likely not even notice. However, a time came when a very troubled defiant girl announced, "I know what I can change...it is my attitude." That statement was uttered during the third session. Later the director of the program shared the nature of some of the challenges the counselors were facing with her. They noted that the short time devoted to RMM accomplished more than 40 hours of one-on-one counseling.

Another participant immediately comes to mind. One of the young men in the group frequently vacillated between soliciting attention, to withdrawing, to becoming openly defiant throughout the first 3 sessions. A few participants mentioned a song he had recently written. When asked to share it with the group, he could not be coaxed into doing so. By the 4th session, he felt comfortable enough to sing it for the group.

His song surprised all of us. Rather than reflecting utter desolation, failure and despair, his words expressed a dream of the basic elements of life that most of us take for granted. In reality it wasn't a song – his verse was the breaking of a shell that had not been penetrated before. Filled with hope and expectation that life for him would one day improve, his song resounded in each of us as a tribute to one's first realization of true potential.

It was also during the third session that I personally felt comfortable enough to share a song of affirmation with the group. It was one that celebrated inner beauty and worth. Two young women immediately responded, and committed the song to memory. The next session, they actually requested to sing it together, and thereafter reported to have sung it daily.

The last session coincided with many participants anticipating a home visit for the holiday. That day the group was no less than exuberant with energetic drumming. For the first time during Inspirational Beats they were able to express appropriate and rational concerns interspersed with anxiety associated with the anticipation of returning home.

The song-writer again shared his song. Hearing it for the second time, I couldn't contain my own tears. As a group, our eyes merged – it was a moment of true connection. In just six short weeks, this rag-tag group had evolved from angry, disengaged, apathetic and defiant teens to a supportive empathetic team that could genuinely share deep-seated emotions while demonstrating a needed sense of caring for each other.

During the sixth and last scheduled session, the young man who had two weeks earlier pounded an angry "gun shot" on his drum jumped to his feet and declared, "GROUP HUG!" At that point, we all "got it!" Within each of us, beyond struggling, fortresses, competition, hurt, anger, distrust and malevolence, common ground set the stage for true connection – at least in the moment.

Six weeks passed, and I continued to reflect on all of our sessions. I will really never know the true impact of this program on each of their lives, nor do I ever expect to fully understand the personal transformations that never would have occurred without these collective experiences. Yet somehow I wanted to learn more – there was so much more to discover on many levels. I feared that the momentum we had achieved would gradually dissipate into oblivion.

As an update, I'd like to share that the pilot group had been extended beyond the original six sessions. This week a new and highly significant door opened for the first time. Our first Inspirational Beats question was: "How does it feel to be out of control of your own life?"

Their frank responses took us to a guarded realm of shattered hearts, broken dreams, injustice and pain. We came face to face with a myriad of trials and tribulations, and allowed each person to reveal themselves without judgment. A broken teen recounted a searing court sentence, and drummed a painful disempowering emotional response. All participants listened intently and responded with similar stories. Several asked, "Did you cry?" A quiet participant sitting next to me murmured, "Of course, we ALL cried."

If that had not been enough to jar each of us, there was no way I could have predicted the responses to the second question: "What one thing can I take control of in order to make my life better today?"

"I can begin to control my angry reactions." "I must learn to control my thoughts." "I need to begin by caring about myself." "I need to learn better behaviors."

"My talents can help me and I will use them better."

A very embittered young man announced, "I will start to control my mouth."

Staring at the floor, a fifteen year old uttered, "I have to control my lying."

As a facilitator, I truly cannot analyze what took place in the hearts of each person this week. Yet it was their genuine heart-felt responses coupled with amazing trust and spontaneity that I will always remember. The unraveling of each person's saga wasn't nearly as relevant as the fact that in their own way, they achieved the courage to face their windmills, and were now prepared to move onward.

Reflecting upon what I have learned as a facilitator, it's apparent that the anticipation of a group's transformation seems somewhat like waiting for a long cold bitter winter to end. It's not surprising that unanticipated storms stand between today and the revelation of Spring. Then one day the earth suddenly reveals its green splendor. While defining that moment is often challenging, experiencing it first hand is a privilege... and I will never be quite the same.

Frank Shaffer is the current Chair of the Percussive Arts Society's Health and Wellness Committee. He is also a classically trained percussionist with the Memphis Symphony, and a trained HealthRHYTHMS facilitator.

My Experience with Drum Circles By Frank Schaffer

I am a relative newcomer to the drum circle experience, having been a professional classically trained percussionist. Several years ago, Ed Murray, a colleague of mine in the Memphis Symphony, presented an Afro-Cuban clinic and drum circle at the West Tennessee Day of Percussion. While I had been aware of the drum circle movement for many years as a member of the Percussive Arts Society (PAS) Health and Wellness Committee, I had never actually experienced one. The participants had a mixture of all ability levels and musical skills, yet the result left everyone deeply satisfied and inspired. It was a great way to finish that Day of Percussion.

When PAS initiated several years of Recreational Drumming: A Celebration of Health and Wellness grants, I organized and participated in these in Memphis and observed how happy they made me and the other participants. There was really something to what they did for people, no matter what the skill level. While I am a timpanist/percussionist and own lots of timpani and the traditional percussion instruments, my prized possession is a beautiful hand made "djembuka" that I bought at Percussive Arts Society International Conference held in 1996. It was literally "Love at first strike". In the event of a fire at my house, it would be the first thing I would try to save.

In 2009, the Memphis Symphony requested that I do more extensive research on drum circles as part of an anticipated music therapy project with a local hospital. In preparation for this, I read Robert Friedman's The Healing Power of the Drum book, consulted with him at PASIC 2009 in Indianapolis and attended one of the evening drum circles there. He also put me in touch with John Fitzgerald of Remo, who encouraged me to come to the Saturday night drum circle hosted by the Drum Circle Facilitators Guild. This particular gathering was absolutely wonderful. I assisted in encouraging newcomers into the circle and got to see first hand all of the wonderful therapeutic benefits of drum circles: the looks of joy on peoples' faces and the general feeling of inspiration, satisfaction and well-being that emanated from the experience.

Full of inspiration, I returned to Memphis and gave my impressions and what I thought we could do. Our grants writer saw a great opportunity to serve the community in the Youth Villages program, providing a more meaningful way to participate in music than the concerts and demonstrations we were providing. Students at Youth Villages have behavioral and psychological challenges that could greatly benefit from drum circles.

Several grants from United Way and International Paper led me to Princeton to the HealthRHYTHMS training sponsored by Remo. I will remember this training as long as I live. It was an absolute turning point in my life. After going through the steps in the HealthRHYTHMS Protocol on Friday, many deep emotions and thoughts came up during the night. Issues that I had been struggling with regarding retirement, wondering how many years as a professional orchestra musician I have left, what post-retirement contributions I could make, kept me awake most of the night. In spite of this difficult time, I was absolutely energized all day Saturday and Sunday. Most of my adult life, I have been looking for a way for ordinary people to experience the transforming power of music and the resulting transcendence that I have felt many times as a performer. I have found it in the Healing Power of the Drum through HealthRHYTHMS. I am very excited right now about being a HealthRHYTHMS facilitator, but I am also very much at peace with myself.

DRUMBEAT
A Music Therapy Program for Australian Youth

I met Simon Faulkner in New York in 2002. It was there that he first shared with me his program DRUMBEAT, a comprehensive music therapy program that has changed the lives of countless numbers of Australian youth and adults. His program was created in coordination with Holyoake Institute. Holyoake is the Australian Institute for Alcohol and Drug Addiction Resolutions. Holyoake presents a range of preventative programs for use by schools and other organizations working with young people.

DRUMBEAT is an acronym for Discovering Relationships Using Music,

Beliefs, Emotions, Attitudes and Thoughts. Simon Faulkner is the developer of the DRUMBEAT early intervention program and an addictions counselor specializing in group work. For 12 years he practiced in the Wheatbelt region of Western Australia working predominantly with young Aboriginal men. The DRUMBEAT program was developed out of frustration with traditional interventions. He is the first West Australian graduate of the Village Music circles accredited facilitator training course and in 2005 was awarded a Churchill Fellowship to study rhythm based interventions with 'at risk' youth across north America.

DRUMBEAT is a 10-week program with one hour lessons each week. The objectives of DRUMBEAT include increased self-esteem, increased collaboration and group cohesion, increased awareness, self-expression, increased musicality, greater understanding of human emotions, and improved cohesiveness in a group. There are numerous instruments used during the program including the Rosenberg Self-Esteem Scale pre and post, a student evaluation form and a teacher evaluation form.

The program is specifically designed for young people who have exhibited 'at risk' behaviors. The average age is 11-15 years old.

Each week students are provided with an evolving curriculum in which they are first introduced to the history of the drum and its mechanics. They are next introduced to the concept of relationship using drumming and dance, followed by an introduction to the concept of harmony, and how the metaphor of blending rhythms relates to create harmony with others. There is constant interplay between the relationship of drums to emotions. Students are provided with an opportunity to express their individuality through the drum. The relationship of maintaining their own beat while focusing on avoiding peer pressure is explored. Students are even provided with an exploration of spirituality, and emotion and how "music touches emotions" and "exploring the rhythm within." The final themes explore teamwork and finding our place in the community around us. The program ends with a public performance. There is a great deal of processing provided for students to explore their thoughts and feelings while learning the drum and to play with others.

Currently over 1300 trained facilitators present the DRUMBEAT program in different settings across Australia and New Zealand.

A number of independent studies have been conducted into the DRUMBEAT intervention that show reductions in alienation, increased emotional intelligence and reductions in anti-social behavior, (reference to www.holyoake.org.au).

Following are essays created by teachers and therapists in a range of settings regarding the efficacy of the DRUMBEAT program.

DRUMBEAT and ADHD

John (pseudonym) attended the DRUMBEAT group at Ellenbrook Secondary College in 2010. He had a history of learning difficulties that included dyslexia and a mild form of ADHD. In the previous term (10 weeks) to the commencement of DRUMBEAT, John had spent significant periods away from school and been suspended 5 times. John would do anything to avoid the shame of being exposed as a slow learner in the classroom and had developed particularly antagonistic relationships with several teachers who saw him as a 'problem child'.

John felt comfortable in the DRUMBEAT group from the start and because the emphasis was always on cooperation, and competition was avoided and seen as destructive in DRUMBEAT, John's confidence grew steadily. Reports started to come back to me in the staff room that other teachers were noticing an improvement in John's level of cooperation and self confidence as well as for some of the other DRUMBEAT group members.

During the term of the DRUMBEAT program John's absenteeism was almost non-existent and he was not suspended at all. His participation in the conversations about relationship issues that are incorporated into the DRUMBEAT program became quite regular and open and showed significant insight. At the DRUMBEAT performance John gave the introduction and personally chaperoned the school principal – introducing him to each of the members of the group.

Although it is clear that there were tremendous benefits for John in this program, there were also significant benefits for the teachers who had already made up their minds about John and also for his parents. John's mother came up to me after the performance saying that the transformation for John had lifted a heavy burden from her, that she was on the point of no return prior to this term and that now she was so proud of him.

Natalie Driver
Ellenbrook Secondary College
Monday 16 August 2009

DRUMBEAT at Schools

Having facilitated a number of DRUMBEAT courses in primary schools I have seen so many transformations. Usually children show marked improvement in self esteem, particularly after performing in front of their peers. Many classroom teachers have commented on the improvement of listening skills and social skills. The course encourages the participants to work together as a team right from the first session. They are given the responsibility of setting and enforcing behavioural boundaries, organising resources (setting up and packing away), participating in discussions and planning the final performance. All individuals are valued members and are listened to both verbally and while drumming. For some students, particularly those who are having issues in their classroom, the opportunity to express themselves and feel safe doing so in the small DRUMBEAT group has produced major transformations.

One student had very low school attendance however he never missed a DRUMBEAT session. We noticed at first that he would never miss a DRUM-BEAT group although he would often leave the school grounds straight afterwards. I was quite concerned about his withdrawn behaviour and inappropriate reactions to different situations at school. I feel sure that his participation as part of the DRUMBEAT program has been an important factor in him relating to me and his peers in a more positive and outgoing manner. Taking part in the DRUMBEAT performance was a very positive experience for him. He now smiles more readily and is beginning to participate more in class activities. After the DRUMBEAT program was completed, the student continued to attend after school drumming classes and lunchtime sessions and his level of attendance at other times has significantly improved.

A very quiet, introverted student changed dramatically after completing the DRUMBEAT course. Her classroom teacher was surprised to see the student speak in front of the school at the DRUMBEAT assembly as she rarely spoke in class. She really enjoyed the sessions and looked forward to the weekly lesson. She was proud to be one of two girls involved in DRUMBEAT. I could see definite growth in her confidence since participating in DRUMBEAT. In class she appears to be less upset with herself over errors and mistakes. She is more confident to take risks in her work. She seems to be more centred in herself. This student continues to perform and speak in front of school and community audiences.

I am very fortunate to have been involved with DRUMBEAT. I know that I have been transformed. My confidence has increased dramatically and I am now taking roles both professionally and personally that I wouldn't have considered in the past.

Michelle Drieberg
Teacher Koondoola Intensive English
Centre School for New Immigrant Children
with little or no English Language Skills

Psychiatric Patients and DRUMBEAT

We have been running DRUMBEAT groups at Sir Charles Gardiner Psychiatric Hospital now for two years. Our patients are all suffering from complex psychiatric disorders often combined with illicit drug use.

The DRUMBEAT program is used as a safe way for our clients to reintegrate back into community life after a period of hospitalisation. We have found this program to be one that patients gravitate towards and the feedback has been that it is a safe way for them to connect or socialise with others, discuss important relationship issues and have fun.

Case Study

Tom is 24 and has major anxiety disorder. Tom has a long history of anxiety and depression often exacerbated by illicit drug use – in particular amphetamine. Tom has had several periods of hospitalisation over the last 12 months. Tom lives with his parents and finds it difficult to form friendships, feels isolated and spend much of his time alone.

Tom participated in the 10 week DRUMBEAT program run by the psychiatric staff from Sir Charles Gardiner Hospital. Initially Tom was reluctant to enter the room. He was supported and encouraged by the hospital staff and eventually took his place in the drum circle. He was told that at any stage, if he felt he needed to leave, he could. In the first session Tom participated for approximately 20 minutes before leaving

Over the next 9 weeks Tom's participation increased steadily to the point where for the last half of the program he was a full time participant. Notable change occurred in his level of mood. Tom became more confident in the use of the drums, and exhibited more spontaneous behaviours over the duration of the program. Tom's facial expression, usually markedly blunted affect, became more animated, including more regular smiling and laughing. Movements became more fluid while engaged in drumming and were integrated into broader movement patterns. e.g swaying to the rhythm, foot tapping etc.

Tom's social confidence improved. Initially Tom would leave the group when it was his turn to perform a simple sequence, or respond to a facilitators question; after attending three group sessions, Tom was able to stay until the end of the session and to perform sequences as part of the whole group.

Cognitive benefits were also observed. For example Tom who believed he had severe cognitive impairment due to his amphetamine use was able to pick up the drumming sequences very quickly. It was pointed out to him that his cognitive skills were still very much intact.

Jane Featherstone
Senior OT Department of Psychiatry
Sir Charles Gardiner Hospital

DRUMBEAT
at Alice Springs Prison

I have been working in the remote central Australian town of Alice Springs, home of the central Arrernte people, one of the worlds oldest surviving cultures (continuous in this region for over 40,000 years). It is always a great privilege to come here and work with the local people, although I work the field of drug and alcohol rehabilitation, which is a huge issue here arising from the clash of cultures and the oppression of colonization.

I have been running the Holyoake DRUMBEAT Facilitator training program for professionals working in this region who come from a wide range of sectors including justice, health & education; but I have also had the good fortune to travel out into remote communities and conduct therapeutic programs for organisations on the ground with local people – the drumming is as always a wonderful conduit into the therapeutic relationship.

This week I have been working in Alice Springs prison – 500 prisoners, 95% indigenous (a horrific statistic). Aboriginal people in Australia are more than five times as likely to be incarcerated as white Australians and out here the liklihood is even greater. Despairing as those figures may be the work in the prison has been joyful for all concerned and a wonderful learning experience.

We have nine men in the group I am working with (implementing the 10 week DRUMBEAT intervention). Of this group seven are Aboriginal and two white. One of the white participants is bi-polar. Three of the Aboriginal men are quite elderly (50-60 years old) and two are tribal leaders, leading law men from their communities and custodians of their country. The other members are younger men between 25 and 40 years old.

Aboriginal men are notoriously hard to engage, trust has been betrayed many times in their past, and there are many cultural barriers, including language, that stand in the way of easy interaction. In Aboriginal society it is not acceptable to look directly into the eye of someone you are addressing; equally it is not acceptable to talk too forcefully about issues as in Aboriginal society decisions are made by consensus. Most therapeutic interventions are ineffective, because they rely so much on dialogue.

But the last weeks have proved to me, the prison authorities and the health department funding our work, the power of the drum to connect people from very different backgrounds; to raise confidence and to loosen tongues. We are running two hour sessions with this group exploring the relationship themes of the DRUMBEAT program through drumming metaphors and analogies and at least half of that discussion. We are having many laughs and making good music, we are sharing experiences across cultures with the central theme of relationships always in the mix. All are learning from each other including us as facilitators – indeed we are probably learning the most.

The men are animated and alive with passion and the drum is accepted, even though it is foreign to their culture and they are wary of cultural dilution. Yesterday at the end of our session, one of the elders started to sing a traditional healing song in his language. As he sang he tapped the rhythm of the song on his drum and slowly the other Aboriginal men joined him – the 'white fellas' in the room stayed respectfully silent but he looked up and asked us to join him – it was a magical moment. I have been running the Holyoake

DRUMBEAT Facilitator training program for professionals working in this region who come from a wide range of sectors including justice, health & education; but I have also had the good fortune to travel out into remote communities and conduct therapeutic programs for organisations on the ground with local people – the drumming is as always a wonderful conduit into the therapeutic relationship.

In addition, here are other training programs which have emerged in the past ten years:

The Therapeutic Drumming Foundation

The Therapeutic Drumming Foundation (TDF) was set up by Barry Wakefield, MA, M.Ed. Barry's background includes drumming, educating, counseling and training. Based in Nottingham, UK, Barry now works with a small team: Hazel Honeyman-Smith, person-centred counsellor and trainer and Ray Watters, drummer and trainer. Other trainers and drummers join in when needed.

The Therapeutic Drumming Foundation exists to promote the therapeutic use of drumming and related activities. We are dedicated to improvement of the human condition in all of its manifestations. The work of the foundation is based on three R's: rhythm, relationship and reflexivity.

The notion is that rhythm is an essential element in our lives and can be used beneficially and therapeutically; and enhanced through the forming of effective relationships, best formed by practitioners who have developed their work through a process of reflexivity.

The Therapeutic Drumming Foundation was formed in August 2000, when after ten years of wondering what his symptoms meant, Barry Wakefield was diagnosed with Parkinson's Disease. He was told that drumming might help him. Having been a drummer in his youth he took no second bidding and acquired a drum. Subsequently he found that there were other studies being carried into the use of drumming for other issues, such as emotional health, which suggested beneficial effects beyond Parkinson's. This led to a period of reflection and research. Barry ran several short workshops in this preparatory stage and integrated the use of drumming into his training work with counselors. There were several brief courses available, mostly in the USA and mostly condition specific, but, surprisingly, no substantial award-bearing training. He developed a diploma that ran for several years before changing to a workshop format.

The TDF now offers a series of workshops to individuals in a variety of fields, who wish to learn more about using drumming therapeutically. It also offers in-house training to organizations wishing to use drums for positive impact. As Barry has withdrawn from delivering these due to his Parkinson's, he has had more time to focus on writing. He is currently working on a book that distills much of his work and ideas.(www.todrumfor.com, barry@todrumfor.com,hazel@todrumfor.com)

In this story, Hazel Honeyman-Smith, program manager for the Therapeutic Drumming Foundation, shares an experience of her program:

> We took a group of students starting out on our Diploma programme to visit a home for elderly people in an advanced level of care. The group spent an hour helping the fifteen elders to engage with the drums and rhythm; for some this meant sitting with a djembe and holding a core rhythm whilst maintaining open eye contact. For others this meant sitting with one person and helping them to make some sounds – with a drum, with a shaker with their hands. One young woman sat for a long time with a woman listening to the memories the drumming brought back of her youth in Yugoslavia. Some of the group walked around supporting people to change instruments, to find something they could actually hold – bells sewn onto tape and fastened around the wrists were the only thing that some could manage. I remember most strongly that one woman who seemed not present managed to hold eye contact and to begin a smile after a long time with one person engaging with her. As trainers it was necessary to support those experiencing this type of work for the first time by encouraging them, and also encouraging the staff to join in.
>
> After the event the Diploma students regrouped to discuss; this event triggered some strong emotional responses for people. To be able to sit and reflect on what was beneficial, therapeutic about this activity, was important. The manager of the home took me to one side before we left to thank me for the experience; she said that it was wonderful to see the residents engaging and looking happier for even a short period as so many of them struggled with pain and discomfort. It was an inspiring afternoon. We look for the human responses of engaging in rhythm and lifting the spirit or expressing some emotion.

Other training programs include:

Developmental Community Music (DCM)

Developmental Community Music is a comprehensive approach, created by Kalani, to designing and leading music-based group experiences. These training courses provide a holistic person-centred approach for recreational, educational, therapeutic, and business settings. DCM training includes various forms of group drumming, rhythm games, movement, song leading, laughter exercises, group process, and program design. (http://playsinglaugh.com).

Drumagination Workshop

Created and presented by drum circle facilitator and author Dave Holland, this hands-on rhythm training is based on the book and DVD by the same name. Drumagination Workshop features basic drum circle facilitation concepts, world drumming techniques and activities designed to create successful interactive rhythm programs. Designed with the music teacher, music therapist, drum circle facilitator and rhythm enthusiast in mind, Drumagination Workshop is both a professional development opportunity and the perfect experience for enhancing your own rhythmic creativity! Find out more about Drumagination Workshop by visiting www.interactiverhythm.com

Healing Power of the Drum Workshop

This comprehensive program focuses on the use of drumming as a vehicle for stress relief, emotional release and psychological empowerment. This rhythm-based training program teaches how to use hand drums and rhythm instruments to foster trust and team-building, increase self-esteem, encourage individual and group creative expression, foster communication and listening skills, identify and express positive emotions, release negative emotions and learn a socially-acceptable skill. Exploration into the use of drumming for various psychological and physiological disabilities will be explored.

This is an appropriate training program for educators, therapists, music therapists, school teachers, personal growth facilitators, music teachers and therapists, health care professionals, group counselors, youth activities coordinators and group presenters. CMTE credits are available for music therapists through the Certified Board of Music Therapists and NBCC credits are available for licensed counselors. This program is taught by Robert Lawrence Friedman, MA. (www.drumming-event.com)

Music Therapy Drumming

Music Therapy Drumming is a professional development program for music therapists and other therapy professionals, by music therapists. MTD includes live instruction, resources, and support for all music therapists, regardless of prior training or experience with percussion instruments.MTD focuses on musical technique, music-centered processes, and clinical practice, making materials immediately relevant and applicable. This approach was created by Bill Matney, M.A., MT-BC, Mike Marcionetti, MT-BC, Carolyn Koebel, M.M., MT-BC, and Kalani. (musictherapydrumming.com)

Rhythm Planet Workshop – A Global Exploration of Instruments, Rhythms and Techniques

Rhythm Planet Workshop, created by two experienced world class percussionists and teaching artists, Dave Holland and Jonathan Murray, is a hands-on workshop for learning about the instruments and rhythms of the world in a fun and playful environment. Participants will learn basic techniques for playing dozens of world percussion instruments and how to create authentic rhythms within an ensemble setting. You will also take away cultural and geographic connections, world folk songs, and other exciting ways to integrate the world of rhythm into your next music class, music therapy session or community drum circle. Rhythms of West Africa, Brazil, the Middle East and the Caribbean are all included in this exciting program. This four-day program will dramatically expand your awareness of ensemble style playing, enhance your rhythmical sensibility and will create connections between cultures, playing techniques and rhythms. Music teachers love the course guidebook as it is a ready-made lesson plan for a school world music curriculum. Music therapists get new ideas for rhythm-based activities that work as enriching activities for their clients. Anyone who is a recreational drummer will get a whole lot out of this program. Visit Rhythm Planet Workshop at www.rhythmplanetworkshop.com

Related Online Training Programs

Online Stress Management Training Program

These online training workshops offer CMTEs and NBCC credits for music therapists and licensed counselors. They are also available for the general public seeking stress management support. It addresses five key areas of life management and client training purposes in the area of managing stress. Five online courses are available including, Balancing Work Family and Self, Humor and Optimism as Tools for Good Health, Managing Work-Related Stress, Conflicts Relationships and Stress and Communication Skills. All courses are eligible for CMTEs for music therapists and NBCC credits for Licensed Counselors. Visit www.stress-solutions.com/generalpublic.htm. This program is taught via Powerpoint and facilitated by Robert Lawrence Friedman.

CHAPTER SEVEN

Drumming with Specific Populations

Children with Disabilities
Blind and Deaf Populations

When a person cannot hear, cannot speak or cannot experience touch in the way most of us do, the drum seems to find a way to transcend the disability and create an opportunity for both a physical and mental victory.

Here is a touching story from drum circle facilitator, Lulu Leathley about her work with children who were blind and deaf.

Dancing Hands and Smiles by Lulu Leathley

One of my most amazing events was at a retreat for deaf and blind children that I did a couple of years ago. I had absolutely no idea of what I could bring to this group but packed up my car with everything, as usual, and took a gulp and went anyway. There were parents and aids with the children, most of whom were in wheelchairs...some even tied to theirs as they would fall out if not!

It was pretty chaotic at first trying to see what would work with this group but after I let go of my expectations it started to gel. I went to each child individually with a bell, a buffalo drum and a clave to see what they would prefer... singing their name and trying each instrument to see how they would react...it was hard to judge! The parent or care giver would know though and eventually we found a sound that resonated with each one. Some were bell kids, others very base drummers but everyone found something. Amidst all the chatter of the care givers we found a common pulse. One little girl with a band around her head to hold a hearing aid closed her eyes and gave a huge smile with her hand up in the air in the only dance she could manage..it was beautiful.

Bob Bloom is the founder and director of "Drumming About You", a participatory drumming program that is accessible to all age groups, and is inclusive of people of challenge.

Drumming Without Sound by Bob Bloom

Established in 1817, The American School for the Deaf in West Hartford, Connecticut (ASD) is the first school for the deaf in the United States and the oldest special education institution in the Western Hemisphere. ASD provides deaf and hard of hearing infants, youth, adults, and their families an education, resources, and services needed to realize their full potential as self-directed citizens.

On November 3rd and 4th, 2009, I was engaged to lead interactive drumming sessions with elementary-grade ASD students who are deaf or hard of hearing, many of whom have cochlear implants. Some of them also have developmental and physical disabilities. I led the students, plus their teachers and other professional providers, to participate in playing beat patterns on a revolving array of hand percussion instruments as the accompaniment to songs. As I sang, a teacher interpreted the lyrics for the students.

One of the boys with multiple disabilities, John, first heard the music of one of the sessions from his classroom two rooms away. He wasn't being aided by any type of amplification, yet he spontaneously began to drum on his desk. His teacher was surprised to see him drumming and relaxed as compared to his usual physical stance. At the following session with his class, the teacher "thought it was amazing for him" that he played along to the music and that he was able to remain relaxed.

Shannon Ratigan has created one of the most useful online tools for drummers and drum circle facilitators, drumcircles.net. It is appropriate that he shares this story on how being online served a child with special needs.

The Value of Technology: Drumming Via Webcam
by Shannon Ratigan

I've been asked a few times about long distance drumming over the web with video camera programs like Skype. My experience, despite some of the technical issues, that it's a very effective way to teach drumming across the country from the comfort of your home.

A family contacted me some time ago that had an 8 year old child with Cerebral Palsy. They had spoken with numerous doctors and specialists about finding ways to help strengthen his weak arm and hand. Because if he could begin using it more at this young age it might help him to work through it a little, or even help it to heal a little bit.

Please keep in mind that this should be approved by the person's doctor. This case was actually a referral from the child's neurologist. While I have seen multiple people improve through drumming, it is certainly not a cure and every one is unique, so the outcomes do vary.

I started by speaking via webcam with the parents about it, and they explained that they wanted to try drumming as a possible solution. I explained that I only teach drumming. I'm not a therapist, and I have no medical degrees. I'm a musician, and I will help to teach him music. Obviously each child, and medical condition has to be approached differently, and that we have to find the right style of drum to suit each individual's needs.

I suggested that we try a couple of drumming lessons and see how things go. If it works out for him, that we could do a webcam drumming lesson once a week, or twice a month. They could continue as long as they felt he was benefiting from it. I've worked a lot drumming with special needs children and adults, both individually and in groups, so finding the right approach and style of drum unique to each person is very important. Most of the time I would just let them choose a drum or percussion item and, later on, suggest they try a different one out.

With this particular child the wish of the parents was to teach him drumming to strengthen the weaker arm. At the time he couldn't really do anything with it, and didn't really want to.

I suggested one of those smaller very lightweight aluminum doumbeks. The reason was he would need to grasp the body of the drum with his weak arm to play it, and he could play with his stronger arm. I figured when it got stronger that maybe a set of bongos on a stand might be the ideal drum. I've seen people at some of the drum circles I hosted with Cerebral Palsy strengthen their weak hand over the course of just a couple of months by playing the bongos.

One person in particular was in a wheelchair and he would just set a drum on his lap and play. I was rather surprised how quickly the weak arm improved and he could begin to tap out rhythms on the bongos with both hands. It happened so quickly that he could play a rhythm as good as anyone else in the group. One of the keys to it was suggesting a basic foundation drum rhythm, and encouraging them to improvise whenever they felt comfortable. This gets them out of their head, and frees them up to not think, and just have fun playing and improvising.

So that was my thinking looking forward going into this. My approach needed to be different than drumming in the room with someone, because they are in New Jersey looking at me on a computer screen, and I'm down here in Florida. With any 8 year old child there is an attention span issue, so my approach was just to encourage him to have fun drumming. I used very basic drum rhythms with word association. I just wanted to make it fun for him so he would enjoy playing and not think about his condition. I gave him a few hand technique suggestions so he wouldn't hurt his hand. I chatted with him a little and found out what his hobbies and interests were so I had something to work with. He liked rock music, and the NY Jets. So examples I used were: "We Will Rock You', "J-E-T-S Jets, Jets, Jets" And we played to those. Just bass and tones. He loved this one: "I like choc-late cake", – (bass-bass, tone tone tone)

With the long distance thing, and attention span, I felt that a 5 minute drum rhythm jam was plenty, unless he wanted to play it a bit longer, but I tried to keep them short so he wouldn't get bored. After each rhythm we would talk for a few minutes, so he could rest, and then try another one out. An hour is a long time to drum with one child, but this ended up working very well. After a half hour he was suggesting jingles, sayings, songs, names, phrases, and raps to play, so that's what we did. We ended up taking turns suggesting them. Again I encouraged him to improvise and play whatever he felt like playing as I held the support rhythm. That first lesson went very well. At the end I asked to speak with the mother for a quick review, and we continued with a 1 hour drum lesson for 4 weeks.

At the end of the fourth drumming session the mom got on the cam and was delighted to tell me that he was now doing tasks around the house with his weak arm. Simple things like opening the refrigerator door, etc. but it was progress they hadn't seen from all the therapies they had tried previously. Keep in mind, he never actually played the drum with his weak arm, he just held onto it while he played with the other one. But this helped to strengthen his arm without him having to do a deliberate task to do it. And that seemed to be the block holding him back.

From there I suggested we upgrade to a set of bongos with a stand. That worked out great. He was excited to play full rhythms with both hands. At first it was barely a curled hand tap, but after a couple of more lessons he was playing some decent beats and now actually playing with the weak hand. I have to say, I was thrilled to see such quick progress with his condition in less than 2 months.

I hoped that he would take such a liking to playing music that eventually he might join the school band like I did. I was a hyperactive child and my parents got me a drum instead of Ritalin. I loved drumming and went on to join the school band as soon as I was old enough.

After that first year, they were planning a Florida vacation to our area, and wanted to meet me to say hello in person. I suggested that we all go to an open drum circle at the beach. They loved the idea, and it worked out great. I piled up the van with drums and my percussion gig bag, we all went down there and had a blast. It was a very pleasing experience for me. Plus, they bought me dinner at a snazzy restaurant I can't afford to even go to. We all said goodbye, and the online drumming lessons continued once or twice a month. He was playing on his own now in-between, but still wanted to hang out and jam now and then.

My goal evolved to the point where he wouldn't need me anymore, as much as it saddened me to think of it. I explained to the mom that's where I wanted him to get to. Coincidentally, soon after that he joined the school band. I was absolutely thrilled. We had reached that point, where they really didn't need me for lessons anymore. He was the percussionist in the band, and was musically way ahead of the other kids.

So it was goodbye. I was happy but also sad. A month later they contacted me because he was going to do a school performance in the school band. The musical director gave them a pretty heavy duty scored piece of instrumental music they had to perform live. The mom faxed it to me and I was surprised how advanced it was for a 10 year old group of kids to play. I didn't see anything like that until I was in high school. I was pleased they were teaching advanced music at such a young age.

But he was stressing over performing it because it was really complicated looking at it from a kids point of view. So we sat down on the computer and went back to the basics. I used word association for musical phrases, we broke it all down measure by measure and slowly put it all back together. It took about 3 lessons to where it all made sense for him, but he got it.

Then I added a little of my experiences with live performances. We talked about how sometimes things do go wrong, about playing with confidence, and working past mistakes if he made one. His block was that he would want to stop altogether if he got lost, or thought he might have played something wrong. I told him to just act like he meant to play the measure that way. There was a lot of pressure on these kids. But I think it was good for the musical director to challenge them like this. And he was reasonably confident to perform in front of a crowd.

I have to admit, I was stressing a little at this point, waiting to hear how it went for him. I so wanted him to do well. I thought about how far he had come in less than 18 months. From not even being able to move his arm, to playing written music with both hands...and now live in front of people. Two longs days went by, and the mom emailed me a short video of the school band performance. It was incredible! That was one of the happiest moments of my life.

John Scalici is an internationally-recognized drum circle facilitator, speaker, musician, clinician, and master teaching artist. His work with special needs groups has been featured nationally on the Hallmark Channel.

Drum Circles at Children's Hospital by John Scalici

I have been facilitating drumming and rhythm based programs at Children's Hospital in Birmingham, Alabama for nearly five years. When I first became interested in facilitating these type of events, I was curious about how I would get permission to do so. All the details of creating and placing a permanent program at a hospital is no small task.

With the vision and guidance of Sherri Van Pelt, Executive Director of VSA Arts of Alabama, I was able to form a strategic partnership with both VSA Arts and Children's Hospital to make this idea a reality. (www.vsaartsalabama.org). VSA Arts is a non-profit organization which provides inclusive opportunities in the arts for people with varying physical and mental challenges.

John Scalici (Photograph by Randy Crow)

We had a plan to secure funding through several donors, including Children's Hospital. It is because of this dedication and vision that we are still there.

My role at Children's Hospital is two fold:

One role is to provide rhythm based programs twice a month on the Adolescent and Child Psychiatric units. This program takes place in partnership with the PT/OT department (physical and occupational therapy).

My second role is to provide open drum circles in the lobby of the hospital during special VSA Arts events. Everywhere you go in the hospital, walls are filled with the beautiful art created by the children both in and outside the hospital. Several times a year, there are fundraisers and awards ceremonies for the artists and the on going drum circles provide the sonic backdrop for the event! It is a beautiful sight and sound.

Winners of some of the arts awards came to drum with their friends and family. All it took was one person to sit down and start playing with us and people started coming from everywhere!

One of the biggest fans of drum circles at the hospital is Mr. Rodney, one of the hospital police. Every time the drum circle would begin, Mr. Rodney made sure he came and played. Seeing a police officer take time out of his day to participate really helped some of the kids with serious illnesses to relax and know that it was OK to have fun.

Since drum circles are an all inclusive and muti-generational activity, it is a great way for the families who have been at the hospital for hours and even days, to relieve some stress and enjoy the calming properties of a properly facilitated rhythm circle.

The drum circles at Children's Hospital helped to calm and comfort when words are not easily found. You see all kinds of situations and hear of the tragedies that are going on all around. Sometimes the best thing is to give a family or individual a smile, a comfortable place to sit and invite them to participate when they are ready.

A skilled facilitator should know when to initiate offering someone an instrument or make sure the volume and rhythm is inviting and comfortable to participants. This is the HEART part of facilitating. Using your inner guide to serve the group.

My work at Children's Hospital is always fulfilling and rewarding. You see families and kids going through a difficult, stressful time and you are able to provide a brief sense of relief for them. It makes you feel gratefulto offer such a simple but powerful means of expression.

Adults with Disabilities
Blind and Deaf Populations

Patricia Hatfield, drum circle facilitator, worked with individuals who are blind and visually impaired, using the hand drum as part of her research project. Here she shares her results:

Benefits of Drumming for the Blind and Visually Impaired
by Patricia Hatfield

I have been leading a drum circle at a Center of the Blind for the past seven years. A few years ago, I wanted to document the benefits the participants had received from their participation in the drumming class, as part of a research project I was working on. I asked them some general questions about their individual experience of participating in the drumming class. I have included excerpts from their responses below and I would like to let them speak for themselves on the profound difference that drumming has made in their lives.

Interview with Woman (Blind) – Age: 46

The feeling of power that I get from drumming gives me a lot of confidence. When I think about drumming – it's the high point of my life. Emotionally I have more confidence and I have a focus.

At first I could not figure out the hand patterns because I had a severe head injury in a car accident and part of my brain is gone (this is when she became blind). I couldn't figure the hand patterns out in my brain. But then I practiced

– I had heard that if I do things over and over – on the right side of my head part of my brain is gone, and even without all those brain cells there, I can still think, because there are neuropathways in my brain and other parts of my brain that will take over for parts that are gone. So a rhythm that was difficult at first, I would practice and it would become simple or at least a lot easier.

I feel like I am the center of a vortex when I drum. I pull energy from the earth. It feels powerful. At times when I feel low, and drumming is coming up, I get excited, my energy level goes up.

A blind man wrote about what he calls "Feeling of Thunder". He loves it when it thunders, because it's the only time when blind people have something over their head. People with sight always have the sky or the clouds or the ceiling overhead.

Drumming fills up the void. We don't have vision – drumming fills up what you are lacking. It makes a space for you to be in – in it and with it – it's all encompassing.

When we drum together we get a true connection. We can't get it through eye connection — we get "ear connection". You experience yourself as group.

Interview with Woman (Macular degeneration/partially sighted) – Age: 82

I was bored about what was happening at the Center. I wanted something that wasn't mental and drumming turned out to be a big asset. I was disappointed that there was so little for our other senses. This is valuable when you have low vision or no vision. If you can hear – the rhythm and so forth is very valuable. Drumming brought liveliness to the place.

My energy level has definitely improved.Before the drumming classes last year, I had been in the hospital a couple of times, had anemia, had surgery and I was not in good shape. The drumming played a big part in raising my energy level in a gradual, good way. I particularly feel it after a drumming class – my energy level goes way up.

People with impaired vision can be very concerned with their egos, and drumming together cools it down. When you lose your sight, your ego gets hurt, kind of out of it – don't let your ego get too hungry. We all get along very well in the context of the drumming together.

Interview with Woman (Macular degeneration/partially sighted) – Age: 64

Drumming satisfies my creative outlet. I'm always in a much better frame of mind when I drum. The drumming is opening up rhythm and movement – allowing me to relax enough to let that come out. I have to concentrate more when I drum. Drumming is a real energizer.

We have a diverse group of people. Everyone comes from a different perspective as far as music, and the group has really melded.

I'm looking forward to more drumming performances for the nursing homes.

Interview with Man (Blind) – Age: 51

I have a mild case of cerebral palsy that affects minor motor skills. Drumming helps. With the drum, a lot of the small motor skills don't come into play that much, but by using those rhythms, it helps the coordination. Drumming requires listening skills. I can deal with rhythm now.

With drumming, I get more physical energy and better coordination.

The drumming group makes people aware that blind and visually impaired, we are human beings. We are not going to drive a car or fly a plane, but there are things we can do. When people see us in a positive framework, it makes participation available.

Interview with Woman (Became blind a few years ago) Age: 56

When you lose your vision, you end up looking for what you CAN do. There is so much that you can't do. The first drum circle opened up a whole new world to me. It's that wonderful feeling of creating. Coming from that sound that you didn't know you had.

For the blind, there are so many people that feel useless, even I grapple with that. I get isolated and I don't want to feel like I'm not producing. Drumming allows me to hold up my end of the bargain. I'm part of the group and no one is relegating me to a corner because I'm too old or not productive.

Senior Citizens with Disabilities
Not Seeing is Believing

There were twenty senior citizens in a circle. We began the drumming circle using shaker eggs. I've found that by combining simple exercises, such as creating imaginary circles or writing the alphabet in the air with the shaker egg, senior citizens can have fun, create rhythm, utilize fine and gross motor movements, and exercise their mind. As I walked around the circle, one woman caught my attention. She had a great big smile and a good sense of rhythm. As I worked with her individually, I began moving my two shakers in unique ways – up and down, in small circles, back and forth. She matched me perfectly as if she were my mirror. I was amazed at her ability to synchronize with my movements, but what made this experience even more extraordinary, was when I discovered, she was blind. She was matching my rhythms, and motions, simply by sound.

Connected through Rhythm by Steve Durbin

During a convention of speakers, I was asked to link up some metaphors and use the drums to demonstrate several speech and presentation concepts. I did this and afterwards an elderly lady, came forward. She was blind and partially deaf."Young man, she began, " I do not suffer fools lightly and I was determined you would not get me, but you damn well did!" She exclaimed, tears were running down her cheeks. I was madly recapping to make sure I had said nothing to offend.

"I often don't connect with others, I know I don't. When I'm speaking, I have to imagine how I'm connecting. I have often thought, damn-it, they can just bloody well listen. I think of it as challenging them. I've been a fool. Today, I couldn't look across the circle to connect with anybody, I felt so alone." I began to interject, "Today you definitely connected with the people around you, you can't fake that connection with drums, you were in rhythm with everyone around you. "

"Do be quiet and let me finish, " She said..I stayed shtum! "That's what I'm getting to, that's what got to me. I connected. There I said it! Thank you. You helped me remember that connection. I was a music teacher 20 years ago. I haven't felt that kind of connection since. Thank you."

"Thank you Leah." This was not an easy gig, I had a spectrum of presentation skills in the audience from beginner pro's to presenting to some serious heavy weights. The feedback was great and this one, lady who was described as 'thorny' provided me with the best verbal feedback I have received.

Drumming with Alzheimer's Patients

Jana Broder is a successful drum circle facilitator who has offered her expertise to other facilitators through her shadowing method. Here she recounts a moving story of working with senior citizens:

A Story of Remembering by Jana Broder

I was asked to drum with a group of seniors at a Tampa Nursing Center specifically for the Alzheimer's residents. I had soon gotten into a routine of monthly visits where I would drum with the residents and sing African folk songs for them.

One day, on my normally scheduled visit, I noticed a woman drumming in the group who had a continuous stream of tears flowing down her face. I was at odds with what I should do. I noticed that at times the tears turned into sobs and during other times she would close her eyes, smile, and cry softly. I looked at the nurses and caretakers in the room for guidance and they just gave me re-assuring looks...as though everything was alright.

After the 35-40 minute drum session was over and all of the residents had returned to their hall, I asked the director about the incident. She told me that this particular senior had spent a good deal of her life as a missionary in Africa and that the songs I sang sparked a memory deep within her of those times. She went on to tell me that this was the first time she had ever gotten any type of response from her. This resident had never participated in any other activity and had never shown any signs of emotion before.

I was reminded how important this work is for the aging population. Until this time, I falsely assumed that what I provided was entertainment. What I have learned is that this work falls into much deeper and therapeutic realms.

Drum circle facilitation has moved from art to a respectable career choice. Numerous individuals have helped thousands and thousands of people using the hand drum and rhythm instruments. Arthur Hull, working through Remo, has trained hundreds if not thousands of drummers. Many individuals have moved from more conventional careers to this new and emerging field, with the purpose of service and soul work. Here are a few stories of a few facilitators and their experience drumming from the insideout.

Dementia and Alzheimer "LuluJam"
by Lulu Leathley

No two "LuluJams" are exactly the same – especially when you're working with dementia and Alzheimer patients at an Intermediate care facility!

Forty three arrived for my event last week and many were unable to remember their names or if they had ever played an instrument before. Fortunately for us all, a "LuluJam" event doesn't need any musical know –how, just a bit of trust and spirit.

As I was bringing in my myriad of drums and percussion toys, there were a few women already in their places in the circle of chairs. They were like toddlers in slow motion – worried about the door being left open, not putting anything on the piano, worried that they'd have to play those....drums!! It wasn't until I started singing and handing out oversized egg shakers that their expressions relaxed a bit.

We started rhythms with participants names, the names of Underground Stations in London and songs from their past. I led them in a Soundscape making sounds of rain on the drums leading into a Story/Song about my dog Rosie. Mary, a worried Scottish lady, backed out of the circle when we started but only moved 6 feet away.She stayed and remained fully engaged, however, telling everyone who passed that we were all crazy! Another woman, Nancy, wouldn't join us at first. "I'm sorry dear, I can't come today, and I'm going to die this afternoon." When I asked everyone to tell me how they felt when we were finished, Nancy leapt to her feet and sang out "I feel revived!"

Every event has its challenges and rewards, especially with this population. I found that the songs from their past helped to bring them out of the fog and into a community making music together. The Activity Director was beaming at the end. She told me that this was the first time she'd seen absolutely everyone participating....mission accomplished!

Randy Brody

Randy Brody has been facilitating drum circles for the past twenty years. In this short but moving story he shares his work with an elderly patient.

Life, Eyes and Miracles by Randy Brody

I work with a diverse population of elders at nursing homes and assisted living homes, and similar facilities. Many of the people I work with have Alzheimers or have had strokes, or suffered from other serious conditions. One woman whom I will always remember, was brought into my drum circles by her husband every time I was doing a program at this facility in Connecticut. She was confined to a wheelchair, and never showed any signs of life, almost like she was in a coma, eyes just staring blankly. Once the drumming started in one particular session, it was amazing to see the life return to her eyes. In a subsequent session, she started tapping her fingers ever so slowly. Her husband, who was there, started dancing around her wheelchair. He was so happy to see some movement. I put a small maraca in her hand and she actually attempted to shake it along with the rhythm of the drums. Her husband, as well as all of the staff who were there that day were amazed and thrilled to see this. Some called it a small miracle. I agreed. This is why I do the work I do.

Kaoru Sasaki has been facilitating drum circles from her native country of Japan. In this thoughtful story, she shares a very "moving" experience.

Standing Up for Rhythm by Kaoru Sasaki

From 2003 through 2007, I used to visit a nursing home every month which was a two hour drive from my home. In one of my visits, I noticed that there was a female patient whom I hadn't recognized before.

As I passed her wheel chair, she grabbed my arm, saying, "I used to dance, I used to dance!". I believed I could tell she was suffering from dementia by the way she looked.

Either: I believed/ or/ I could tell... Later, I was told she couldn't recognize her dear family any more.

At first, I thought she was pulling my arm, but, actually, she wastrying to stand up. I understand that she hadn't been walking foryears. Sometimes, as she was drumming, she would slightly shuffleher legs, as if she were dancing.

I asked the nurses and caretakers of the facility to support herbody. She almost stood up! She was holding me as if I was herdance partner, and she started to swing.

I asked her, "Am I supposed to be your partner? Then I will be theman, though I never danced the men's part!" She said it didn'tmatter and kept swinging, with shiny, dreamy eyes. No one knewthat she used to dance. As she listened to the drums, she seemedto be back in her younger years again having a wonderful timedancing to the rhythms!

I had no idea whether it was waltz, tango, fox trot or cha-cha, but I decided not to worry about it.

After a while, I asked her to sit down again so I could facilitatethe group's groove, and she reluctantly did so. After that, everytime I passed nearby, she tried to grab my arm again, reaching outto try and stand up to dance.

When the drum circle was over, a young volunteer came to me to tellhe was a student and in the ballroom dance club of the university.I told the lady, "Wow! Did you hear that? This young handsome mancan always be your dance partner whenever you wish from now on,and he will be often around. Lucky you!" Then she told me, "No.It's got to be you!"

The drum circle on that day gave me even stronger confirmation that rhythm can 'uncover' the joy that was in someone's precious lifeso that it can be remembered and shared — so it can be remembered and shared again.

Rhythm also opens new doors to relate to that person, and enhance their quality of life. It also confirmed that rhythm can "ignite" someone's motivation, just like that old lady trying to stand up again to dance.

Nathan Brenowitz, a gifted drum circle facilitator shares a story of drumming and stroke survivors:

Drumming and Strokes A Small Movement – A Great Delight
by Nathan Brenowitz

The Brain Trauma Center in Kingston, NY was always just a building to me. It wasn't until I was asked to do a rhythm circle there that I began to realize the people in the building, before their stroke or accident, were just like me.

After working out the details and agreeing on a date, my assistant Laurie and I showed up with our collection of drums and various percussion instruments. I often say that most of what I get paid for is schlepping.

As the health care workers began to wheel in all of the participants I realized that I had a huge challenge in front of me. How were we going to get these incapacitated people involved in banging the drums. Most of the patients were victims of severe accidents and their blank expression showed the degree of their particular disability.

We handed out all of the instruments. Many of the people were barely able to hold an egg shaker in their hand. For those who could only tap their foot we placed a tambourine on the floor next to them.

I gave my introductory rap and then started with the same simple rhythm I begin all of my circles with. My assistant, Laurie kept a strong steady beat going on the djun-djun.

Usually I hear lots of sounds as the participants begin feeling their way in. This time it was different. It was more what I saw than what I heard. As the rhythm progressed, everyone, in his or her own way, attempted to participate. Some could only move their shaker while others simply moved their had back and forth.

When Laurie and I demonstrated a drum conversation I could feel everyone's energyintently focused on us. As we worked our way around the room to interact with each person individually, the responses were amazing. No matter how severe the disability, people gave us something – maybe a small tap, a quiet drumbeat or a rhythmic eye movement. Everyone who participated, wanted to do whatever it took to make the rhythm happen.

"It's time to dance," I announced. As I picked up the tempo on my conga drums, Laurie moved around the room dancing in front of almost everyone.I was amazed to see patients, who were motionless when we began, now doing whatever they could to create movement somewhere in their bodies. Smiles and soft laughter began to emerge and patients and staff seemed to be enjoying each other's efforts.

As we packed up to leave, the people gave us nods, touches, and any other way they could muster up, to show their appreciation. The Program Coordinator, who had worked with us on setting up the day, told me that this was the first time she had seen such a degree of focus and participation from this group.

Personally, I was not at all surprised. The rhythm never fails. No matter who, no matter where and, no matter what the circumstance, once the drumbeat begins, a transformation takes place. As long as one's heart is beating the rhythm's going to get you. The Brain Trauma Center proved no different.

Drumming at a Rehab Institute

When I began facilitating drum circles at a local rehab institute, an elderly patient would sit outside our circle and curse at the loudness of the rhythms. Yet she remained. Each week, she would sit five feet away and curse. When nurses would ask her if she wanted to move to another area, she would decline, and curse at the sounds of rhythm. About four weeks in, I noticed something curious: she sat in the circle and didn't curse. But she didn't play either. She just listened, and when I asked her if she wanted to join us, she said, "no, keep moving". About eight weeks into our drum circle, she asked for a drum. Now what has replaced her cursing is her drumming. Watching the evolution of this woman was enjoyable and gratifying—especially when I learned that she was 104 years old.

Jonathan Murray has been a professional drum circle facilitator for the past ten years working with diverse populations. In this essay, he shares his experience working with senior citizens.

Impactive Drumming by Jonathan Murray

One of my favorite groups to work with are seniors. In my area, I offer continuing programs at different senior centers, nursing homes and rehabilitation centers.For most of the seniors I work with, drumming is a completely new activity, but most take to it with great enthusiasm. I have been privileged to witness drumming facilitate joy, wellness and interaction amongst the senior groups I have worked with.

In one program, I was facilitating a series of several drumcircles for an anniversary celebration of a local senior center. In each of the groups I had from 15 – 35 participants. At the beginning of the second drumcircle, a gentleman came into the room and said that he wasn't feeling too well, but that he wanted to try playing the drums for a while. During the drumcircle, I had half expected this gentleman to get up and leave, but he stayed and played and was having fun. At the end of the circle he came up to me enthusiastically and said how he hadn't been feeling too good – that his body had been hurting and he hadn't planned on staying very long at all. However, now he said he was feeling good – his pain was less and he was feeling better about himself and everything. He told me he was going to go get his wife and come back for the last drumcircle, which he did. They both stayed and played for the last drumcircle and had a lot of fun. At the end, they both came up to me and thanked me for the fun time and told me how good they felt. The gentleman who first entered the room and the one who left with his wife could have been two completely different people. The man who had first slowly shuffled into the room was leaving standing taller and moving easier, with almost a bounce in his step. The drumcircle had revitalized them, giving energy, joy and a powerful connecting experience.

One of the local senior centers where I have been leading monthly senior wellness drumming programs for the past two years has had a very strong and enthusiastic group of senior drummers. One of the pleasures of my profession is getting to know these people on an individual basis. One gentleman – Fred came to almost every program I offered at the center. He along with his girlfriend, a beautiful Filipina lady (later to become fiancé) would regularly attend the drumming sessions, and Fred would always play the big African bass drum I would bring. It kind of became his thing. Every session I knew I had to make sure to bring that drum for Fred. The interesting thing was that about 2/3 of the way through each program Fred would fall asleep and doze off for a while, still with his mallet on the drum. The group would continue to play and he would eventually wake up when we would change the rhythm or start singing. Fred and his fiancé were regular regulars at the senior center drumcircle. This summer there were a couple of months when I didn't see this regular couple, but figured they might be on vacation or something. One day when I was setting up for the senior center drumcircle, Fred's fiancé walked in alone. She told me that Fred had passed away, just weeks before their wedding. She was obviously still grieving and in pain. I was stunned when she told me, and saddened to know that this all happened just before they were to be married. She had come to the senior center that day just to tell me what had happened. I asked her if she would stay and help us honor Fred in our session that day. As first she didn't want to as she felt it would be too upsetting, but I encouraged her to play if even for a little while. When I pulled out Fred's drum and handed it to her, she had tears in her eyes. As the group played, I asked us all to remember Fred and send him some good music. We drummed for Fred and through our drumming, our group was able to celebrate Fred's life and offer our support to his fiancé. We still miss Fred, but before each circle I have done since his passing, I remember to think of Fred and always offer him the big drum.

My life has been truly touched by the path I have taken. I have been able to offer the gifts that group drumming can deliver to so many groups; leaving a wake of joy, connectedness and wellness behind. To be able to deliver powerful experiences from such a fun activity is a true blessing. Our culture is only just waking up to remember our connection with rhythm – one of the most sublime forces of the universe, and drumming – our legacy gifted from our earliest ancestors. As a drum circle facilitator, I feel fortunate to be able to have a humble role in the rhythmical empowerment of our world.

Jonathan continues sharing his thoughts on his experience with Parkinson's patients.

Drumming and Parkinsons Disease by Jonathan Murray

In 2006 I was asked by Heather MacTavish of the New Rhythms Foundation to help her coordinate a renewal room at the International Parkinson's Conference. Her idea behind the Renewal Room was to have a physical – Location at the conference where people could go for a break – for respite. The conference was attended by people living with the disease and their families, in addition to medical and research professionals.In the renewal room I coordinated several local and other facilitators who came from out of state to help run a 2 hour long drumcircle. Some people would come and go, but there were many who stayed and played for the entire time. At the end, one gentleman approached me to thank me. He was effusive with his praise, and had clearly been touched by the experience. While we were playing I had noticed that despite his muscle spasms and tremors he was in perfect rhythm with the group. In fact, while he was playing the drum, you couldn't see any of the manifest symptoms of his disease. It was only when he stopped playing that you could see some of the signs of Parkinson's. He thanked me profusely for the drumming experience, and told me that for the first time in years he had been able to forget about his condition. In the few hours he had been drumming was one of the few times when his disease wasn't in the front of his mind, where he had been able to feel like a 'normal' person, who was just there to drum and play – not a patient who needed care. He was very thankful about having been able to drum and forget his cares for a while. Imagine your every waking moment is filled with focus on your disease; whether because of symptoms or pain or because you are absorbed in trying to find treatment or a cure. From speaking with him, I came to realize what a powerful gift he had been given by the drumcircle.

In this moving story, Arthur Hull shares another of his thoughtful stories.

Story, My Left Foot by Arthur Hull

I was in Birmingham Alabama doing a series of outdoor family friendly community drum circles at it's down town festival called City Stages. A man in an electric wheelchair came to the edge of every circle that we did. I facilitated five circles that summer day.

The circles were always full and with five concentric rows deep of excited players, so it was not easy to get out to him. When I saw him at the edge of the first circle that we did that day, it was the end of the event and there was no time to greet him. When he showed up to the second circle the circle groove was a little shaky so I knew that I could not spend too much time with him before I had to get back into the circle to steady the group rhythm.

As I approached him with frame drum and a mallet he held up his arms as if to receive the instruments. But his wrists were bent at an odd angle and his fingers were all gnarled and twisted into themselves. I tried to hand him the frame drum but it soon became clear that he couldn't hold onto it. So I placed the drum in his lap and tried to hand him the mallet. He couldn't hold the mallet.

As I was attempting to accommodate him, he was moving his mouth and sounds were coming out but there were no words that I could discern. I did not know what was wrong with this person but his actions seemed very similar to those of advanced Parkinson's Disease. He could not control his involuntary head movements and his chest and torso would jerk around a lot.

The shaky rhythm in this transient drum circle was calling me back to facilitate the groove, so sadly I had to abandon the man in his wheelchair to go serve the circle. By the time I could put my attention back to him he had gone.

The man in the wheelchair showed up during the middle of the third drum circle and waved to me from outside the circle. This time, when I was able to approach him, I figured out that he was trying to talk to me. The low groans and mumbling sounds that were coming out of his mouth as his head bobbled around on its own accord, were a concentrated effort to say words. His tongue was actually getting in the way of his ability to speak. All of that, coupled with the booming rhythm of the 150 person drum circle surrounding us, made it hard to understand his words.

As he was trying to speak to me and I was trying to listen, the shaky rhythm groove of the circle called me back once again. Apologizing to him, I told him that I had to go back and serve the circle. I could see he was frustrated and disappointed and so was I. I asked him to stay after this event or to come to the next circle before it started and I could give him the attention that he deserved.

It made me sad to see him wheel away in his electric wheelchair as I facilitated the circle.

He showed up early for the fourth drum circle of the day. Before the event started, I had a chance to sit down next to him and take the time to listen to the words he was trying to force out past his noncooperative mouth. It took a long time for him to get the words out, but by listening very carefully to him I could finally understand what he was saying.

"Put it at my foot!", was all he was trying to say. That was it. Put the drum under his foot. That was it.

So I got the biggest frame drum I could find and took it to the back of circle to his wheel chair. I pushed his left wheelchair foot pedal out of the way and placed the frame drum on the ground under his foot. He stretched his leg out so that he could reach the drum with his foot to tap it, and he played the drum.

Here was a person who was totally incapable of holding onto a drum, let alone play it with his hands, but he was not incapable of playing it and he knew it.

Before the people started arriving I removed a chair from the outside row next to an isle way, and pushed him and his wheelchair into its place placing the drum on the ground under his foot.

A short time later the drum circle was full of people and in full groove, he was happily tapping his drum in rhythm with the group. Sometimes he wasn't totally in rhythm with the rest of the players, but it didn't matter to him... or me. What mattered was the he was now a contributing part of our community drum circle.

The man came back the next day for the final day of drum circles at the festival. All day long he sat in his wheelchair in the outside row of the circle and tapped on the big frame drum with his left foot.

We did not talk to each other much that day. It was a lot of work for him to fight his way past his impediments for him to be able to speak. But my belief is that, even though he could not say the B, he said his name was Bill. I knew for sure what " Annnk uuu" meant. The constant smile on his face, that even advanced Parkinson's Disease could not suppress, said it all.

Of course, I wouldn't let him leave on the final day without taking the frame drum with him.

I put it in his big backpack on his wheelchair. It had become his drum. It had his left foot print on it.

Drumming and Burn Survivors Drumming at the World Burn Congress

She was a meditator. She had been meditating her entire life to create calmness within. She shared with me that on this day, as every other day, she set the small tealight on the floor, preparing to sit next to this gentle light, and began to meditate.

On this day, though, she wore a long dress. Unusual for her, and a grim mistake.

As she lit the candle, and stood up, she realized the candle was just below her, and she felt some heat at the back of her leg. She looked down, and saw that the candle had caused her dress to catch on fire. She told me that her mind at that moment didn't work the same way anymore. Instead of rolling on the floor, she walked a few steps towards the bathroom to douse herself with water. It didn't work that way. Within just two steps, the oxygen caused her dress to become completely enflamed.

With her dress in flames, she walked into the bathroom. The shower curtain caught on fire as she walked into the shower. Unfortunately, earlier in the day, she had her faucets replaced, and she didn't know which was hot or cold. Completely in flames now, she looked at the faucets, trying to remember which one was hot and which was cold. She didn't want to scald herself, she thought. Finally, after a few moments, she decided it wouldn't matter as she turned the knob. It was scalding hot water, but the fire was going out. She walked out of the shower, and decided to call her husband who worked a few minutes away. She didn't realize the extent of her injuries until she watched her husband's face turn pale. She looked down and saw her skin falling off her body. He called the ambulance and she collapsed into shock on the gurney. When she woke up, she was listening to her doctor tell her that she would need to be put into a two month medical coma; she would need 22 skin graft surgeries that could be painful enough to cause a heart attack. Burn surgeries are the most painful. When she woke up two months later, 75% of her body was burned, from the neck down. She was missing an arm and had scars on most of her body. Even more shocking is that she said she was grateful for the experience.

What amazed me, as the room of 900 burn survivors began drumming together, was that hers was the brightest smile. She jumped up and down in glee as she drummed. I wondered how so many of us get caught up in our worries and fears, and how debilitating this can be. How someone who went through this type of trauma could live her life with gratitude and joy, serves as a reminder for all of us that it is possible—even in the worst physical pain imaginable—to live a positive, joyful life.

I was invited to a three-day retreat for Burn Survivors in North Carolina. It was a powerful experience.

Drumming at the Burn Retreat

One man walked in with no fingers and one leg. A woman had a face disfigured by acid. One had lost a leg in a car accident, when the motor crushed it. Fifteen victims and their spouses came to this idyllic North Carolina retreat. For three days, I was to work with them to support them.

As they shared their stories, each case seemed so random. One man driving 50 miles an hour found that his steering wheel stopped working. In another instance, a man in a house was behind a door and the fireman didn't realize he was there.

Yet each of them, who at one point or another made the decision to overcome their challenges, their disfigurements, decided they wanted to have hope and attend this retreat.

As a man with disfigured hands attempted to hold a simple canister of salt, I watched his frustration as he had to use both stubbed hands to grip it.

As the weekend progressed, each survivor became a little more comfortable. They demonstrated their vulnerability, in actions more than words. Artificial legs came off and rested on the floor, shorts bared disfigurements.

We began our drumming session on the last day of the program. As the burn survivors began playing, I looked around the room and began to see smiles.

As I invited them to play each other's drums, and create a community of drumming, I noticed the man without hands, playing his drum with intensity. He was hitting his drum with his fists, and for the first time that weekend, he too began to smile.

Over the weekend, these survivors came together to become parts of a larger community with more hope and rhythm.

Augie "Doggie" Peltonen lives near Atlantic City, New Jersey. He is a retired art teacher and a percussionist. He is a certified drum circle facilitator with Arthur Hull's Village Music Circles and is a member of DCFG (Drum Circle Facilitator's Guild).

Chemo Patient by Augie "Doggie" Peltonen

My neighbor Jean was diagnosed with breast cancer. She chose to have a lumpectomy followed by chemotherapy and radiation treatments. At our weekly community drumcircle on the beach in my resort town, I announced to the group that Jean, who has attended our circles before, was undergoing treatment for breast cancer. I asked if the group wouldn't mind sending some "healing vibes" her way since she was in the hospital and couldn't be with us. At this same time, there was the horrible oil spill in the Gulf of Mexico. I asked the group to send out some "healing vibes" to our ocean which was being severely contaminated. I asked the group to look at our clean ocean here in Jersey, which had a full moon rising above it at the time, and send out some good vibe intentions. Our next drumming piece would be for both Jean and the "mother ocean." We started with the "heartbeat" groove and morphed it into high volume, fast tempo, frenzied full groove. I went to the center of

Augie "Doggie" Peltonen

the circle and lowered the volume so they could hear my voice. I took out some Buddhist temple bells, some Vietnamese finger bells, and a large gong. While the circle was playing low volume, I mentioned Jean's name three times, playing the bells, then I mentioned mother ocean three Times while also playing the bells. We slowed the groove down along with the volume to "fade out" stop which ended with the vibration of the large gong. It was a powerful ending which sent chills up my spine. The following week Jean showed up at our drum circle. She looked a little pale and her hair was starting to thin out a bit. I asked the group if they would mind sending out some healing sound vibes to Jean. Jean smiled and said she appreciated that and was feeling much better this week. I also found out that the oil spill in the Gulf had been stopped. Jokingly, I told the group, "now you can see how powerful this group drumming can be; we sealed the leak in the gulf and Jean feels much better." Everyone had a good laugh about the comment and we started the next groove under the full moon on the beach. Jean continues to feel better with her treatments and continues to come to drum circles and be on her road to full recovery.

Rehabilitation Hospital Drum Circles
by Augie "Doggie" Peltonen

I was hired to do a drum circle for people on the mend at The Bacharach Rehabilitation Hospital in Pomona, New Jersey. The patients were mostly recovering from hip and knee replacement surgery. Some were recovering stroke patients. Mostly all were wheelchair bound. I placed them in a large circle; it had to be fairly large since the wheelchairs take up a lot of space. My assistant helped pass out a variety of small percussion instruments and I set up an assortment of frame drums with soft mallets that could be played on the patient's lap while they were in the wheelchairs. I also had some free standing tubanos that are placed on the floor next to the folks who want to play them with stick mallets.We went through the usual routine of a community drum circle with "drum call"; ie. introductions, non verbal signals for "rumble", "volume up – volume down," etc. We started with some simple rhythm games like "echo" (call and response), "say your name – play your name" and "pick a beat from one to four" (on a four beat count). Eventually we morphed into full grooves and everyone seemed to be enjoying themselves. I could measure my success by the look on the faces of these patients. When the full effect of group drumming occurs, there is a look in the eyes of the drummers; that of being on a "natural high." What actually happens is the brain waves shift into the alpha stage which releases endorphins which release stress. This is where the healing takes place. One elderly lady yelled out during the drumming session, "I can't believe it; I don't feel any more pain since we've been doing this drumming." Well, it could have been the pain medication she was taking or perhaps the drumming was her pain medication.

At the end of these hospital sessions, which usually last about an hour, the patients have a wonderful smile on their faces as the nurses wheel them back to their rooms. I do these once a month and the patients really look forward to them.

In another story one lady came to my community drum circle who was scheduled to have pelvic surgery the next day. I asked her if I could announce it to the group and we could send out some special "healing vibes" her way. She told me that is the main reason she showed up for the drum circle. This drum circle was held indoors at a local Elks Lodge. We dimmed the lights to create a nice atmosphere and started the circle as usual. About a half hour into the drumming, I made an announcement that Melissa, was to have some pretty serious surgery the next day and asked the group if they wouldn't mind sending out some "vibes of healing intention" her way as we played. The group was more that eager to help her out. We started with the "heartbeat" groove that is used in a lot of serious intention drumming. As we did, I asked that we become aware of our own heartbeats and send some vibes toward Melissa. I slowed the beat down and lowered the volume. I went over to Melissa with some Buddhist temple bells and started playing them over Melissa's head and body. These bells have a distinctive high pitched vibration to them and send a powerful sound wave through the body.

Then I walked in the middle of the circle and played them the same way above each person. There were about twenty people in the circle.

We eventually went into full groove from the heartbeat with volume up and tempo up to high energy levels. After the circle was over, we all wished Melissa good luck with the surgery. Later we came to find out that she did extremely-well in surgery and everything turned out as was intended. Whether or not the drum circle promoted her success in surgery will never be known, but group intention with sound vibrations can be a very powerful thing when it comes to healing.

Drumming with Psychological and Psychiatric Populations

Patricia Hatfield is a Health Rhythms Facilitator and Certified Cross Cultural Music Healing Practitioner. She shares her experience working with schizophrenic patients.

Pathways to Possibility by Patricia Hatfield

Through a serendipitous series of events, I was invited to come to Becker House to share my love of music and drumming with the residents there. At the first meeting, I asked Rita, the Director, about the condition of the residents and what she thought would be the benefits for them of drum circles and music. She informed me that the residents were schizophrenic, and she explained that Becker House had started as a pilot project in which they had taken on the most difficult cases, people who had been institutionalized and basically unable to function for, in some cases, years. Over time, the staff of Becker House had been able to bring each resident into a positive place emotionally and psychologically, and at the time of my meeting, they were all participating in one or more daily activities outside of the residence. All the residents were taking medications, and along with the activities and support they got from the staff, they were able to manage their symptoms.

Rita explained that the residential program at Becker House was intended to have the residents move from being in their own world to being more socially aware and capable of being out in the world engaging with others. The main intention was to move to a board and care situation that was more independent than Becker House.

Rita surmised that the drum circle could have the potential to enhance the social rehabilitation of the residents, develop their awareness of others, support them in developing coping skills, develop a sense of community and perhaps even lead to a spiritual support for them. We agreed that it could bring fun to the house. We decided that I would lead a drum circle for the residents once a week on Wednesday afternoon from 3:30 to 4:30pm.

Creating The Drum Circle

The first few sessions of the drumming class were an education for me. Instead of just focusing on teaching drum rhythms and techniques, I became aware of the necessity to create and build a relationship with each person and take the time to get to know them and become sensitive to what limitations or difficulties they might be experiencing. I became much more aware of the drumming as a vehicle for relationship and getting to know people.

We began with humming together. I explained that it is a way to relax and that they can hum for themselves when they feel themselves getting anxious. The more we continued to do the humming the more comfortable the residents became with it. Don Campbell points out in his book The Mozart Effect (page 272), "The US Alcohol, Drug Abuse and Mental Health Administration reported the results of a study in which schizophrenics proved less likely to hear hallucinatory voices if they hummed softly...They found that humming the Mmmm sound very quietly resulted in a 59 percent reduction in auditory hallucinations in hospitalized patients with the disease. "

Then we worked with the drums. Whenever I work with people for the first time with the drums, I take the time to show them how to make a good sound on the drum.Once people can make the basic sounds on the drum, we can begin to play rhythms together. I taught an African rhythm called "Shiko" to the residents and staff. There are three parts, and everyone learned to play all three parts. I divided the group and had 2 or 3 people play each part until all were able to play the three parts together. It sounded great! I also taught them an African song of gratitude called "Oya Pu". They all learned to sing it, and it always raised the energy and people's spirits.

I discovered that it is most important is that no one gets overwhelmed with my trying to teach too much too fast. People's self-confidence with drumming can grow, but it needs to be based on small successes, and the learning gradient has to be appropriate to the students. Acknowledging each individual as we play, letting them know how great they are doing, particularly pointing out something they do well makes a big difference in their participation and satisfaction. It impacts the energy level and deepens relationship. A very important component of this kind of work is making sure they know they are noticed and acknowledged for doing well, both as individuals and as a whole group when we are playing well together.

Benefits And Outcomes From Our Drum Circle

An extraordinary performance:

Rita offered the Becker House drum circle to perform as the "opening act" at a presentation by professional musicians for a public fundraiser for the National Mental Health Institute. At my invitation, the staff played with the residents for the performance. We chose to perform "Shiko", the three-part African rhythm, and the African song of gratitude called "Oya Pu".During the weeks of rehearsing, the residents' attention would waiver, people would make mistakes, and people would forget their drum part. Still, the more we practiced, the better we got. Then the night came for the performance and something shifted for all, staff and residents alike.

When we settled into the drum circle onstage, each resident was awake, aware, fully engaged and connected. The song, which we had orchestrated with shakers and drums, was sung and performed beautifully."Shiko" was played powerfully. We brought the house down! It was a fabulous performance and the audience loved it. The Becker House residents were enlivened and animated and so happy with themselves and one another.

Breakthroughs:

The staff let me know some breakthroughs that had occurred for individual residents out of their experience of the drum circle and also out of our public performance.

a. One resident, a 33-year-old woman, suffered from chronic depression. The staff reported that the first time they ever saw her smile was during the first drum circle she participated in with me, and they were very surprised. They said that drumming was the only thing she responded to positively since her arrival at Becker House. During the performance she also became animated and enlivened.

b. Another resident, a middle-aged woman, used to be a concert violinist and had ended up homeless before living at Becker House. Although she seemed nervous and unsure at her first drum circle and spoke very little, she quickly became competent with learning and keeping a rhythm and provided a strong foundation to the group.She would never talk about her experience of playing violin, but just prior to the performance, she began sharing with a staff member about her fears performing with the violin, how much pressure was put on her as a performer and how she never felt like she was good enough. She said that this performance with the drummers was much more fun; she wasn't afraid and she had a great time playing and performing with the group.

c. One of the male residents at Becker House also had a breakthrough during the performance. During the drum circles at the house, he would often play very enthusiastically, then withdraw with an unhappy face and stop playing. But during and after the drumming performance, he became a happy, social butterfly, and did not withdraw. The staff said they had never seen him like that before.

d. Another middle-aged female resident began to exhibit a major attitude change, according to the staff. Formerly "the Queen", manipulating whatever she could for her own interest, she began sharing more with the other residents and fostering positive conditions with the other women. Not long after the drum circles began, she asked if she could help me bring in the drums and proceeded to help bring all 8 of them into the class. By the conclusion of the circles, she had taken on more and more responsibility including, at her own request, helping with the recycle program at Becker House.

I believe that drumming opportunities like these just begin to tap the potential for therapeutic intervention.

Drumming and Schizophrenia

Tony Scarpa is a New York State licensed creative arts and music therapist who received his master's degree from New York University. He works at the Partial Hospitalization Program (PHP) at North Central Bronx Hospital in New York City, running music therapy groups and individual sessions with mentally ill patients. Tony states that playing the drums with patients can aid them by helping adjust to their internal world via getting in touch with their inner feelings. They also learn to interact better socially.

Tony writes this account of a music therapy session he had with M, a woman in her early 20's who suffers from schizophrenia. To avoid revealing her identity, her personal details have been changed and fictionalized so that her character is actually a generic composite. But the real music therapy interventions are told as they actually occurred in order that the reader gets to experience what a music therapy session using the drums is like. Here is an account of these music therapy sessions using the drum as the vehicle to an improved state of well-being written by Tony Scarpa:

Schizophrenia is a debilitating illness that causes a person to hear and see things that aren't real. It affects a person's most primitive and basic levels of existence. People who have schizophrenia have ego boundaries that are completely permeable and diffuse. There is a hallucinatory blurring of these boundaries between inside and outside, between dream and reality, a failure to establish a grounded physical self clearly differentiated from the environment and a failure to establish internalized self-images clearly differentiated from internalized object images. They can't easily tell where their body stops and the physical environment begins. They have difficulty differentiating their emotional self from that of others and as a result they narcissistically treat others as extensions of themselves and others are constantly invading and disrupting their fragile boundaries.[2] They project their feelings and emotions onto others, fusing their feelings and emotions with the emotional world of others. There is hallucinatory wish fulfillment in images which causes their sensations, sensorimotor cognitions and impulses to be perceptually distorted and fused with the environment. There is omnipotence of thought.

They have hallucinations that are often accompanied by religious insights that are interpreted through magical thinking which can sometimes lead them to believe that God is speaking directly to them or that they are God. This is not in the mystical sense where one sees God in all, but in a narcissistic sense where the individual sees themselves alone as God.

These hallucinations create a serious conflict in the patient's mind between

---

[2] Wilber, K. *Integral Psychology*. Boston: Shambala 2000 116

logical and illogical thinking. The patient is torn between logical and illogical thoughts which both seem real. This inner conflict between their rational and irrational thoughts can cause an overload, flooding their minds and leading to a psychotic breakdown.

Their hallucinations can often command a person to perform illogical actions which can be dangerous to themselves and others. They can have archaic, masochistic thoughts leading to literal self sacrifice: "Since the world doesn't understand me, since, in fact, they are out to get me, I should get myself first". The only treatments that seem to really work for schizophrenia are pharmacological or custodial.

When M first came to PHP (Partial Hospitalization Program at North Central Bronx Hospital) she was withdrawn and isolated herself from others. She was extremely guarded and suspicious of everyone. Her body was as stiff as a board and she walked with her arms completely rigid and straight by her side. She gave no eye contact to anyone. As she sat slumped in her chair her eyes looked to be rolling to the back of her head. At times she seemed to be in a catatonic state. It seemed that she couldn't tell where her body stopped and the chair began.

At first it was recommended by one of the staff psychologists that M not be accepted into the program, as the psychologist believed that M's level of functioning was too low for her to benefit from the program and her disturbing appearance might distress the higher functioning patients in the program. But during her first music therapy group, even though she sat motionless and didn't participate, I caught a momentary determined look in her eye as she heard the others in the group play the drums in a spontaneous clinical drum improvisation that led me to believe that she would be motivated to respond to the therapy offered at PHP. Based on this she was accepted into the program for six weeks.

During her stay at PHP, M attended six groups a day run by psychiatrists, psychologists, social workers, and dance and art therapists as well as four music therapy groups per week and an individual music therapy session per week.

During her first few days at the program M was desire less, choice less and was fearful. She trusted neither staff nor peers. At her first music therapy session I placed a drum in front of her hoping that she would hit it at least once in order to create a sensory motor response. M just turned away and wouldn't even look at it. Most of the other patients in the group had been in the program a few weeks and were advancing in their therapy. After a few days of sitting in the music group and watching these other patients enjoy themselves playing the drums, M raised her hand and hit the drum.

At first she just hit the drum one isolated strike at a time, without creating any specific rhythm, playing with a rather blunt expression on her face. Her playing was instinctual, impulsive and id like, as if she wasn't differentiating herself from her surroundings or like she was unaware that her own tension was coming from within her own body. If you have compared her rhythms to language they would have sounded like an infant's gibberish. I encouraged her to strike the drum in this way to see if it would lead to her increasing her emotional affect and sense of satisfaction. I felt she needed to decrease her inhibitions in order to allow emotions to be immediately discharged. After the first week I was able to see that this exercise was helping M to release tension. She began to be able to get in touch with her feelings so that now where she previously cut herself off from her physical sensations she began to experience pleasure from experiencing the rhythmical feelings in her body. This led to her developing a more positive attitude towards the drum. The sensations that she had from playing the drum were a positive experience and helped her to increase her perception which was the process of attaining awareness and understanding of sensory information. This is what Piaget would describe as the sensorimotor level[3].The purpose of this exercise being that the sound of the drum would stimulate her lower or image mind and h form mental pictures by using only images in her mind created by the sound of the drum.

During the second week I encouraged her to advance her drum rhythms by playing in a specific tempo opposed to playing isolated strikes. This was a way to help her to sustain and experience rhythmic time in the immediate present. It was noticeable that she was playing the drum with a brighter affect and the sustained drum patterns were helping her experience sustained emotions in the immediate present.

She was beginning to open herself up to a new reality. Over that second week her drumming continued to become more expanded over longer amounts of time. These extended rhythms worked to expand her sense of the present moment, even though her rhythms were still random and not to a specific beat. As she played it could be seen that her body was becoming more relaxed, she was smiling more and she began to develop a sense of trust between staff and peers. At this point, each beat no longer sounded isolated to the one before it, as the way she previously played, but now began to sound more related to the one before it so that now when comparing her rhythms to language her playing no longer sounded like gibberish, but sounded more like developed vowels and consonants.

She was now playing similarly to the state of development that Piaget would refer to as preoperational thinking. This is thinking that uses images, symbols and concepts but not yet complex rules and formal operations. She was able to play rhythms that reminded her of images from her past but not able to play by the rules of counting out drum rhythms in a specific time signature or

---

[3] Piaget, J. *The Essential Piaget*. Gruber & Voneche (Eds.). New York: Basic Books, 1977 118

any other formalized music theory. She was also beginning to be able to play the drum symbolically which means playing beyond simple images, therefore the mental images created by the sound of the drum could be represented by her verbal thoughts such as labeling her drumming as being good and bad, right and wrong. This act of translating her drum rhythms symbolically was a more difficult, and more sophisticated cognitive operation. She was also playing more conceptually which meant that she wasn't just playing isolated sounds but she was grouping the sounds together to create actual beats. This was an even more difficult cognitive task. But the thing that she could not do was fit in with the playing of the other members of the group because she was still unable to take the role of others. She expected the other group members to mirror her playing because in her mind it was her playing that was special, unique and perfect. When the others failed to mirror, what she believed to be, her perfect playing she became humiliated. She was still very egocentric.

Over the third week M's rhythms became more and more evolved. Her increasingly structured rhythms now began to reflect moments from her past as she was creating rhythms that reminded her of her youth and were attached to unorganized images of her younger days. As M's rhythms began to become more attached to people, objects, memories and experiences of her past, they started to evoke the same types of emotions as the original experiences did. These more extended and sustained rhythms resulted in prolonged emotions and feeling tones. They also brought up feelings of anxiety and fear as she connected more to her unconscious. These feelings and images that arise in patients are threatening to their ego and thus are split off from consciousness where they become the shadow and distort the self-concept (the ego) and leave the individual with a false or inaccurate self-image (the persona). Freud also believed that a person's needs and motivations are unconscious as well. He believed that because a person's real desires are unconscious the person is never fully aware of them and they are never adequately satisfied which leads to neurosis and mental illness. Carl Jung called this form of repression the personal unconscious "shadow". He believed that the ego is split and is partly repressed. The shadow which was part of the ego is projected as foreign, alien and disowned. The shadow is a person's ego potentials with which they have lost contact, forgotten and disowned and so believe that they are not theirs and belong to other people. They appear to exist in the environment. They then turn on the person and threaten their existence. In the words of psychiatrist G.A. Young, "In this process the individual will make themselves less than he is and the environment more than it is."[4] As Fritz Perls, founder of Gestalt Therapy, puts it, "Once a projection has occurred, or once we have projected some potential, then this potential turns on us."[5] Instead of being angry at

---

[4] Wilber, K. *The Spectrum of Consciousness*. Wheaton, Ill.: Quest, 1977
[5] Frederick S. Perls. *Gestalt Therapy Verbatim*. Lafayette: Rea People Press, 1969, p.99.

someone, a person feels the world is angry at them. Instead of momentarily hating someone, they will sense that the person hates them. Instead of rejecting a situation they will feel rejected. They project their negative tendencies onto the environment and thus populate their world with imaginary but quite frightening boogey men, devils and ghosts. They then become frightened by their own shadows. They give their valuable potentials away, consequently feeling that they lack them and instead see them as belonging to others. They then feel worthless and the world appears to be populated with people who are talented, important and awesome in their eyes.

Patients will also project their negative qualities and project them onto others. These undesirable aspects of themselves are denied and pushed out of their consciousness and seen in other people. When this happens communists are under every bed and the devil is waiting behind every corner. They will deny this but the aggressive denial is the proof of their projection because if they didn't deny they wouldn't be projecting. In the words of Dr. Perls: "Much material that is our own, that is part of ourselves, has been dissociated, alienated, disowned, thrown out...I suggest that we start with the impossible assumption that whatever we believe we see in another person or in the world is nothing but a projection".[6]

One of the aims of music therapy is to reunite the persona and shadow so the higher-order integration of the total ego can be established. But the problems that M was experiencing were not so much from her emotional self having been repressed but by the fact that it hadn't been fully emerged and stabilized. Her emotional boundaries were still too fluid and shifting, and so the aim in her therapy wasn't to uncover anything as it was to build up a distinct and individuated sense of self using techniques that would build structure known as structure building techniques.

With this in mind I then redirected the sessions in a way that would increase her bodily pleasure by having her play more involved rhythms on the drum in order to reduce her anxiety. At this point her playing was making more musical sense, so when comparing her playing to language her playing sounded more like developed words instead of nonsense sounds or simple vowels and consonants.

As the fourth week began, M's playing was still rather impulsive, physiological and mostly involving somatic bodily processes within the sensory motor realm. When comparing her playing to chakra psychology we would say that she was playing from the third chakra. This is the level of aggressive power. She was still hitting the drum and not necessarily playing it. So I focused on getting her to learn new rhythms and beats on the drum. The unique thing about M was her strong motivation. This motivation helped her to continue to improve her drumming so that now at this point in her music therapy sessions

---

[6] Frederick S. Perls. *Gestalt Therapy Verbatim.* Lafayette: Rea People Press, 1969, pp. 67, 100

when comparing her musical rhythms to language they were starting to sound more like actual minute phrases opposed to isolated words.

M still didn't have clear boundaries between herself and not-self as these were still fused which is a common trait with psychosis. She was not well aware of the separation between her mind and body. Working with M was different from working with someone with neurosis who I would try to help create a feeling of oneness between their mind and body using musical uncovering techniques. With psychoneurosis there is some sort of conflict or repression within the self-structure (the ego, for instance, represses some id impulse). A strong self structure can repress, disassociate, or alienate aspects of its own being. The self has strong tools such as elaborate concepts and beginning rules which forcefully repress the body and its feelings, displace its desires and create reaction formations. The uncovering techniques are designed specifically to bring these unconscious aspects back into awareness, where they can be re-integrated with the self.[7] These techniques were developed by music therapists who studied the writings on psychoanalysis by therapists like Greenson[8], much of Gestalt therapy by Perls[9] and the integrating-the-shadow aspect of Jungian therapy[10]. The treatment would be to relax and undo the repression barrier, re-contact the repressed or shadow feelings and reintegrate them back into the psyche. The treatments therefore are uncovering techniques because they attempt to uncover and reintegrate the shadow. Wilber states "This regression in service of the ego temporarily returns consciousness to the early trauma (or simply puts it back in touch with the alienated feelings drives or impulses), allows it to befriend and reintegrate the alienated feelings, and thus restores a relative harmony to the psyche. With a person suffering from schizophrenia there is little repressed material to uncover, because the self has not been strong enough to repress much of anything. It is of little use, for instance to try to integrate the shadow with the ego self if there is insufficient ego-self to begin with. The types of treatment modalities are characteristically different and often functionally opposed." In neurosis, for example, resistance is usually confronted and interpreted as a sign of repression and the goal is to contact and befriend shadow feelings, but in psychosis it is often encouraged and assisted as a sign of separation-individuation. Sources for such differential diagnosis and structure building techniques include Kernberg[11], Gedo[12], and Blanck & Blanck[13].

---

7 Wilber, K.; J. Engler; and D.P. Brown. Transformations of Consciousness: Conventional and Contemplative Perspectives on Development. Boston: Shambala. 1986.

8 Greenson, R. The Technique and Practice of Psychoanalysis. New York: International Univ. Press, 1967.

9 Perls, F. Gestalt Therapy Verbatim. New York: Bantam, 1971.

10 Jung, C.G. The Undiscovered Self. New York: Mentor, 1957. 121

11 Kernberg, O. Object Relations Theory and Clinical Psychoanalysis. New York: Aronson, 1976.

12 Gedo, J. Advances in Clinical Psychoanalysis. New York: International Univ. Press, 1980.

13 Blanck, G. & Blanck, R. Ego Psychology II: Psychoanalytic Developmental Psychology. New York: Columbia Univ. Press, 1977.

The aim of these therapies is to help complete the separation-individuation stage so that the person emerges with a strong self and clearly differentiated-integrated emotional boundary.[14] This would be similar to object relations therapy,[15] psychoanalytic ego psychology,[16] and self psychology[17] and involve strengthening boundaries.

With M it wasn't that a self repressed the body, but that there wasn't enough of a strong self to begin with. There was too little self-structure to perform repression. On the contrary, the self structure (or self system) was weak and under developed. With patients like M their self system is so fluid that the self and object representations merge and fuse. The self is then overwhelmed by world-engulfment or fears of annihilation and treats objects and persons as mere extensions of its own grandiose world fusion self.[18] M's boundaries of her "self" were vague fluid and confused. Her world seemed to emotionally flood her as she was volatile and unstable.

At points M would become merged with the drum. I tried to help her make more of a differentiation between herself and the drum and help her realize that she was in fact performing a physical operation on the drum in order to stabilize object constancy and help her become more aware of her muscular coordinated physical operations, increase her musical structure and sophistication and for her to coordinate her physical rhythms on the drum. To build up the self's boundaries and fortify ego strength.

Working with a person with psychosis this way is different from working with neurosis when a music therapist might want to encourage the person to become one with the drum opposed to differentiating oneself from the drum. This is because the neurotic has a more developed ego that the music therapist is helping to try and relax, where with psychosis the ego is more fractured without clear boundaries and the therapist is building up the ego. With M, differentiating herself from the drum was important for her because in doing so she was actually transcending the drum in order to better operate upon it using her sensory motor body. At this point I was still trying to improve her boundaries by creating more of a separation between her and the environment and help her become more identified with her biological body or body ego. This is different than working with someone who is at a higher functioning level who I would want to help become more connected to their environment. I didn't want her to become one with her environment as he hadn't fully yet successfully separated from her environment the way healthier minded

---

[14] Wilber, K. *Integral Psychology: Consciousness, Spirit, Psychology, Therapy.* Boston: Shambala, 2000

[15] Winnicott, D. *Collected Papers.* New York: Basic Books 1958.

[16] Mahler, M. *On Human Symbiosis and the Vicissitudes of Individuation.* New York: International Univ. Press, 1968

[17] Kohut, H. *The Analysis of the Self.* New York. International Univ. Press, 1971.

[18] Blanck, G. & Blanck, R. *Ego Psychology II: Psychoanalytic Developmental Psychology.* New York: Columbia University Press, 1979.

people do. Her inside and outside worlds were confused causing most of her problems.

This confusion was heard when M spoke of her drumming. She referred to playing the drum as if it was a magical experience and that she was gaining a special magical power over the drum, as if it was a sort of ritual. She also spoke of the drum as if it was alive with personal qualities and a mind of its own.

Although M was capable of being aware of the playing of the other members in the group, I realized she was incapable of playing along with them. I then began to encourage M to play her rhythms more tightly with others in the group in an effort to help her to become more aware of the world surrounding her. Soon she was reacting to the playing of others but she was still not able to consciously conform to their playing. She was still too self-centered and narcissistic in her playing.

During the fifth week M showed much improvement and she began speaking more. Her speech showed that she was moving away from magical thoughts, magical thinking and magical imagery. She was adapting better to her medications and they were working to limit her hallucinations. At this stage I worked on increasing the duration of time of her drum rhythms and also pushing her to make her rhythms more sound, organized and adjusted. I encouraged her to play her moment to moment feelings and impressions in an effort to help free her from being chained to the present and help her expand her consciousness through the vehicle of the drum. The goal at this stage of therapy was to allow her drum beats to create a perceptive space quite beyond mere sensory input. She was still feeling a lot of anxiety and tension as she was still aware of her separateness and vulnerability, but her playing was improving and she was now developing rhythmic patterns that when compared to language sounded more like actual full sentences.

By the sixth week it was obvious that playing the drum rhythms was allowing M to combat her impulses by recalling and establishing a fuller world of time. She could understand the past and future on abstract terms and playing the drums was allowing her emotions to run freely through the world of time evoking more and more emotions. She was more able to picture sequences of things and events which weren't immediately present to her body senses and her rhythms when compared to language were now sounding more like extended sentences. She was now playing from the fourth charka.

Playing the drums was a way for her to transcend the simply present world and to anticipate the future. She was now able to delay her bodily impulses as drumming became her substitute for mere discharge reaction. It helped her create a period of time between stimulus and response. She was able to postpone the immediate and be less impulsive to her simple biological drives. She was no longer dominated by instinctual demands but to a better degree was able to transcend them. She was able to emerge from her body and emerge as a mental being. Drumming helped her delay her body's immediate discharges and postpone her instinctual gratifications. Her more advanced playing allowed sublimation for releasing emotional energies creating a healthier ego.

Now that M was in more control of herself she was now open to praise and self praise resulting in a sense of pride within her. In a way she transformed herself from a hopeless child into her own parent and began to create a persona to facilitate social interactions. Mental illness doesn't exist only in a person's mind but also between themselves and their environment. For this reason many psychologists believe that there should be an emphasis placed on social conditioning. Alfred Adler, Otto Rank, H.S. Sullivan, Karen Horney, and Eric Fromm all gave more attention to sociological factors. Rank emphasized social relationships in the etiology of emotional distress. Sullivan's "interpersonal therapy" claimed that the process of becoming human is the process of becoming socialized and Fromm detailed the vast interrelationships between psychic make-up and social structure.[19]

In the music therapy groups that M participated in social factors influenced her interaction or transaction between herself, her peers and her environment. In her individual sessions her focus was on "I". In the groups her focus was on "I and them". The way that she experienced reality and subsequently herself was influenced by the group's structures, social systems and the implied and unconscious rules of interaction between herself and her peers. These social conventions such as culture, logic, the group rules, and the group's ethics, its goals, plans and common sense assumptions were all symbolic relationships that distinguished the group and were eventually internalized by M.

M had to mold her prior awareness and perceptions into forms that were acceptable to the group and edit her reality into expressions that were acceptable by the group. She had to transform her experience to be socially meaningful in order to fit in with the group. She became accepted by the group when she successfully internalized their rhythms. She became part of the group when the group became a part of her. She learned to respond to the group as she believed the group members believed she should. This conventionalization to the group's reality entailed connecting her rhythms to the rhythms of others. She had to learn to play in a way that was conventional to the group in order to fit in and be understood. When her rhythms were too harsh, loud, fast, noisy or unmusical she just didn't get along with them very well. Eventually she was able to take her drum beat, which had little meaning by itself, and make it into something that was meaningful to the group. By themselves her drum rhythms pointed to, signified and meant very little. It

---

[19] Wilber, K. *The Spectrum of Consciousness.* Wheaton, Ill.: Quest, 1977 124

was the act of playing them with others that gave them meaning by making a socially verifiable connection with others. Her sound gained more meaning when combined with the sounds of others. The group's rules served to mold M's awareness into something meaningful to the group and all of those aspects of her reality which didn't conform were screened out and repressed by virtue of the group's rules. The group became M's filter of reality. In other words social factors molded M's sense of existence. Experiences that didn't play the game or follow the group's laws were outlawed and as psychoanalyst R.D. Laing states "If our wishes, feelings, desires...do not correspond to the law, they are outlawed.[20]

As the week went on she was able to dialogue on the drum with me and her peers with increased affect gaining more will power, self control and self esteem. Although her playing still wasn't very creative or imaginative she started to imitate the playing of others and began to take the role of others and understand some of the basic rules of playing with others. This opened up in her a new dimension of object relations, with a new sense of self and a new moral sensibility. Soon, I could hear her matching her beats to the rhythms that the group was playing. I could hear her desire to fit in, to belong, to find her musical place in the group among her peers, to understand the rules and conform. This helped her to develop a more positive view of her outer world and to connect and communicate with others. Her playing became heartfelt. She was now playing from her fourth and fifth chakra.

Playing the drum for longer lengths of time, more spontaneously with fewer inhibitions helped provide M access to the entire conventional world of extended temporal realities. She began to become more self actualized, integrated and autonomous and grounded in the present moment and more intellectual and intuitive. She was becoming more socially adapted, mentally adjusted, ego integrated, syntactically organized and conceptually advanced. Her more advanced rhythmic playing helped raise her above the fluctuations of the simple, instinctual, immediate impulsive ego to be able to visualize that which wasn't immediately present to the body senses, giving her a means of dealing with the non-present world and transcending the simply present world.

Expressing herself in time through rhythms helped her to anticipate the future and plan for it. Playing the drum helped her to delay and control her present bodily desires and activities. This is, as Fenichel explains, "a gradual substituting of actions for mere discharge reactions. This is achieved through the interposing of a time period between stimulus and response".[21] M was able to postpone and challenge the otherwise immediate and impulsive dis-

[20] R.D. Laing, *The Politics of the Family*, New York: Pantheon, 1971, p74
[21] Fenicle, O. *The Psychoanalytic Theory of Neurosis*. New York: Norton, 1945

charges of simple biological drives. She was no longer dominated by instinctual demands but was able to a certain degree transcend them and differentiate herself from her body and emerge as a more mental self which was able to work with her body using her own mental structures as tools delaying her bodies immediate discharges and postponing her instinctual gratifications, allowing a sublimation of her bodies emotional energies into more evolved activities using the tools of representational thinking. This is what Piaget calls "concrete operational thinking" or thinking that can operate on the concrete world.[22]

When working with a patient who is suffering with psychosis and whose verbal communications are somewhat confused, the developmental stages such as those discovered by Piaget and other developmental psychologists can often be seen more clearly and more directly in therapies that use non-verbal activities, such as music therapy than therapies that rely only on verbal language alone. This is why the developmental psychologists that discovered these stages did so by using activities such as playing with blocks or filing objects with sand and liquids rather than just speaking with the subjects. Watching the subjects perform actions on these objects provided these developmental psychologists with a clearer and more direct view of the stages of development as well as a better measuring stick for discovering the stages of development then just talking with them could do. Likewise directing the patient forward developmentally can often be done with a greater degree of accuracy with music therapy because the physical and mental actions when playing music can be used to more accurately see where the patient is developmentally and the direction they need to go in order to progress. It must be realized that the goal is not limited to moving the patient vertically through the stages as these stages take a very long time to move through. It must be realized that the average healthy person may only move through four or five stages in their entire lifetime which means when thinking of moving a person through vertical development it can take a period of five years or more. But the patient can immediately progress horizontally increasing their capabilities and level of functioning at the stage that they are currently at.

This occurs with the help of the theory of eros and thanatos. Eros being an integrating, consolidating, pulling together or preserving force and thanatos as an aggressive, differentiating, separating, dissolving, or negating force. Both eros and thanatos are phase-specifically necessary for overall development. Freud stated that the aim of eros "is to establish ever greater unities at the stage at which the person is at and to preserve them". The aim of thanatos "is, on the contrary, to undo the connections to that stage" or to dissolve

---

[22] Piaget, J. *The Essential Piaget.* Gruber and Voneche (eds.). New York: Basic Books, 1977

and negate them[23]. Hienz Hartman believed that differentiation, or separa-
tion-negation, is necessary with synthesis, or integration-preservation)[24].
The synthetic function being libido or drive (eros) and differentiation being
destruction (thanatos). Preservation (eros) occurs when the identifications
and object relations are being built and strengthened at the level allowing
increased and better functioning at that level. Negation (thanatos) helps by
dis-identification, separation and transcendence at the current stage so that
there can be transcendence to a higher stage. Eros helps a person better function at their current stage and thanatos helps the person disconnect from
their current stage and transcend to a higher stage.

Transcending through these musical emotional stages or lines aids the person in other areas of their lives as the different areas are interrelated or connected. For example when a person is given a medication which changes their
brain chemistry, this has an effect on the thoughts which than effects the way
the person relates to others which affects their social life. Likewise when a person's thoughts change to ones of either anxiety or depression these thoughts
will create changes in the person's brain chemistry as well as the way that they
relate to others affecting their social life. And thirdly, changes in a person's
social life, such as falling in love with another or getting into an argument,
will affect their thoughts which will then affect their brain chemistry. It is the
process of these interrelated connections that allow development in these
musical emotional stages to affect changes in other areas of their life such as
their thoughts, the way they relate to others and brain chemistry.

M began to become increasingly creative as she played. She was connecting to other group members by matching and imitating the rhythms that they
were playing and taking on their perspectives. But her mirroring was becoming excessive. She was copying the rhythms of others to avoid the fear of playing her own rhythm and being guilty of ruining the sound of the group. I then
took the opportunity during her individual session to work with her on drum
exercises that would help her to find the courage to not only imitate the playing of others but to create her own rhythms and thus allow her to think for
herself and still fit in without becoming anxious. Soon she was also able to
separate her rhythms from those played by her peers by playing with them in
a call and response style. She was able to listen to what they played and then
answer them with a completely different rhythm. She was imagining more
possibilities. Her playing wasn't as dry and abstract as in previous weeks but
she was now playing with more feeling. Also, the individual sessions that we
did over the past six weeks gave us the opportunity to talk more personally

[23] Freud, A. *The Ego and the Mechanisms of Defense*. New York: InternationalUniv. Press, 1946
[24] Hartman, H. *Ego Psychology and the Problem of Adaption*. New York: International Univ. Press, 1958

than we were able to in the group. In the individual music therapy sessions we were able to talk about her sensitivity to criticisms made by peers about her playing and how she became hurt and angry when peers in the group refused to mirror her playing (narcissistic mirror transference). How she would sometimes overly flatter my skills as a therapist stating that I was the best therapist at PHP (splitting)[25]. We also spoke of her avoidance of making close friendships with peers at PHP for fear of being swallowed up or smothered (fear of engulfment) and her fear of leaving PHP and her request to stay longer (fear of separation.)

The work we did during the groups, her individual sessions on the drum and talking about her problems helped her to become more introspective. She was able to activate herself. Her motivation to get well was increasing and she was becoming more confident and relaxed. She was also developing a beautiful smile.

M is still suffers from schizophrenia. She must take medications daily and work with her mind so that she continues to progress forward and not regress. But after leaving PHP she was been able to return to college and pursue her career as her inner and outer beauty emerged.

Most of the patients that I work with at PHP have lifelong chronic illnesses, and it would be unrealistic to believe that they could be totally cured of these serious illnesses by just playing the drums in music therapy sessions. But what music therapy does is improve the quality of the patient's life. It helps ease the anger, guilt, fear and resentment that these patients have to deal with on a daily basis. It teaches them that because they have mental illness they don't have to think of themselves as failures. After all, these are people with hopes and dreams, and loves and children. Music therapy doesn't just treat mentally ill patients who are people, but rather treats people who only incidentally have mental illness.

As Dr Khatija paperwalla, Director of PHP states: "Therapy is more than just talk and medication, but it encompasses a broader range of modalities including music, art and dance. Patient M was able to make great improvement during her stay at PHP in large part due to her ability to engage in playing the drums in music therapy. Just like different learnings styles, patients may have differing therapy styles that they respond to, and excel with,as already seen with patient M. I freel strongly that creative therapies are an important aspect of healing that are often underutilized. I am very fortunate to see how they enhance patients' recoveries on a daily basis, whether it be improvement in connecting themselves to reality, or allowing them to lessen or better control a symptom or side effect. These types of therapies are aiding patients move forward in their lives, and there is no better gift a therapist can give."

---

[25] splitting is dividing the self and the world into "all good" and "all bad" representations.

In this next piece, John Scalici, Occupational Therapist, Drum Circle Facilitator describes his experience providing his program to psychiatric patients:

Rhythm Establishes Connections by John Scalici

Drumming and rhythm can be a powerful tool for reducing stress and anxiety, while simultaneously satisfying many of the goals of the occupational therapist during a given session.

In June of 2005, I was contacted by VSA Arts of Alabama (a non-profit organization which provides opportunities in the arts for people with chronic illnesses) to facilitate outcome-based rhythm and drumming activities with adolescent and child psychiatric patients at Children's Hospital in Birmingham, AL. I initially met with Michelle Puckett, MS, OTR/L and Lauren Hansell, MS, OTR/L, to discuss our goals and activities. These goals include:

• Establish positive peer interaction
• Learn sequencing skills
• Develop social skills
• Learn appropriate self expression through the drum
• Attending to task

Because our groups frequently change, by size and diagnosis types, we have established a protocol that gives us some consistency in measuring results.

Before each session, we have a briefing of any new dynamics that may be going on within the group. I gather as much information from this short meeting as possible.

To start the session, I introduce an ocean drum, a two-headed, thin instrument with metal beads inside, which when held level, will produce the soothing sounds of the ocean. This activity establishes a few key concepts as we pass from person to person:

Positive peer interaction

Sequencing and coordination skills (taking the drum from one person, holding it balanced, experiencing it for an appropriate length of time then passing it on.)

Using the metaphor of balance. This is a teachable moment to comment that when our emotions and feelings are in balance, then our lives come into balance. With the help of our OT team, we reinforce the idea of healthy expression of emotion to achieve balance. For some, attaining this balance means taking medication or continuing counseling.

Next, small percussion instruments are laid out inside the circle. Patients choose from instruments such as shakers, rattles, finger cymbals, bells, and wooden frogs. As this is done, there is some chaos—another teachable moment! This is a good time to introduce some visual/verbal cues to help us control our "new voices" as well as practicing turn taking and appropriate peer interactions.

As we proceed with the activity, I explain that we will create a rhythm or sound with our new voices one at a time, upon me making eye contact with the first person to my right or left. As I play a simple rhythm on my drum, I look to the person next to me, inviting them to play along with me. Because I am the one creating the steady beat, there is no need for the others to maintain a steady rhythm. The activity becomes about building eye contact and social skills and learning how to function as a group.

When that person has played for a brief moment, they make eye contact with the next person, signaling that it is their turn to play. This continues around the circle. Next, I asked them to play "together", creating a bit of "controlled chaos".

I use body language to signal them to play quietly (which I can do because I have spent time establishing trust and building rapport with the group). The activity ends by me asking the group to collectively fade out their sounds. With this simple activity, we have achieved several goals:

- Non-verbal communication skills (making eye contact)
- Auditory sequencing
- Creativity as an individual and as a group
- Accountability and responsibility

The final activities utilize hand drums.

Drumming and Family Practice

Jim Anderson, MFT is a Licensed Marriage and Family Therapist in Private Practice in Temecula, California. Over the past two years Jim has worked at the Childhelp Merv Griffin Village with abused and neglected children, where he has designed and implemented a new innovative Music Based Therapy Program which uses music, drumming and songwriting as a therapeutic tool for growth and change.

Drumming and Relationships in
Therapeutic Practice by Jim Anderson

Why would someone want to use drumming in therapy practice?

I think the answer is best summarized in the following statement made by a 13 year old boy I recently worked with in a level 12 group home:

After a very difficult morning, Joe ended up in my office in crisis. It wasn't unusual for him to be in crisis, but it was my first time working with him. He had assaulted a peer and was threatening a teacher when he had to be restrained after being assessed as a danger to self and others. Diagnosed with Bi-Polar disorder, he sat in my office so upset and full of rage that he couldn't even talk.

I told him that we didn't have to talk and that talking was over-rated. I instead, handed him a pair of drumsticks and asked him to play his anger for me on my digital drumset. The intensity of the rhythms he played took me on a long journey through his childhood and what it felt like the abuse and torment he experienced as a young boy. The sadness in his beats mirrored and traced the outlines of the 25 failed placements he had experienced over the past 10 years in the foster care system. After this release, his beat changed to an almost celebratory march. It was a like a slice of heaven for him in those moments he played with happiness.

As quickly as it all started, he suddenly stopped and with a tear in his eye gave me a very heartfelt thank you. He told me that coming to my office and drumming together was the only real break he had ever felt from his own mind. He said it was like a new part of him had been born and that he felt released from the sadness he experienced living in group homes. He said that drumming was like traveling somewhere else, maybe to a different time and a different dimension. He said it was like taking the best journey he had ever taken, to a place where he was finally free from all of his anger he felt inside.

As I watched him walk back to school, I realized that something very profound had happened that day. Drumming had changed his life in those moments! It was like a journey through his past that cemented a deep connection between us. Joe and I continue to play drums together in his treatment and he is making remarkable strides in dealing with his past abuse, his anger and his depression.

CHAPTER EIGHT

Drumming and Societal Challenges

Drumming and Conversations

The two young adults sat across from one another, with a Remo djembe drum between them. The entire group felt their stares, as both clenched their hands. These two men were beginning "Drumming Conversations" as a way to resolve some of their differences. The Hudson County Detention Center provided the framework. The goal was to provide a tool for these men to displace their emotions, vent them so that rather then express their anger through hurting one another, they would take their anger and play their drums. The room was silent, but the stares were palpable. Jim (name changed) hit the drum first, then James (name changed) hit his. Their only instruction was to feel their feelings as they played their drum, and to have a drumming conversation. No words could be spoken once the exercise began. Amazing how an entire room can feel the tension of two individuals. James hit his drum right back. Suddenly, both detainees' hands were flying as they expressed their anger through the intensity of their drumming. I monitored their playing, making sure that they didn't hurt themselves in the process. Suddenly, something happened. Amidst the flurry of drumming, a beat emerged. James starting playing a steady rhythm, hitting his drum, in a constant 4/4 rhythm. Jim, then began playing against James beat, and suddenly what was an aggressive intense, exchange of displaced violence, became a rhythm song. As the two men continued to drum, the entire room began to clap along with this unexpected rhythm song, as the other detainees joined in. The two men started smiling.

Othaday shares how the highs of drumming spread all over the land.

"Join Us" (Drumming and the Community) by Otha Day

I met Linda through an article written about me in a local newspaper. She asked me to assist her in finding her rhythm. Totally spontaneously and fortuitously Linda and I met for our first session at a health food store/restaurant. As my car was full of drums, I suggested that our first lesson be on the sidewalk outside the restaurant.

I took out about 10 drums, tambourines, claves, shakers and we set up on the side-walk....after 5 minutes, a couple of homeless men joined us, then a couple of folks from the restaurant came rushing out, then a number of other passersbyers joined in.....IT WAS FANTASTIC!! I LOVED IT!! It was in great part the spirit and joy that she had that showed me how to open that part of me up to folks in that circle.

After that, Linda made a beautiful sign that said simply "JOIN US!" and we continued this pattern of going to a new town/city and setting up, putting out our sign a couple of times each week for about 6 weeks (never asking for money, of course)...and just as Arthur says, these gigs led to a number of wonderful other opportunities that were paying: a large drum circle for a church as an opening for a benefit for a Rwandan girl, a wonderful totally spontaneous drum circle for about 40 "Emerging Leaders" teachers as the very last event on the very last day of a state-wide summer teacher conference, a corporate gig and on and on...None of those gifts to me were planned.

Drumming Out Drugs – Research from Dr. Michael Winkelman[26]

Another area of research has been the use of drumming for addictions. In his research paper "Drumming Out Drugs", Dr. Michael Winkelman, PhD, MPH found that "shut-down, disenfranchised youth came alive as drumming gave them an avenue of expression." In his research, Dr. Winkleman shared a number of programs that use drums for addictions. One of these involved Mark Seaman and Earth Rhythms. In Seaman's program, he begins by drumming as the individuals enter the room. He follows this with warm-up exercises, teaching them how to hit the drum. He asks the group to play spontaneously and to play how they feel. Seaman describes the drumming as a "letting go" process. He ends with visualizing, to focus on connecting to a higher power. Seaman found that drumming pulls a group together, creating community. One of the challenges of working with individuals with addictions is that they tend to be "self-centered, disconnected and feel isolated, even around other people. The drumming produces a sense of connectedness that they are desperate for. Drums penetrate people at a deep level."

Wilkinson next describes Ed Mikenas and the Lynchburg Day Program. Mikenas is a substance abuse counselor and drummer. Mikenas shared that drumming emphasizes self-expression, "teaches how to rebuild emotional health, and addresses issues of violence and conflict through expression and integration of emotion".

---

[26] Winkelman, Michael. Complementary Therapy for Addiction: "Drumming Out Drugs" *American Journal of Public Health*; April 2003 Vol. 93 No. 4

Mikenas taught his group basic skills, and complex dances. Mikeas used Afrocentric traditions, and Afro-Cuban and Brazilian rhythms. He found that drumming draws people in and alters their consciousness; they discover their potential and learn to lead.

Through drumming, people go from chaos to an orderly sense of feeling. They address "unhealthy emotional reactions" and stimulate pleasurable feelings without drugs. They glow. Drumming teaches nurturing, respect in relationships, and honesty.

Myron Eshowsky's Shamanic Counseling Approach

Eshowsky is trained as a shamanic counselor and has worked with drug and alcohol addicts. Working with storytelling, journeying, healing work and dance, he found that drumming and shamanic journeying calmed them. Those in the program used drugs less, and there was a dip in drug-related violence. It's also proven useful with street gangs.

In summary, Dr. Winkelman found that "drumming produces physiological, psychological and social stimulation that enhances recovery processes. It induces relaxation and produces natural pleasurable experiences, enhanced awareness and release of emotional trama. It also helped those in attendance to reintegrate themselves. It addressed "self-centeredness, isolation and alienation", all qualities of addiction.

"Drumming circles and other shamanic altered state of consciousness activites can address multiple needs of addicted populations. These include physiological dynamics, inducing the relaxation response and restoring balance, psychodynamic needs for self-awareness and insight, emotional healing and psychological integration, spiritual needs for contact with a higher power and social needs for connectedness and interpesonal support." He believes that drumming "may reduce addiction by providing natural alterations of consciousness."

CHAPTER NINE

Where Have We Come, Where Are We Going?

When I first wrote the *Healing Power of the Drum* there were fourteen drum circle facilitators listed in the reference section, no training programs, and only a handful of research had used drumming as a vehicle for wellness.

As demonstrated by the reference section in this book alone, the number of facilitators available to provide support in this arena has skyrocketed, and continues to grow. There are over seven training programs available now for individuals who are seeking this path, and the field is certainly expanding as more and more information and evidence demonstrates the reality that hand drumming has health benefits.

In this writer's opinion, based on both the anecdotal stories presented in this book and the clinical data found, there can be no doubt that the drum is a healing vehicle. Something positive consistently happens, whether it is stress relief, emotional release, creative expression, or as Arthur Hull so eloquently shared, the quality of release.

We cannot separate the healing power of the drum from what it inspires; dance, song, and other instruments also demonstrate how music heals. Musical expression bares the soul.

In this essay from the father of the Drum Circle Movement, Arthur Hull shares where we have been and where we are going:

Drum Circles Then and Now

There are healthy free-form anarchist drum circles all over the world. They are like the ones I encountered in the late 1960s: a beautiful combination of freedom and spirit. Culturally specific drum circles existed then as well, but except at a few universities in the U.S., these circles were focused mostly on Afro- Cuban and Brazilian rhythms.

Back then, all that existed was free-form drumming circles and culturally specific drum circles. Now, drum circles range from the study of specific African, Caribbean and South American drumming cultures, to rhythmacultures from around the world, including Polynesian drumming, Japanese Taiko drumming and Balinese gamalong music.

Even the free-form drumming community now has many variation and forms of expressions, from the rainbow type of drum circle to the different types of modern earth worshipping pagan drumming circles such as the Fire Tribe and the Phoenix fire drumming community.

The family friendly Paralounge Drum Gathering, created by Clint Tipton, is a good example of the evolving free-form drumming community. It is a place where free-form drummers and culturally specific drummers can come together, exchange ideas, rhythms and play with each other in a supportive environment. At the Paralounge, oil and water can mix.

It is 43 years since the Summer of Love and that vast wasteland between free-form drumming and culturally specific drum circles is being filled with gender-empowerment circles, drum programs in schools, hospitals, corporate meetings, prisons, and family friendly community drum gatherings.

Now, wherever people gather, there is an opportunity to use rhythm based events for team building, community building, message delivery, stress relief, and just plain old in-the- moment music-making fun.

Population shifts from 60s to today

What started as a drumming fad has become a worldwide movement used by all types of professionals that serve a wide range of constituencies through facilitated rhythm-based events.

For the last 17 years I have been traveling to at least 10 countries a year, teaching drum circle facilitation training to over 7,000 people so far. In each country, when I first arrive, the population of a Village Music Circle Facilitators Playshop sometimes is dominated by one particular type of job description, such as drum teachers in Germany, kids at risk counselors in Australia.

But by the fourth or fifth time I had returned for another session in these countries, the population demographics of the training had shifted and evolved to include all types of job descriptions. These people have discovered that facilitated rhythm-based events are a powerful tool that they can use in the community they are serving.

Major reason for growth

A community drum circle is a celebration of life through the spirit of rhythm and drumming. Participating in a drum circle is a healing experience for hearts, minds, and bodies.

"This is fine for the drummers," you might think, "but I am a musically challenged rhythm dork!"

That is the big lie that our culture has put on us as we were forced to "grow up and act our age," or put into the dumb section of the school chorus and told to whisper, or taught by an oppressive music teaching system that we never want to pick up a musical instrument again.

The big lie is that our western society is a rhythmically challenged culture.

We are all rhythmic beings who have a rhythmic spirit that can be facilitated to express it to its fullest in group drumming situations.

After facilitating thousands of rhythm based corporate events under the guise of team building, culture change or diversity, I know that even the most rhythmically challenged person can successfully contribute their rhythmic spirit as a part of an "in the moment" collaborative rhythmic and musical event called a drum circle.

A group of any size playing together will create a positive group consciouaness. A drumming event creates a kinesthetic massage that goes to all the heads, hearts, bodies and souls of the people within close proximity of the circle. This group rhythm massage goes to the places in each individual that need it the most, and creates emotional, mental and physical "release."

When we contribute our rhythmic spirit to the group's music making, we merge our consciousness through the sharing of our rhythmic bliss.

That experience naturally takes us way beyond looking for the One in the music. We come to that place where we are one with each other as well as with the music.

There are rhythm evangelist pioneers doing their work in populations all over the world, from schools to parent- teacher meetings, to church services to hospitals and clinics, and so on.

All my students eventually become my teachers and I continue to learn and grow from their experiences.

Future of the drum circle movement

Babatunde Olatunji predicted that at some time in the future there would be a drum in every house hold. When I first heard that prediction 20 years ago, I scoffed at the enormity of his vision.

After watching Baba follow his mission, share his spirit and help birth what is the foundation of the recreational drumming movement in America today, it is obvious that his prediction will someday become true.

As more cultures are absorbing the use of facilitated drum circle events as a tool for healing and unity in many parts of their community, I and many other rhythmic evangelists like me will help fulfill Babatunde Olatunji's dream and legacy.

Drum circles are not a fad. They are a lifestyle.

(Reprinted with Permission from *Drum Circle Magazine* (www.drumcirclemagazine.com)

Drums are indeed here to stay, but we still need more research to prove what the anecdotes of this book make clear.

Music Therapy vs. Drum Circle Facilitation

As a psychotherapist and drum circle facilitator who straddles the world of therapy and music, I think it is important to differentiate the world of the drum circle facilitator and the music therapist.

As shared by the Drum Circle Facilitators Guild (www.dcfg.net) a drum circle facilitator is:

"an individual who makes an interactive music making experience "easier" for the participants. A facilitator creates a space for the expression of community by empowering the group of participants with a safe and fun atmosphere and tools for expression, enabling them with technique and encouraging them with fun. Trained professional facilitators recognize the need for empowering each individual as the consciousness of the entire group evolves into a musical composition. Drum circle facilitators act in service to the group, helping individuals achieve greater personal potential, shared joy, and interdependent group dynamics. A facilitator develops a rapport with the participants and through various techniques is able to assist the music into various compositions unique to the population.The drum circle facilitator may come from any number of fields, education, counselor, music, nonprofessional, and receive training to be facilitator of drum circles. The major difference of the music therapist is that the music therapist has received specific therapeutic training that requires music therapy licensure,and they are able to diagnose and treat illnesses that fall within their venue."

When a drum circle facilitator works with a therapeutic population it is recommended that they work with a music therapist or therapist who may be better suited to assist clients when there are emotional issues that arise.

Tony Scarpa, music therapist and licensed creative arts therapist shares his thoughts on music therapy:

The musical techniques used in music therapy sessions I do are based on musical structures. Structures in music are formed by the musical elements such as harmony, rhythm, and the types of musical instruments that are used and so on. There are two types of musical structures: surface structures and deep structures. The simplest way to understand these musical structures, without having knowledge of music theory, is that the deep structures are the structures that allow you to tell the difference between different types of music. In other words, the reason that classical, jazz and popular styles of music are different from each other is because of their deep structures. Surface structures allow you to tell the difference between two songs that are within the same style. In other words classical music sounds different from jazz, country, rock or folk music because of their deep structures, but two pieces of music within the same style, such as two classical pieces, sound different from each other because of their surface structures. This would hold true for all styles of music such as jazz, country, hip hop, R&B, and rock or folk. We can also approximate what the music of hunter gatherers 40,000 years ago sounded like because of our knowledge of its deep structures. For example, we know the types of instruments that were used back then as a result of archeological findings, and the types of instruments qualify as one example of the musical elements. But we don't know the music's surface structures because we have no written or recorded samples of their music. In other words we never actually heard it. But we do know the surface as well as the deep structures of pop, rock or classical music because we can currently listen to them.

The music therapist helps the patient develop both the surface structure and deep structures of their music. Working with a patient on surface structures would be a form of horizontal development. Working with a patient on deep structures would be a form of vertical development. The best way to understand the difference between horizontal and vertical development would be to think of a 10 story building. Improving the floor of a building by doing repairs on the floor would be an example of horizontal development. Moving from one floor to the next would be a form of vertical development. In other words horizontal development is a way to improve or make a person feel better at the level of development that they are at. Vertical development on the other hand is making a more radical life change to another stage of development in a person's life. In music therapy horizontal change would make improvements in self esteem, confidence, improved concentration, focus and attention span. Vertical development would lead to self-actualization, transformational growth and healing.

Working with a patient's musical structures leads directly to changes in their behavior, especially in the social realm. This is because the musical structures have direct correlates with social structures as our social interactions also have similar structures to that of music. These surface and deep structures in music and socializing are similar as they both involve interacting with others. Music and socialization are similar enough so that when the musical structures are developed the social structures also become developed. As previously stated – changes in a person's inner thoughts and feelings create changes in a person's social life and vice versa.

Since working as a music therapist I find the drum to be a most powerful tool for its ability to connect one to what Freud calls our archaic heritage or what Wilber calls the archaic-unconscious.[27] "Freud had once thought that our thoughts could be traced back to real life experiences, but he came to see that many of our thoughts could not possibly been generated by personal experiences. He stated "In them the individual...stretches out...to the experience of past ages."[28] This "archaic heritage" includes besides instincts "abbreviated repetitions of the evolution undergone by the whole human race through long-drawn-out periods and from prehistoric ages". This is in full agreement with Jung who speaks of images which he called "archetypes". "Man inherits these images from his ancestral past, a past that includes all of his human ancestors as well as his pre-human or animal ancestors. These racial images are not inherited in the sense that a person consciously remembers or has images that his ancestors had. Rather they are predispositions or potentialities for experiencing and responding to the world in the same way that his ancestors did".[29]

Generally speaking, the basic rule of thumb that I recommend is that in any intentional drum circle focusing on releasing emotions or which has a psychodynamic focus, it is recommended to have a music therapist or psychotherapist present to assist in providing support.

---

[27] Wilber, K. *The Atman project: A transpersonal view of human development.* Wheaton, Ill.: Quest. 1977
[28] Freud, S. *A general introduction to psychoanalysis.* New York: Pocket Books, 1971
[29] Hall, C. *A primer of Jungian psychology.* New York: Mentor 1973

Resources

Music Therapists

Kalani, KALANI MUSIC
11862 Balboa Blvd. Suite 159
Granada Hills, CA 91344
www.kalanimusic.com
www.playsinglaugh.com
www.musictherapydrumming.com
www.worldpercussiontracks.com
SKYPE/iChat: kalanimusic
Face Book: Kalani Percussionist
Kalani uses music and music-based experiences to help groups of all kinds reach their goals in education, recreation, therapy and various areas of personal and professional development.

Tony Scarpa, MA, LCMT
tonehealer@optonline.net 516-581-2320

Christine Stevens, MSW, MT-BC
christine@ubdrumcircles.com
www.ubdrumcircles.com 970-310-8010

Additional music therapists in your area can be located through:

The American Music Therapy Association: phone: 301-589-3300
www.namt.com

Family Therapists

Jim Anderson, MS, MFT
Family Therapist
JimDrumz@aol.com
www.DrumsAndPercussion.com
p. 909-549-9400 f. 909-549-0549

Drum Circle Facilitators

UNITED STATES
Don Allen
Drum 4 Wellness LLC
www.drum4wellness.net

Bob Bloom
bb@drumming-about-you.com
www.drumming-about-you.com
860-429-9280
Bob Bloom is the founder and director of "Drumming About You", a participatory drumming program that is accessible to all age groups, and is inclusive of people of challenge.

Jim Boneau
Bluepoint Leadership Development
Seattle, WA
www.bluepointleadership.com
206-853-3628
At Bluepoint we believe we can accelerate the natural development of leadership skills in teams, managers, and leaders at all levels of all organizations. We combine one on one coaching with dynamic experiential workshops that challenge, engage, teach and grow leaders through Bluepoint's unique style of growth and development.

Nathan Brenowitz, MS
life@ulster.net
www.maximal.nu/brenpp
914-679-6855

Jana Broder, Drum Magic
Apollo Beach, Fl
www.drummagic.com
www.corporatedrummagic.com
www.drumcirclemagazine.com
janabroder@drummagic.com
Drum Magic brings interactive drumming to groups throughout the United States. Populations served include School aged children, senior citizens, at risk youth, developmentally handicapped adults/children, corporations, and college athletes.

Randy Brody, Weston, Connecticut
Sound Directions/Drum-N-Dance
www.sounddirections.net
rbdrumguy@sbcglobal.net
203-544-7085
Group drumming and rhythm-based programs for staff development, team building, wellness, recreational therapy, special education and community events. Graduate of HealthRHYTHMS® and Unity With a Beat, and certified Music for People facilitator.

Michelle G. Cappellieri, CSC, CPLRC Circle Rhythms, 203-767-2397
michelle@circlerhythms.com
Circle Rhythms hosts transformational rhythm and music circles at our urban farm sanctuary in Stratford, Connecticut.

Robin Cardell, Oshkosh, Wisconsin
Oshkosh Rhythm Institute
www.oshkoshrhythm.com
robinc@oshkoshrhythm.com
920-379-2217
Offering regular community drum circles, Health Rhythms programs and professional facilitation of rhythm based activities and events in NE Wisconsin. Programs for schools, church groups, folks facing various challenges, and private parties, as well as, team building, leadership, and diversity workshops.

Pete Carels, Rhythm Expedition,
Drum Teacher Oxford, Ohio
carelspe@hotmail.com 513-523-8614
Specializing in groups of 10 to 50 participants, all ages.

Michael Clark, Drumatic Innovation Inc
6037 Sunrise Beach Rd NW
Olympia WA 98502
Michael@DrumaticInnovation.com
208-485-7501
DrumaticInnovation.com

Chuck Cogliandro, Kumandi Drums
p. 404-577-6842 f. 404-289-5726
www.kumandi.com
chuck@kumandi.com
Populations: corporate, conference, schools, churches, well elderly, healing, spiritual, learning disabled

Ken Crampton, Eyeclopes / Everybody Drum, 620 Charlotte Street
Fredericksburg, Va 22401
(540) 371-9040
www.everybodydrum.com
ken@everybodydrum.com
Drums and percussion are as diverse as the individuals playing them. Programs developed with Everybody Drum fit individual organizations needs for education, icebreakers, team-building and community building.

Steve Durbin, Playworks® M 0431 369 197 steve@playworksoz.com

Pete Ellison, One World Rhythm, Inc.
United States, Burbank, California
oneworldrhythm.com
pete@oneworldrhythm.com
(818) 332-0679, (818) 848-3512
Pete is a professional Drum Circle Facilitator and Motivational Speaker/Consultant working in Los Angeles California. Pete's company *One World Rhythm* specializes in kid's rhythm programs as well as general population drum circles. Pete is a Remo Artist & Member of the Vic Firth Educational team.

Lori Fithian, Drummunity!
4889 Birch Lane Dexter,
Michigan 48130 734.426.7818
lorifithian@mac.com
www.drummunity.com
I am a full-time facilitator based in Southeast Michigan. I travel all around with my van-load of drums and percussion and serve any and all community groups: Schools, Libraries, Camps, Wellness Centers, Faith Communities, Festivals, Workplaces, Conventions, Retreats, Family Celebrations, etc. Pre-schools to Nursing homes, every age, every ability.

John Fitzgerald,
Manager of Recreational Music Activities for Remo Inc, Freelance percussionist, Healthrhythms Trainer
jfitzgerald@remo.com
Facilitates with a wide range of populations for the purpose of celebration, empowerment, team cohesion and community building are central to John's interests and passion.

Robert Lawrence, Friedman, MA, CPP
Stress Solutions, Inc.
Drumming Celebration™
Drumming for Teambuilding
Drumming Away Stress™
Drum Circles For Wellness™
New York, New York, 718-520-1794
e-mail: stress.solutions@gmail.com
www.stress-solutions.com
www.drumming-event.com
http://shop.stress-solutions.com
718-520-1794
Robert creates local, regional and international rhythm-based events for corporations, conferences, retreats, health care institutions, family reunions for the purpose of stress management, leadership development, teambuilding, celebration, teambuilding and providing greater health and wellness.

Kat Fulton, Sound Health Music
San Diego, CA
Kat@SoundHealthMusic.com
www.RhythmForGood.com
Rhythm For Good is an online resource with tips, videos, and articles on making music in medical, wellness, and recreational settings with people across the lifespan.

Jordan Goodman
Jordan's Drum Studio/Beat Well Blog
Baltimore, MD
www.jordansdrumstudio.com
jordansdrums@gmail.com
Jordan Goodman is a dynamic drum and percussion educator, facilitator and performer. He has bridged his passion for rhythm in his Clinical Psychology Master's program, using the drum specifically with ADHD and anxiety disorder populations.

Jim Greiner, Hands-on!
Drumming Programs
jgreiner@cruzio.com
www.handsondrum.com
831-462-3786
Jim Greiner is a nationally-known touring percussion and educator who leads team-building, drumming events and celebrations for corporations, conferences and communities through his company, Hands-On! Drumming Events.

Ed Haggard, The Love Drums
USA
info@thelovedrums.com
www.thelovedrums.com, 615-727-2724
Ed Haggard and The Love Drums facilitate drum circles for corporate, church, youth, and spiritual groups. They provide performances for festive and ritual occasions of all types. Ed has taught thousands of drum classes for youth and adults. Ed is also a team building facilitator on ropes courses and in other settings.

Bonnie D. Harr
P.O. Box 345, Youngstown, PA !5676
QuietPsalm@aol.com, 724-539-0536

Patricia Hatfield,
Harmony Drum Circles
Santa Rosa, California
plhatfield@earthlink.net
www.harmonydrumcircles.com
Patricia Hatfield is a drum circle facilitator, sound healing practitioner, and senior programs consultant who offers individual and group sessions for personal growth, teambuilding, empowerment and transformation, with experience serving diverse populations, including Seniors facility residents, the visually impaired, community drum circles and special circles.

Derek E. Hemenway, Ed.S., NCC
Trained HealthRhythms Drum Circle
Facilitator Positive Path Solutions
1361 Lawndale Road
Tallahassee, Florida 32317
(850) 541-2633
Derek.Hemenway@yahoo.com

Nellie Hill, Playful Spirit Adventures
Drum Circle Facilitator and Coach
Located in Maryland/ Washington,
DC metropolitan area. Serving all
populations, consultant to music
educators everywhere
www.playfulspiritadventures.com
playfulspirit@mac.com, 301 776 2382

Dave Holland
Beatin' Path Rhythm Events
Atlanta, GA
www.beatinpathrhythmevents.com
info@beatinpathrhythmevents.com
404-819-4053
Beatin' Path Rhythm Events provides high energy performances, workshops and drum circles in community, educational and corporate environments! Whether it's a rhythmic storytelling session for preschoolers or a conference opener for a major corporation, we are committed to sharing the power, magic and creative possibilities of interactive rhythm making!

Arthur Hull
Community Building in Community
Festivals, Spirit-Building in Colleges
and Conferences, Team-Building in
Corporations, Unity Through
Diversity Village Music Circles
Facilitators Playshop
drum@drumcircle.com
www.drumcircle.com, 831-458 1946
Arthur Hull, author of *Drum Circle Spirit and Drum Circle Facilitation*, is recognized as the father of the community drum circle movement.

Lee Kix
HealthRHYTHMS Facilitator
Costa Mesa, CA
www.circlethedrums.com
714-323-7332

Joseph Lorincz and Steve Caulkins
One Heart Community Drummers
7308 Coldwater Canyon
North Hollywood, CA 9605
www.oneheartcommunitydrumming.org
oneheartcommunitydrummers@yahoo.com
Our "Drum Circle to Go" program offers innovative, interactive, and experiential facilitated drum circles. Business and corporations find our facilitated drum circles fantastic for team- building and leadership training. In addition community events, personal growth workshops, corporate and private parties create an enviornment that allow people of all ages, regardless of skill levels or experience to participate together as one.

Toni Kellar, Roots To Rhythm
24718 Lakeland Road
Senecaville, OH 43780
www.rootstorhythm.com
info@rootstorhythm.com
740-838-1343   *continued*

Roots To Rhythm offers interactive development programs and rhythm events for conferences keynotes and breakout sessions; business, workplace and team development programs; and community groups including youth, festivals and health and wellness.

Neysa Lettin, HealthRHYTHMS
Provider Heartbeats to Drumbeats
Centennial, Colorado 80121 njldrums@comcast.net

Jaqui MacMillan, Drum For Joy!
Westminster, MD
www.drumforjoy.com, 410-346-6884
drumforjoyjaqui@gmail.com

Solange Monette, M.A. & Sinde Rubiner
Facilitators
Rhythm for Change, LLC
3143 E. Kleindale Rd, Unit 3
Tucson, AZ 85716 p. 520 325-2212
RhythmForChangeAZ.com
info@RhythmForChangeAZ.com

Jonathan Murray
FunDrum Rhythm Circles
'Celebrating Community Through Rhythm'
www.fundrumrhythmcircles.com
http://fundrum.blogspot.com
410 964-DRUM (3786)
fundrum@verizon.net
FunDrum Rhythm Circles facilitates rhythm-based events designed for team-building, wellness and celebration. Jonathan regularly works with professional groups (for- profit companies, state government and non-profit corporations) and community institutions (schools, churches and nursing homes). Jonathan also teaches adult and children's classes in world drumming.

Jorge Ochoa, OTR
Occupational Therapist
TamboRhythms: Wellness
Through Rhythm
San Antonio, Texas
Community, Educational, Corporate,
and Health &Wellness Events
www.tamborhythms.com
tamborhythms@yahoo.com
210-289-7100

Jim Oshinsky
MusicforPeople.org
ReturnToChild.com
jim@musicforpeople.org
Music Improvisation workshops
Jim has worked alongside cellist David Darling in the organization Music for People for over 20 years, and he is the author of "Return to Child," a book about personal and ensemble improvisation (and how to teach it). Jim is available for drum circles near his home on Long Island, NY, and for consultations on facilitation training.

Othaday, Drum To The Beat
www.DrumToTheBeat.com
1568 Massachusetts Ave.
North Adams, MA. 01267
413.884.5088
OthaDay@DrumToTheBeat.com
Otha facilitates fun and lively drum/rhythm circle events from the deep belief that rhythm has the power to build community, promote well-being and create joy. Working with groups of participants from 4 to 400, he supports awareness of the presence of rhythm in every act of living knowing that "your HeartBeat is the rhythm of your soul."

Augie "Doggie" Peltonen
Augie Doggie Drumcircles
203 11th St. North Brigantine,
New Jersey 08203
Augie4doggie@hotmail.com
Augie mentors facilitator trainings in Oahu, Hawaii with Arthur Hull's Village Music Circles Playshops. He also facilitates drum circles for youth at risk, healing circles at the local rehabilitation hospital, and does drum circles at the African American churches in Atlantic City.

John Scalici
1012 55th St. South
B'Ham, AL 35222 p. 205-222-6998
www.GetRhythmPrograms.com
Founder of Get Rhythm!®. He facilitates rhythm based events, including leadership and team building programs, innovative programming for special needs adults and children, and rhythmic development workshops. The mission of all Get Rhythm!® programs is to empower people to realize their full human potential through the power of rhythm.

C.Barry Skeete, Drum With Me
United States, Largo/Clearwater, Florida
www.drumwithme.com
www.bluejayrhythms.com
barry@bluejayrhythms.com
727-235-7228
Drum circles for everyone, Power of Sound Workshops

Christine Stevens
UpBeat Drum Circles
Ashti Drum REMO
HealthRHYTHMS™
info@ubdrumcircles.com
www.ubdrumcircles.com
Upbeat Drum Circles is the premiere company for drumming and wellness, keynotes and diversity training. We offer products and services for the daily drum lifestyle, facilitation training and private coaching.

Scott L. Swimmer
drumSTRONG™ DrumsForCures, Inc.
725 Providence Rd. Suite #210
Charlotte, NC 28207
scott@drumstrong
org www.drumstrong.org
704.375.7177/704.996.9170

DRUMSTRONG presented by
DrumsForCures, Inc.
www.drumstrong.org
725 Providence Rd. #210
Charlotte, NC 28207

704.375.7177
¡*Drumming to BEAT cancer!*
Raising awareness and funds for important cancer initiatives globally through rhythm

Cameron Tummel
Santa Barbara, California
ct@camerontummel.com
www.camerontummel.com
(805) 455-2599
Djembe teacher, Recording artist, Rhythm event facilitator. Interactive rhythm events for communities, colleges, kids, families, festivals and corporations, in areas including teambuilding, stress management, celebration and leadership training.

John Yost, Rhythm Revolution
5218 W. Carmen Chicago IL 60630
www.drummingcircle.com
drumcircle@juno.com, 773-802-0605
Rhythm Revolution works to connect participants with themselves and their communities in all types of settings with all populations.

Gregory Whitt, Drum for Change
Raleigh, NC p. 919-696-0883
www.drumforchange.com
Gregory@drumforchange.com

Marilyn Wilson and Lynn Curtin
Blondes Drum 2
1518 Birkdale Lane
Ponte Vedra Beach, FL 32082
www.blondesdrum2.blogspot.com
blondesdrum2@yahoo.com
904-334-5290
Blondes Drum 2 brings rhythm, drumming, song, and performance to every occasion. They are committed to bridging communities and individuals while healing body, mind, and spirit of all. DCF, Chicago IL USA, John Yost, Rhythm Revolution, www.drummingcircle.com

John Yost, Rhythm Revolution
Chicago, Illinois
www.drummingcircle.com
www.chicagoparkdistrict.com
www.oldtownschool.org
drumcircle@juno.com, 773-802-0605
Facilitation of all populations, author of best selling DVD John Yost teaches West African Rhythms, Performer in Dahui and Kaiju Daiko rhythm based ensembles

AUSTRALIA

Steve Durbin, Director Playworks®
www.playworksoz.com
M 0431 369 197
Melbourne Positive Psychology based interventions with activities, games and drum circles

Simon Faulkner, Holyoake Institute
Perth, Australia
www.holyoake.org.au
drumbeat@holyoake.org.au
Simon is the Manager of the DRUMBEAT Therapeutic program, and has a history of working with alienated young people affected by alcohol and drug misuse.

CANADA

Lulu Leathley, LuluJam
Vancouver, BC, Canada
www.lulujam.com
lulu@lulujam.com, 1-604-263-8640
I work with people of all ages and backgrounds, from birth to 106. I do a lot of work in the Special Populations area: welderlies, cancer patients, dementia patients, Parkinson's patients, deaf/blind children, mentally handicapped, at risk youth and adults, teachers, recreational directors and people going through life trauma.

Pamela Lynn
Heartbeats to Drumbeats.com
World Percussionist/ Singer/Workshop Facilitator
Canada, Vancouver Island, British Columbia
250-618-6051
www.PamelaLynnMusic.com
Pamela@PamelaLynnMusic.com
Specializing in World/New Age Music, Empowerment Drumming For Women, Rhythm Workshops

Leyshya
Midland, Ontario, Canada
One Tribe (soon to be HeartSongs)
www.heartsongs.ca
onetribe@csolve.net or hearts@csolve.net
1-705-527-6038
Leyshya provides quality musical/drum experiences for others that are coupled with movement, chant/song and other expressive modalities that guide others to discover their inborn treasury of creativity. Leyshya has worked with various clients which includes the general population, children and adults of all ages. In short, she goes to wherever the song of the drum is needed!

ITALY

Diana Tedoldi, Drum Power
Treviglio, Bergamo province,
North Italy.
www.drumpower.net
info@drumpower.net
I facilitate drum circle within corporate training, team building and energising events, community groups, special needs people and schools.

MALAYSIA

Bill Lewis, Lewis Global
Kuala Lumpur, Malaysia;
Abu Dhabi, UAE

bill@lewisglobal.com

+6 019 3152942

Delivers programs on communication, leadership, team working, creative thinking, EQ, selling and negotiation skills for corporations. Also presents community building and personal development workshops. Applies principles and techniques from NLP, Brain Gym®, Multiple Intelligences, Improv, Interactive Rhythm Based Learning and Laughter Yoga in his programs. Bill is a certified laughter yoga teacher (CLYT) and a certified Corporate Coach.

MEXICO

Cultura Ritmica, Mexico City

www.earthsoundz.com

deluix@hotmail.com

Tel-Fax 0052714 1509

Mostly working with business groups, spas, schools and detention centers.

UNITED KINGDOM

Steve Hill

England, Leeds, Yorkshire

Daftasadrum www.daftasadrum.co.uk

www.drumability.co.uk

skyking@daftasadrum.co.uk

p. +44 (0) 113 252 3205

f. +44 (0) 113 252 3205

Freelance Drum Circle Facilitator bringing rhythm to anyone: schools; festivals, fun days and galas; Scouts and Guides; groups with special needs and mental health issues; companies public and private – team-build, away days and conferences; refugees and asylum-seekers; young offenders

Steve Parker, Oliver Parker

Active Rhythmology

www.activerhythmology.co.uk

active@rhythmology.biz

p. 0113 2589330   f. 0113 2288377

Active Rhythmology provide a fun indoor team building exercise, away day activity, conference energiser, business training, meeting ice breaker, school workshop, party or community fun day. We rhythmologise almost any group of people in the UK and help them to relax, reduce stress and have fun.

John Walter, DrumCrazy Ltd,

United Kingdom

1 magdalene Totnes Devon TQ9 5TQ

www.drumcrazy.co.uk

44(0)7501 222779

DrumCrazy is a team of facilitators led by John Walter who has trained alongside Arthur Hull pretty consistently since 2000 and coordinates his United Kingdom Training events. We work in schools of every type for every population including all types of special needs. We take part in a number of community events, parties and celebrations. We run corporate training events

Drum Teachers

Steve Hill

England, Leeds, Yorkshire

skyking@daftasadrum.co.uk

p. +44 (0) 113 252 3205

f. +44 (0) 113 252 3205

Drums You Teach: Djembe Any specialty/styles you teach: African-style

Jonathan Murray

www.fundrumrhythmcircles.com

http://fundrum.blogspot.com

410 964-DRUM (3786)

John Yost, Rhythm Revolution

Chicago, Illinois

www.drummingcircle.com

www.chicagoparkdistrict.com

www.oldtownschool.org

drumcircle@juno.com, 773-802-0605

Organizations

drumSTRONG

drumSTRONG™
http://drumstrong.org
the power is in your hands
Scott Swimmer, DrumsForCures, Inc.
Founder and President
725 Providence Rd. #210
Charlotte, NC 28207
scott@drumstrong.org
www.drumstrong.org
Donations are tax deductible to the extent of the law and greatly appreciated. They can be mailed to:
DrumsForCures, Inc.
725 Providence Rd. #210
Charlotte, NC 28207

Holyoake

75 Canning Highway
Victoria Park, WA 6100
p. (08) 9416 4444, f. (08) 9416-4443
Holyoake is the leading drug and alcohol counseling and rehabilitation service in Perth, Western Australia. It presents a range of preventative programs for use by schools and other organizations working with young people. Programs include drug education courses as well as others tailored to address social skill deficits, including anger management, problem solving, communication and relationships. It is recognized that students that exhibit anti-social behavior at schools are at greater risk of dependent drug use in later life.

Music for People

David Darling
MusicforPeople.org
Goshen, CT
mfp@musicforpeople.org
1 877 44 MUSIC
Group programs for all instruments and voice; how to improvise in an ensemble; how to solo in a powerful and sensitive way; how to contact your inner muse and make your own music; how to share that music with others; how to teach improvisation in an accepting and encouraging way. All age groups from school children to elders

Products Magazines

Drum Circle Magazine (drumcirclemagazine.com) *Drum Circle Magazine* was created for all drum circle enthusiasts across the world. Its purpose is to connect the enthusiasts with the knowledge and resources to follow their own rhythmic path. The magazine is filled with articles and photographs from professionals and enthusiasts alike. Readers can learn more at www.drumcirclemagazine.com and purchase a copy right there.

Drum Magazine, drummagazine.com

Books

Judy Cormer, *Freestyle Community Drum Circles*

Robert Friedman, *The Healing Power of the Drum* (Whitecliffs Media, 2000) *How to Relax in 60 Seconds or Less* (Healthy Learning, 2010) (http://shop.stress-solutions.com) (www.stress-solutions.com) (www.drumming-event.com)

Mickey Hart, *Planet Drum* (Harper San Francisco, 1991)

Dave Holland, *Drumagination – A Rhythmic Playbook for Music Teachers, Music Therapists and Drum Circle Facilitators* BOOK/DVD

Arthur Hull, *Drum Circle Spirit: Facilitating Human Potential Through Rhythm* (The original 1998 edition of the comprehensive handbook with CD.) Drum Circle Facilitation Book—Building Community Through Rhythm, www.drumcircle.com

Kalani, *All About Hand Percussion* (2008) *Together in Rhythm – A Facilitator's Guide to Drum Circle* Music. (Book and DVD – July 4, 2006) *The Amazing Jamnasium – A Playful Companion to Together in Rhythm West African Drum & Dance – A Yankadi-Macrou Celebration.*

The Way of Music – This book strengthens the student's musical foundation, introduces intra- and intermusical techniques, and explores dynamic strategies within partner and group settings. Although it is aimed at music therapists, the contents applied across a range of professions and applications. (http://playsinglaugh.com)

Dennis Maberry, *Drum Circle Grooves*

John Marshall, *Hand drums for Beginners* (book andCD) (Paperback 2000)

Bill Matney, *Tataku: The Use of Percussion in Music Therapy* (includes DVD). Sarsen Publishing. 2007

James Oshinsky, *Return to Child: Music for People's Guide to Improvising Music and Authentic Group Leadership* Publishing info: Music for People, 2004

Bill Matney, M.A., MT-BC, *Tataku: The Use of Percussion in Music Therapy Sarsen,* Publishing – 2007, www.sarsenpublishing.com

Music Therapy Drumming, www.musictherapydrumming.com, Percussion Training Program for Therapists

Jim Oshinsky, *Improvisation Curriculum Book for Musicianship and Leadership*

Shannon Ratigan, *A Practical Guide to Hand Drumming and Drum Circles* (Kindle-Feb. 12, 2009) www.drumcircles.net

Christine Stevens, *The Art and Heart of Drum Circles Book/CD,* (May 1, 2003) *Body Beat Cards*: Body Beat is an innovative card deck for educational, recreational, and corporate groups. The 36 sound cards can be used to make six different games for anywhere from 4 to 70 people. There are SURPRISE cards that will get your group loosened up, like the "Go Wild" cards. There are also some SERIOUS cards that will give the rebels a responsible role, like the "Beat Keeper" cards. Body Beat does not require any musical experience. In fact, there are no notes or time signatures to read. The five simple body percussion sounds make different rhythms that sound GREAT together and inspire your group to groove. www.ubdrumcircles.com

Will Schmid. *World Music Drumming – A Cross-Cultural Curriculum* (Paperback – April 1998)

CDs

Chuck Cogliandro
A Call To Drum
In the Circle
West African drum and vocal CD
T.H.E. Percussion Choirdirected by
www.kumandi.com

Julie Corey
How to Play the Djembe
Level 1 for Beginners
www.thevillagedrum.com

Dahui, Ensemble du Rhythm
West African based
djembe and dunun music
www.drummingcircle.com

Robert Friedman
Innerflight
http://shop.stress-solutions.com

Dave Holland
Drummin' Songs and Jam Alongs
www.beatinpathrhythmevents.com

Arthur Hull
Dancers Journey
www.drumcircle.com

Arthur Hull with James Asher
Sounding the Stones
www.drumcircle.com

Pamela Lynn
Essential Rhythms For Personal Empowerment

Mike McElya
Sunshine Drumming
Traditional West African Rhythms
to play along with
www.sunshinedrumming.co.uk

Oshkosh Rhythm Ensemble and Drumming Community Phoenix
Creative Community Rhythm Reborn.
www.oshkoshrhythm.com

Christine Stevens
Drumming up DIVA!
Women's empowerment drumming

play-along CD, UpBeat Drum Circles
DRUM! Reviving Rhythms play-along
CD, UpBeat Drum Circles Guided
Imagery Drumming CD, REMO
HealthRHYTHMS Hal Leonard
www.ubdrumcircles.com

DVDs

Kat Fulton
Drumify dances for Older Adults
Learn how to use popular, live music to
dance on the drums with your groups
Rhythm for Good.com

Mike McElya
instructional DVD for the African Djembe drum.
www.sunshinedrumming.co.uk

Robert Lawrence Friedman
Drumming and Wellness for Children –
Provides valuable information on how
to use the hand drum to work with your
child. Including emotional release and
creativity. (Healthy Learning, 2004)
Drumming and Wellness for Adults – How
to use the hand drum to work with
adults in areas such as stress relief and
creative expression. (Healthy Learning,
2004)
Rhythms of the Drum – Join Robert L.
Friedman in learning to drum and
improvise. (Healthy Learning, 2004)
Managing Stress – The latest techniques
in managing stress anytime and
anyplace. (Healthy Learning, 2004)
Balancing Work Family and Self – *How to
Create a Healthier Life Balance* (Healthy
Learning, 2004)
Being the Best You Can Be – Staying
Motivated – Tools for creating a happier
life(Healthy Learning, 2004)
Relaxation On-Demand Software – 24/7
Stress Management Coaching System
(http://shop.stress-solutions.com)

Jim Greiner
Community Drumming For Health
& Happiness: hand drum and hand percussion instruction with a drum circle play-along section. LPV115D – distributed by Latin Percussion Instruments (www.lpmusic.com)
Play Shekere – beginning to intermediate instruction on Shekere: distributed by Jim Greiner (www.handsondrum.com)
Rhythm Power® – DVD Series by Jim Greiner: hand drum and hand percussion instruction with inspirational Life Lessons – distributed by Jim Greiner (www.handsondrum.com)

Arthur Hull
How to Facilitate A Drum Circle
www.drumcircle.com

Christine Stevens
The Art and Heart of Drum Circles DVD, Hal Lenard
www.ubdrumcircle.com

John Yost
John Yost Teaches West African Rhythms Instructional
www.drummingcircle.com

Drums, Rhythm Instruments and Rhythm Games

Aromatherapy Drum, Created by Remo, this unique drum is the first stress management system integrating the life enhancing benefits of healing music, aromatherapy and therapeutic drumming. (remo.com) "The aromatherapy drum is "a fragrant, musical intervention for connecting the notes of your life through memory, focus and intention..." Bonnie Harr, MSN, MA, RN

Body Beat Cards: Body Beat is an innovative card deck for educational, recreational, and corporate groups. The 36 sound cards can be used to make six different games for anywhere from 4 to 70 people. There are SURPRISE cards that will get your group loosened up, like the "Go Wild" cards. There are also some SERIOUS cards that will give the rebels a responsible role, like the "Beat Keeper" cards. Body Beat does not require any musical experience. In fact, there are no notes or time signatures to read. The five simple body percussion sounds make different rhythms that sound GREAT together and inspire your group to groove. www.ubdrumcircles.com

Boomwhackers – tuned percussion tubes; Boomwhackers www.boomwhackers.com

Drums and soundz, Earthsoundz, www.earthsoundz.com

The Healing Drum Kit, Sounds True, 2005 Body Beat, UPBeat Drum Circles, Christine Stevens, www.ubdrumcircles.com

Adult Scat Cards –Used by facilitators and educators around the world, both as an icebreaker and for teambuilding, Scat Cards™ are a laminated deck of 35 cards of nonsensical words that provide an easy and fun experience of rhythm. Each Scat Card includes a specific rhythmic phrase using nonsensical words. These colorful and laminated cards will induce laughter, create team spirit and begin the process of recognition of each person's inner drummer!

Kids Scat Cards – Same as above but for children ages two to five years old. Robert Lawrence Friedman, (http://shop.stress-solutions.com)

Related Products

Arthur Hull, SHIPPING BOXES for the Facilitator, www.drumcircle.com

Scott Swimmer, Playmore Design Corp., Recycled Plastic playground equipment and instruments featuring: Re-Percussion recycled plastic percussion alternatives for Classrooms, Playgrounds & Community Drum Circles Virtually indestructible, high quality rhythm instruments with professional attributes www.playmoredesign.com 725 Providence Rd. #210 Charlotte, NC 28207 704.376.PLAY (7529)

Resources

Shannon Ratigan, Dunedin, Florida, www.drumcircles.net, Resources for drum circles, hand drummers, facilitators, and teachers.

InteractiveRhythm.com, www.interactiverhythm.com Designed by world percussionist and teaching artist Dave Holland, InteractiveRhythm.com is an online resource for music teachers, music therapists and drum circle facilitators. At InteractiveRhythm.com, you'll find many rhythmic resources, instruments and workshops designed to bring intention, interaction and fun to your next class, therapy session or community drum circle!

www.playworksoz.com, Melbourne Positive Psychology based interventions with activities, games and drum circles, M 0431 369 197

Drum Centers

Remo Recreational Center is dedicated to providing an atmosphere where people of all walks of life, of all ages, with our without a musical background, can experience making music with others in a welcoming, friendly, non-challenging, environment and experience the benefit and joys of making music (remormc.com)

Websites of Interest

www.drumcirclemagazine.com – Magazine featuring drum circle facilitators www dcfg.net –Drum Circle Facilitators Guild

www.drumchannel.com – Terry Bozzio breaks down the Basic Permutations of Ostinatos

www.drumcircles.net – Current listing of drumcircles around the globe.

www.drumlnks.com –Quality drum links on any drum subject

http://drumstrong.org – Website for Scott Swimmer's organization

www.djemberhythms.com/roots.htm – Traditional West African drum rhythms and hand drum improvisations

www.pas.org – Percussive Arts Society

Drumming Mailing Lists

drumcircles@yahoogroups.com – Hand drumming Listserv with emphasis on Arthur Hull's teaching methodologies

rhythmhealing@yahoogroups.com- Focuses on the use of drumming and healing

Drumcircles in the United States

The following list was compiled by Shannon Ratigan, who put ten years of her life into providing a resource for individuals seeking drumcircles around the globe. His website is www.drumcircles.net. It is recommended that you contact the individual/ organization running the drum circle prior to attending, to determine restrictions, fees, if any, current – Locations, any requirements for that particular drumcircle, as well to avoid the journey in case the drum circle has been discontinued.

ALABAMA

Birmingham – Location: Winter—Children's Dance Foundation (1715 27th Ct. S., Homewood, AL 35209) Fall, Spring, Summer—Railroad Park (1600 1st Avenue South, Bham, AL 35223-2316) When: Once a Month Contact: GetRhythmPrograms. com or 205-222-6998 Bring your drum or percussion instrument—all people, all levels are welcome! Hosted by John Scalici. (Featured in *The Healing Power of the Drum*) Due to my schedule, please call – email for exact Drum Circle dates. or go to GetRhythmPrograms.com to join my e-newsletter list!

Huntsville – Location: Big Springs Park (near Huntsville Utilities) When: Sundays 4pm Contact: http://groups.google.com/group/drumcirclehsv Contact: email – drumcirclehsv@googlegroups.com

Mobile – Location: 3 LightBridge Way-251 645 9081 Contact: drums@mysticmerchant.com

Scottsboro – Location: The Aruni Jam Festival When: Start playing at 4:30. Contact: www.arunijam.com Phone: 256 657-5125 Email: josh_johnson_21@yahoo.com

ALASKA

Anchorage – Location: Abbott Loop Elementary School – When: Tues, Wed & Fri 6:30–9:00pm Contact: 907-522-3596 – imedance@juno.com Ouman-Taf, Djembe Master Drummer from West Africa

Anchorage – When: 1st Wednesdays, 7pm Contact: wrldtree@alaska.net

Eagle River – Location: Grass Roots by REI! When: Every 2nd and 4th Sunday from 2pm–4pm

ARIZONA

Kingman – Location: 418 E Beale St. When: First Friday, 7pm – Location: Open Drum & Belly Dance Clinic When: Saturday afternoons, 11 a.m.

Location: Park Burbank & Beverly Street Contact: (928)-681-7309, porthos_the_pirate_2000@yahoo.com

Phoenix – Location: 7th Ave and Montecito. It's free! Facilitated: Frank Thompson, Rhythm Connection When: First Friday of every month, 7 pm Contact: Frank@azrhythmconnection.com

Pinetop – Location: On the New Moon Contact: Jeri at Whispering Wind Store, j10629@cybertrails.com

Tempe –
  Location: New Moon Drum Circle – off Mill Ave and 5th street. When: Saturday
  nights after last flick Contact: 602-555-8908
  Location: Himmel Park (1 block south of Speedway Blvd. and 1 block east of Tucson
  Blvd.). When: Every Sunday, 2–5 pm, between Hippie Hill and tennis courts.
  Location: 2132 N. Treat Ave. (Studio behind home) Contact: 520-326-1263 – bbird@
  aztarnet.com

ARKANSAS

Fayetteville – Location: Rose Garden on Dickson Street. When: Every Wednesday
  night. Contact: arkansasrainbowfamily@yahoo.com
Hot Springs National Park – Location: Manataka American Indian Council. Contact:
  drumsociety@manataka.org or amanda_morningstar@hotmail.com
Little Rock – Location: Wesely Foundation on 32nd street just east of the University of Arkansas at. When: Meets every Tuesday from 8:30–10:00 p.m. (with the
  exception of the Tuesday between Christmas and New Year) Contact: More info call
  Thompson Murray, director at 501-661-1153
Norfork – Location: Drum circle at the Hemp Store. When: 1st Sunday every month
  from 2 to 4pm.
Paragould – Location: Harmon Park 309 Northend Avenue. When: Every Sunny Sunday at 2pm

CALIFORNIA

Berkeley – Location: Ashby Ave. Ashby BART Station. When: Saturday 2pm Bay
Brea – Location: The Enchanted Fairy Box When: 1st Thursday
Bwhana Aptos – Ongoing Hand Drumming Group Workshop with Jim Greiner-
  When: Wednesday 7pm
Costa Mesa – When: Sunday Nights at The Camp (corner of Bristol/Baker) 7:45pm
  Contact: 949 842 4051 or kimma949@yahoo.com Website: campdrumming.com
  Location: Visions & Dreams When: 4th Friday Drum Circle, Saturday
Concord – When: 7:00 pm Contact: Spitzer Music 510-676-3151
Culver City – Location: 2921 La Cienega Blvd., Culver City Contact: 888-419-0515
  When: All Women's Drum Circle, every Sunday 7–9pm
Encinitas – Location: Monthly Drum Circle 101 Artists Colony Encinitas, Second
  Tuesday CA facilitated by Frank Lazzaro frankdrums.com
Fernando Valley –
  Location: African Corner, 16511 Brookhurst Street, Contact: Jennifer or Rich at 818-
  893-8337, www.deirfamily@aol.com When: Sunday 5pm Drum Circle
  Location: Los Caballeros Racquet Club Complex: 17270 Newhope St., When: Every
  Wednesday night – Time: 7:00–9:00pm
Huntington Beach –
  Location: Pier drum Jam north of the pier on the beach When: Sunday 12 noon
  Location: Huntington Central Park When: Saturday 11 a.m.
Idyllwild – Location: 54750 North Circle Drive When: Saturday from 4–6pm Contact:
  (951) 659-3191 Website: chakrachack.com

Irvine – Location: 17881 Sky Park Cir, #E When: Women Only Dates: 7–9pm Contact: Melinda Rodriguez 1-800-N-TEMPLE

Laguna Beach – Location: Drum Circle Main Beach When: Sunday 4pm til dusk

Location: Laguna Niguel Mission Lutheran Church: 24360 Yosemite Rd. When: Every Sunday afternoon 3:00 Contact: Niguel 949-306-3734

Long Beach – Location: Long Beach – The Phat Drum Circle: When: Every Sunday afternoon in summer only – 4:00pm Facilitator: Marcus Tucker-marcust Contact: 949@sbcglobal.net Time:

Los Gatos – Location: Drum Circle Unitarian Fellowship When: Wednesday 7:30pm Contact: Spiritual 408-358-1212

Marin County – Location: Golden Gate Center of Spiritual Living Corte Madera Contact: For more information, email jaygustafson@netscape.net.

Montclair – Location: Vista UUC 9185 Monte Vista Ave.. When: 4th Wednesday of each month at Monte Contact: 909-626-3066 – MonteVistaUU.org

Mountain View – Location: 324 Castro St Contact: 800.909.6161

Napa Valley – Location: Unity Church When: Sunday 12:30pm

North Hollywood –
Location: Griffith Park When: Sunday Afternoons.
Location: Remo RMC Recreational Music Center. 7308 Coldwater Canyon When: Tuesday & Wednesdays from 7pm to 8pm Contact: Jerry Zacarias e-mail: jzacarias@remo.com, (818) 982-0461

Oak Park – Location: On the corner of 33rd st. and 4th Ave. When: Starts at 6:30pm Fourth Friday

Palo Alto – Location: Henry Hoover Girl Scout House When: Friday 7:30pm Contact: Lou 415-964-4826

Pleasant Hill – Location: The Winslow Center When: 3rd Thursday 7pm

Pomona Drum – Location: The International Center 757 N. Garey Ave When: Every Fourth Sunday at 2pm Contact: (909) 629-5277 ext 3014 Circle with Ron Powell Ron Powell, percussionist for the Kenny G Band

Princeton-By-the-Sea – Location: Half Moon Bay Yacht Club When: Wednesday 7:30pm

Santa Monica – Location: Drum Dance Church in Ocean Park When: 1st Saturday 8pm

Sacramento – Location: Mckinley Park – 3330 McKinley Blvd When: Every Sunday at 1pm, drumcircle.meetup.com/15/

Sacramento –
Location: East West Books 2216 Fair Oaks Blvd (At Howe Ave.) When: First Friday of the month Starts at 7pm-9pm Contact: 916-920-3837
Location: The CHA Center, 2862 Arden Way, Suite 215c When: Last Sunday of each month, 6pm – Contact: chacenter.com
Location: East West Books 2216 Fair Oaks Blvd (At Howe Ave.) When: First Friday of the month, Starts at 7pm-9pm Contact: 916-920-3837
Location: Full Moon Drum Circle Paradise beach (over the river levee from Glen Hall Park) When: Bi-monthly Contact: Ravencoyotesong@aol.com for more info.
Location: Fair Oaks Park at Fair Oaks & Madison When: 2nd Saturday 4pm Drum Circle

San Diego –
  Location: San Dieguito Park (lower entrance, eastern end) When: First Saturday of every month
  Location: Full Moon Drum Circle Blacks Beach When: Tuesday 5:30pm
  Location: Side of Balboa Park When: Sunday afternoons
San Jose –
  Location: Moitozo Park at Rio Robles and N. First St. (one block from Tasman) When: Every Friday (weather permitting) 12pm – 1pm
  Location: Healing House 1460 Koll Circle, Suite C San Jose, Ca 95112 C When: Every Tuesday at 6:30PM Contact: Healing House
San Francisco – Location: Hippie Hill, Golden Gate Park, San Francisco When: Now on Saturdays as well!
San Luis Obispo – Location: Cuesta Canyon Park When: 1st Sunday 12noon Contact: 805-543-0338
Santa Ana – Location: WIZE PLACE (Women Inspired, Supported Empowered) When: 1st Sat. of the Month. Arrive by 6:30pm, DRUM CALL- 7pm to 9pm Facilitated by David Van Dorn-
Santa Barbara – We meet on the seasonal quarters & cross quarters, earth religion holidays style, but drum Native American style with frame drums, flutes welcome. When: Circle meeting dates, times, places are posted on our site. Contact: handsandhearts.wordpress.com/ Contact Cerena Childress: 805-898-7888
Santa Cruz & Monterey Bay Area – Ongoing Weekly Hand Drum Circle with Jim Greiner Santa Cruz, CA Hands-On! Drumming® Percussion Center Wednesdays, 7 to 8:30 p.m. (subject to Jim's drumming/travel schedule) 831-462-3786 jgreiner@handsondrum.com, www.handsondrum.com Jim has conducted this circle for over 20 years
Monthly Benefit Community Drumming Circle with Jim Greiner Santa Cruz/ Monterey & San Francisco Bay Areas, CA – Location varies from month to month, depending upon fundraiser recipient One Saturday afternoon each month 831-462-3786 jgreiner@handsondrum.com www.handsondrum.com Jim conducts this monthly circle as a fundraiser for area non-profit groups
Rhythm Power® Drumming Circle with Jim Greiner Santa Cruz/Monterey & San Francisco Bay Areas, CA Hands-On! Drumming® Percussion Center & various – Locations One Saturday afternoon or Saturday evening each month 831-462-3786 jgreiner@handsondrum.com www.handsondrum.com Jim conducts Rhythm Power® events monthly that use hand drumming as a vehicle to reinforce positive Life Rhythms & Life Skills Contact Jim about bringing his Drum Circles and Drumming Workshops in your area! (Featured in *The Healing Power of the Drum*)
Santa Monica – Contact: www.seasons-on-montana.com.
Sebastopol – Location: Women's Drum Circle Sound Lounge (inside Teen Center at 425 Morris St.) When: Saturday 7pm Sebastopol
Sherman Oaks – When: 1pm –3pm Dance and Drum Circle Anisa's School of Middle Eastern Dance When: 12noon Drum class on Basic Arabic Rhythms Anisa's School of Middle Eastern Dance

Sonoma County – Contact: For more information visit pulsewave.com

Stanford – Location: New Guinea Sculpture Garden When: Friday 7pm Drum Circle

Thousand Oaks – Location: Rhythmotomy Drum Circle Conego Creek Park When: Sunday 1:30pm

Three Rivers – When: Every Sunday around 8pm to 10pm at the Cort Gallery. Contact: kaweahriverdrumcircle.blogspot.com/

Venice Beach – Location: Center for Spiritual Living 1195 Clark St San Jose CA 408.294.1828x115 When: Quarterly Drum circle Saturday and Sundays.

Ventura – Location: Mission Park When: 2nd Sunday 12noon

COLORADO

Bellvue – Contact: Judy's home 970-482-5091 When: 2nd Wednesday Contact: 970-221-2728

Berthoud – Location: Wildfire Community Art Center When: Every Wednesday Night 8:00–9:30pm Contact: Keith Hancock & Gwilda Wiyaka keithha@mindspring.com.

Breckenridge – Location: S. Park Street Riverwalk Center When: Thursdays – 7 pm Contact:Lisa, lisatunnell@hotmail.com

Broomfield – Location: Moon Drumming 3218 W. 11th Avenue When: 3rd Sunday 5:30pm Contact: 303-439-8816

Colorado Springs –

Location: Immanual Lutherian School. When: We drum each Thursday nite fron 7–9:30 Contact: drumcircle.meetup.com/279.

Address: Small Circle Imports 1139 Francis St. Contact: 303-682-5080 Contact: hotweelshippy@yahoo.com

Location: 846 East Pikes Peak Colorado Springs When: First and third Sunday at 7:00pm Contact: 719 964 8031 Facilitated by Andy Wuenschel Contact: andy@televiso.com

Denver –

Location: CUUPS Drumming Circle First Unitarian Church When: 4th Friday 7:15pm Contact: 303-295-0515

Location: 1400 Lafayette When: 7:00 pm at the Unitarian Church, CO. Contact: For info, DianaMapesDenver@aol.com

Fort Collins – Location: 5213 Arrowhead Lane When: 1st, 3rd & 5th Weds at Contact: Keith at 970.207.1139

Frisco – Location: Summit County Senior and Community Center

Lakewood – Location: Full Moon Books and Coffee 9108 W. 6th Ave, When: Tuesdays from 7:15 to 9:30

Longmont – Location: Community Drum Circle Small Circle Imports When: 1st Sunday 8pm

Manitou Springs – Location: The Organic Earth Cafe 1124 Manitou Ave When: Monday Nite from 8–10pm

CONNECTICUT

Avery Point – Location: Groton Campus Univ of CT When: 7:30pm Contact: 204-445-3494

Bristol – When: First Saturday of the Month, 6–9pm, Contact: 860-940-9437

Guilford – Drum Journeys For Women When: second Friday of each month at 7:30pm in. w/ Melinda Alcosser Contact: maps12@sbcglobal.net

Hamden – Location: 700 Hartford Turnpike When: First fridays 7:30–9:00pm Contact: mark.z@att.net for more info

Hartford – Location: Immanuel Congregational Church, 10 Woodland Street When: Second Saturday of each month. 7:45 p.m. to 9:30 p.m. Facilitated by Bob Bloom. (Located at the corner of Farmington Avenue. Contact: 860-429-9280 Contact: bb@drumming-about-you.com. (featured in *The Healing Power of the Drum*)

Ledyard – Location: Dragon's Egg Shewville Rd, CT When: First Sunday of each month 5–7 Contact: 860-536-3370

Manchester – Location: Samadhi Yoga Studio 983 Main Street, When: 3rd Wednesday of every month 7:30 to 8:30 p.m. Contact: (860-916-9914) drummingworks@cox.net

Newtown – Location: Homemade Soup Supper When: Saturday September 12th (& monthly) at 6 p.m. Contact: 203-270-8820 Location: Sticks and Stones Farm Retreat – 201 Huntingtown Road Contact: sticksandstonesfarm.com

Southington – Location: 1273 Queen St Route 10, CT When: Every Thursday evening from 7–10pm Contact: 860.747.1100

Tolland – Location: More Yoga Studio Colonial Square 68 Hartford Turnpik When: 1st Friday every month

Waterbury – Location: St. John's Episcopal Church, 16 Church Street When: Second Tuesday of Every Month, 7pm Contact: Jean-Claude NAICISUMOl@yayoo.com

West Hartford –
Location: Natural Medical Service When: Sunday 7pm Contact: 413-584-3022
Location: Mansfield Center, 549 Storrs Rd. Mansfield Center When: Monthly circle, September to May.
Facilitated by Bob Bloom. info@drumming-about-you.com Contact: 860-429-9280 or bb@drumming-about-you.com

West Haven When: 2nd Friday 7pm Contact: 203-387-2490

Weston – Location: Drum-N-Dance at the Norfield Grange, 12 Good Hill Rd., When: Third Monday of the Month Contact: 203-544-7085 rbdrumguy@sbcglobal.net Contact:sounddirections.net or rbdrumguy@sbcglobal.net Facilitated by Randy Brody (Featured in *The Healing Power of the Drum*)

Windsor – Location: South Windsor Community Center 150 Nevers Rd South, CT 06074 When: Second Thursday of the every month 7:30 p.m.–9 p.m.

Woodbury – Location: Woodbury Drum Circle, CT Mattatuck Unitarian Church When: 1st and 3rd Sundays – 6 to 7:30pm Contact: sage-center@sbcglobal.net Facilitator: Bob Werme -

DELAWARE

Newark – Location: Phillips Park 276 E. Main St When: Every Tuesday, 4th (sometimes 3rd) Friday Contact: tnewarkartsalliance.org/ and delawarebellydance.org/ drum.html

FLORIDA

Bunnell – Location: Merlin's Mercantile 202 N. Railroad St. When: Wednesday 8pm

Cape Coral – Location: Jaycees Park When: Sunday 6pm

Clearwater – Location: Ringside Studio –1575 S. Missouri Ave. When: Thurdays nights at 7:30 to 10:30pm

Clearwater Beach – Location: Pier 60, Clearwater Beach, FL When: Weekly and Saturday Nights 9pm – 11pm

Coconut Creek – Location: Broward Drum Circle Fern Forest Nature Park, 201 S. Lyons Rd., FL When: Every Saturday, 2:30-4:45pm Contact: 954-984-4183

Crystal River – Location: Citrus County drum circle at Crystal River When: Second Sunday of the month. Contact: keyccrazy@yahoo.com.

Deerfield Beach – Location: Key Largo Framing, 817 S. Federal Hwy., FL, When: 7:30-9:30pm, Saturdays

Deland –

Location: Merlin's Vision 100 S Woodland Blvd Deland, FL 32720 When: every Saturday night 7 to 9. Contact: 386-738-4056

Location: 17-92 and Hwy 44 100 South Woodland Boulevard When: 7pm to 9pm every Friday night Contact: (386) 738-4056

Dunedin – Location: 937 Douglas Avenue, Dunedin. 34698 When: Every Tuesday Night 8pm–11pm

Gainesville – Location: 519-E NW 10th Avenue When: Friday Night 6pm–8pm Contact: (352) 338-8302

Hernando County – Location: Brooksville Community Drum Circle When: Last Saturday of the month. Contact: 352.584.1966 or chris@glyndower.com

Hollywood – Location: Waterfront Tower, 801 Johnson Street When: Every 2nd and 4th Sunday at Holland Park – Contact: Kirsten: 954-889-8615

Jacksonville – Location: Riverside Park Drumcircle Corner of Park and post next to Five Points Village When: 6:30pm:

Jacksonville Beach – Location: Renaissance Healing Center. 228 N. Third Avenue When: Second Sunday of each month. 6:15pm, Contact: heart2heartcircles@yahoo.com

Jupiter – Location: Corners bar and grill When: Thursday, Time: 8:30pm – 11:00pm.

Jupiter Beach – When: full moon of each month 8 p.m. – 1 a.m., Contact: Check the site before leaving: Yahoo group – JupiterBeachFloridaDrumCircle (join group to access the site)

Lakeland – Location: Mitchell's Coffee House, 235 N Kentucky Ave When: 7:30-10:30pm Contact: Sheeba – zargarita@yahoo.com

Lawn at Mirror Lake – When: 1st Sunday of the month 2:30 to 5:30 Contact: Jen at znjenyoga@hotmail.com

Naples – Location: Cambier Park When: Every Saturday night Contact: Facilitated by SayerJi SayerJi@gmail.com Contact: drummingishappiness.googlepages.com/home

New Port Richey – Location: Starbucks Street: 5220 Little Rd. Contact: phyrestorm08@yahoo.com

Orlando –
    Location: 618 N Thornton Ave When: Next date – New Moon: Contact: centralfloridadrums@gmail.com
    Location: 604 North Thornton Ave When: Mondays – Contact: 407-595-3731
    Location: Native American Women's Medicine Wheel Circle 750 North Thornton Ave When: Once a month (based on the date of the full moon) Contact: 407.677.1467

St. Augustine – Location: Davenport Park drum circle When: on "every full moon" Contact: Daniel – dsampiero@gmail.com

St. Cloud – Location: The New Day Café-3195 13th Street – Highway 192 When: 407-891-2100

St. Petersburg –
    Location: 1620 Park street N. St Pete, When: First Monday of every month. Contact: drumquest.com
    Location: Beach Drum Circle When: Weekly Sundays Starts several hours before sunset.
    Location: Unity Campus When: Held once a month at Contact: drumonfire.com
    Location: Wings Bookstore! 4500 4th Street North When: First Fridays at 7 pm Contact: wingsbookstore.com

Tampa –
    Location: Sweetwater Organic Community Farms When: First Saturday of the month. 7:30 pm start
    Location: Yoga Lotus Pond When: Every Sunday evening. Contact: kdennis47@yahoo.com
    Location: Gandy Bridge When: Sunday nights Contact: lopmanu3@aol.com
    Location: Public beach at the Davis Island seaplane basin When: every Sunday at 5pm Contact: linda.parrish@HCAHealthcare.com When: Monthly Native American Contact: 727-343-4638
    Location: 3 Palms Restaurant, 8203 N. Armenia When: First Wednesday of each month

Treasure Island – Location: Port Richey Unity Church of Port Richey 5844 Pine Hill Road 34668 When: last Sunday of every month.

Palm Coast – Location: Merlin's Mercantile St. Joe Plaza 234 St. Joe Plaza Dr. When: Every Wednesday at 8pm Contact: 386-445-9092

Pompano Beach – Location: Fern Forest Nature Park When: Every Saturday 2:30 – 5pm – Contact: FaceBook page: broward drumcircle

Pompano Beach Pier – Contact: browarddrumcircle.webs.com/fullmoondrumcircle.htm

Sarasota – Location: Siesta Beach When: 1 hour before sunset

Sebring – Location: Highlands Hammock State Park When: Third Sunday of the month Contact: primalconnection.org

Venice Beach – Location: Nokomis Beach When: Every Wednesday and Saturday before sunset

Ft. Myers – Location: Centennial Park (under the gazebo) When: Every Saturday night from 6:30 to 10

New Smyrna Beach –
  Location: 200 Julia Street When: First Friday of every
  Location: Mainland Shuffleboard Clubhouse When: 7pm Contact: Drum4p@aol. com

Orlando – When: Saturday 11pm Contact: 407-210-2002

Sebring – When: Each full moon 6pm Contact: 863-655-4637

Stuart – Location: Shepard Park FL. When: Sunday 2 hours before sunset Contact: Tim Brown at Timsdrums@aol.com or call 772-486-4671

Virginia Key Beach – Location: 4020 Virginia Beach Drive When: Every 3rd Sunday – starts between 2:00 and 3:00PM Contact: HVKBEvents@gmail. com – 305-960-4600

GEORGIA

Albany – Location: 612 N Slapppey Blvd When: 229-438-5878 Contact: Stephen_and_Rheana@hotmail.com

Alto – Location: Golden Hills Community Center When: 1st & 3rd Tuesdays, 7:00-9:00pm Contact: 706-839-1323

Atlanta –
  Location: Blue Mist Rising/ Woodstock, Marietta & Cartersville When: 2nd Saturday of each Month at 7:30pm
  Location: Atlanta Lake Claire Land Trust When: Saturday – 1st & 3rd at Dark
  YMCA When: Sunday 12:30pm Contact: 404-635-1177
  Location: 500 Chandler Park Dr NE, Thump, GA When: Tuesday 8pm Contact: 404-378-8564
  Location: 425 Clifton Rd Atlanta When: Tuesday 3pm Contact: 404-377-0764
  Location: 371 Kings Bridge Road When: Every Thursday Night Contact: 706-729-1776

Augusta – Location: Celtic Crossings Drum Circle & Band, GA 30901 Building When: 9pm–11pm Contact: CelestialHolistics@mail.com

Decatur – Location: Decatur Healing Arts (109A New Street, Decatur, GA 30030) Contact: Rhythm Synergy facilitators drummingatlanta.com When: Saturday 5:30pm Contact: 404-761-8287

Robins – When: 3rd Friday of each month Contact: wiccan.meetup.com/39/

Tucker – Location: 2329 Main Street When: Thursdays Contact: Rae Sirott 770-493-8880

HAWAII

Honolulu – Location: Magic Island Drum Jam Magic Island Beach, HI When: Tuesdays 7pm Contact: (808) 737-3786

Kailua-Kona – Location: Holualoa School When: 2nd Tuesday of the month 7-8:30pm Contact: 808-325-7489

Kona – When: Monday 6:30pm Contact: 938.5869

Maui – Location: Makena Beach Makena, HI When: nightfall, sunset Contact: 8088761978 / zuma@malibumusic.com

IDAHO

Pocatello –
Location: 303 North 12th Ave When: 2nd & 4th Fridays 6:30pm Summer
Location: Whole Heart Health Cooperative Pocatello When: 2nd and 4th Fridays, beginning at 6pm. When: 2nd Friday: Spiritual Meditation & Singing with Frame Contact: 251-2400/234-9309 cretemamachen@earthlink.net

ILLINOIS

Bartlett –
Location: Active Senior Centers 1101 W. Bartlett Rd. IL Rita Lopienski RMT When: Monthly
Location: Blue Island Drumjam at Hustlers Blue Island 2146 Vermont St., IL Contact: Atheleas@comcast.net 773-330-2753

Chicago –
Location: 2650 W. Petersen(6000 N.) between Western and California, IL When: every Friday night from 7:30 to 10 pm Contact: Rhythm Revolution Chicago Facilitated by John Yost Community drum cicle
Location: Green Briar park. Outside if weather permits, inside field house if cold or wet out. Contact: 773-286-0605
Location: Touhy Park 7348 N. Paulina When: 3rd friday of the month 7:30-9:30pm Contact:meetup.com chicago drum circle, drummingcircle.com
Location: 4740 N. Womenspirit Drummers (Women only) When: 1st Friday 8:15pm
Location: Landfill Of Northwestern University Stone Circle Fire-Pit When: Friday 7:30pm

Evanston – Location:SHE DRUMS the Women's Drumming Community 607 Lake Street Church, IL Contact: 773-549-3026 shedrums@earthlink.net

Fox River Grove – Location: 314 Northwest Highway When: 3rd Friday of each month 7:00pm to 10:00pm Contact: 847-462-8951

Naperville –
Location: Percucitis Drum Circle North Central College When: Sunday 1pm
Location: 1550 N. Route 59 When: Saturday 10 AM

Palatine – Location: (Countryside Church Unitarian Universalist) 1025 N. Smith Road When: 2nd Friday of every month Contact: Journey-Inward.com

Richmond – Location: Howl at the Moon Gems & Jewelry 5628 W Broadway When:2nd Sundays from 3 to 5pm, Contact: Howlatm.com

Woodstock – Location: Square Drum Circle at The Square When: Impromptu – at least once a month Contact: launch.groups.yahoo.com/group/squaredrumcircle/ our drum circle is called Square Drum Circle.

Willow Springs – Location: Old Willow Center – 3rd Level 8695 Archer Ave When: Every Saturday 6 p.m.

INDIANA

Chesterton –
  Location: Indiana Dunes State Park When: Every Sunday, 2 hours before sunset
  Location: Indiana Dunes National Lakeshore (next to the pavilion) When: Sundays
  at 5pm Contact: Tim at myspace.com/wavebeats
Fortville – Location: Fortville Park When: 1st Sat. of every month Contact: 317-331-
  5520 runlikeanantelope420@yahoo.com
Goshen – Location: 1700 South Main Street When: First Thursdays of each month
  from 6 pm Contact: 574-535-7361 deblk@goshen.edu
Indianapolis –
  Location: 8481 Bash St. Suite 1100 When: Every Thursday Night Contact: 317-595-
  9065
  Location: Broad Ripple Park When: Thursday Contact: ryanta1972@yahoocom
  Location: 420 Kratom Avenue When: Evening before each full moon Contact:
  brightwingdrums@lycos.com
South Bend – Location: Morris Performing Arts Center When: Tuesday Contact: Eric:
  scopolian@yahoo.com
Madison – Location: 108 E Main St (2nd Floor) Blue Spirit Drumming Circle Indiana
  When: first and third Friday of every month Contact: 812 265 4446
Muncie – Location: Muncie Drum Circle -Located In Front Of WISHBONE GIFTS –
  210 S. Walnut St. When: Saturday Evenings – 7 to 9pm
South Bend – Location: St. Joe River Howard Park Contact:210-1804 SouthBend-
  DrumCircle@yahoogroups.com
Terre Haute – Location: Darkfires Drummers Rose Hulman University When: Every
  Friday, starting at 19.00 hrs
West Lafayette – Location: Memorial Mall, Purdue University Campus, Purdue West
  Lafayette When: Every Sunday at 4:30pm Contact: granola@purdue.edu
Vendor – Location: Drum Circle Village When: 3rd Friday 7pm

IOWA

Davenport – Location: Coffee Dive 226 West 3rd When: Saturdays 5 – 7pm
Des Moines – Location: 1700 Woodland Ave – Location: Ancient Ways When: Mondays – monthly – near full moon Contact:Jo Von Stein / 515-280-3375
Iowa City – Location: Unitarian Society When: Wednesday 7pm Contact: 319-338-
  8524

KANSAS

Topeka – Location: 117 SE 6th Downtown When: Tuesday 7pm Contact: Derek 785-
  235-3786
Wichita –
  Location: Warren Theater on Mead St. When: Every Friday and Saturday 7 till 10
  Contact: Yahoo group called wichita_hand_drumming
Location: Amira Productions Dance Studio on West Douglas When: Saturday
  4–6pm

KENTUCKY

Bowling Green – Location:Alive Center drum circle 1818 31-W By-Pass When: Every Wednesday 7pm to 8:30pm

Crescent Springs – Location: Lifepath Academy of the Healing Arts When: Saturday 7pm

Louisville –

Location: First Unitarian Church corner of Fourth Street and York Street When: 2nd Sunday of each month 4:00 to 5:30 Contact: mamajo16@yahoo.com / Liz Haeberlin at lizimages.blogspot.com

Location: 1924 Newburg Road When: 7:00 Contact: doug@dougvanhouten.com

Nicholasville – Location: Unity Drum Circle Wilmore When: Every other Friday, starting October 18th. Contact:(859)887-3175 solflwr@hotmail.com

LOUISIANA

Baton Rouge – Location: Our Lady of the Lake Regional Medical Center, Tau Building When: First Tuesday of the month 12:15 Contact: (225) 765-6041

Lake Charles – Location: Bor Du Lac Park Gazebo When: Every 2nd and 4th Sunday 3:00 pm Contact: (Ask for Damon) 337-491-9763 / doctort63@communicomm. com

New Orleans – When: Wednesday night Contact: Ty at thegumbowitch@yahoo.com/ meetup.com/noladrum Location: The Mystic Heard Of Nutrias Farbourg Center When: Thursday 8pm Contact: 504-949-0369

Ruston – When: Sundays 2pm Contact: pbickham@woodard.LaTech.edu

MAINE

Bangor – When: Thursdays at 5:30pm Contact:Mark Hedger / 1-207-989-7631

Brunswick – Location: Fort Andross Contact: Tim Hladky / prof.funk@yahoo.com

Saco River – Location: Yoga Studio, 12 Pepperell Square When: 1st Friday of every month Contact: 207-229-9965 acoriveryoga.com

Yarmouth – Location: First Universalist Church 97 Main Street, Maine When: Meets first Sunday and second and fourth Fridays of the month 6:30pm Contact: synthrick@hotmail.com

MARYLAND

Adelphi – Location: Paint Branch Unitarian Church, 3215 Powder Mill Road When: First Sunday of every month, 7:00 – 9:00pm

Annapolis – Location: 333 DuBois Ave, When: 3rd Tuesday of every month from 7:45 to 9:30 pm

Baltimore –

Location: Women's Circle First Unitarian Church When: Friday 7:30pm Contact: 410-426-9231

Location: 4711 Harford Rd, 2nd Floor When: 3rd Fridays of the Month 8:00-9:15pm Contact: greatsoulwellness.com

Location: The Resurgam Gallery When: Wednesday 7:30pm Contact: Resurgam Drum Jam 410-324-1084

Bethesda – Location: The Mindfulness Center, 4963 Elm Street, Suite 100 When: first and third Friday of every month, 7:30-9:00pm. Contact: (301) 986-1090 themindfulnesscenter.com

Columbia – Location: United Columbia Reiki Center, MD When: Wednesdays 7:30pm

Finksburg – Location: Cedarhurst Unitarian Universalist Church When: 3rd Saturday of every month from 7 to 9 pm, Contact: Laurie: lprecht1@verizon.net

Location: 2912 Clubhouse Road When: 4th Saturday of Every Month, 7:30 Contact:Stu Needel, Office/Cell (443) 845-1715

Frederick – Contact: shantileigh@hotmail.com and ask to be added to the drum circle list

Contact:Frederick Community Drum Circle on Facebook. 195

Location: Unity in Frederick Church, 1 West Ninth Street Frederick, Maryland When: last Saturday of the month 6:30pm to 8:30pm

Fulton – Location: Lime Kiln Middle School, 11650 Rte 216 When: 4th Tuesday of month 8:00-12:00am Contact: 301-776-2382

Hagerstown – Location: MCC 40 West Church Street- across from City Market When: last Friday of the month 7:00-8:00pm with the exception of, Jan 30, Feb 27, March 27, April 24, June 26, July 31, Aug 28, Sept 25, Oct 30, Nov 27, Dec 18, 2009 – Contact: David 301-302-5767

Hagerstown – Location: UUCH on Cearfoss Road. When: Every 4th Friday of the Month 8pm Contact: BMacW20705@aol.com onecircle.net/1000drumcircles / Stream at 301-949-8984

MASSACHUSETTS

Amherst – Location: Amherst Common, Munson Memorial Library Building When: First Friday of every month 8:30-11:30p.m.

Boston –
Location: The DrumRoom, 50 Tufts Steet Contact: 781-648-0066, Alan Tauber alan@drumconnection.com / drumconnection.com
Location: Unitarian Universalist Church, AREA DRUMMING, Boston When: Sundays 6:30 p.m. 617-261-3427

Cambridge –
Location: First Church, Boston Drum & Dance with the Earth Drum Council When: 8pm Contact: 978-371-2502
Location: First Parish Cambridge Unitarian Universalist 3 Church Street, Harvard Square, Cambridge, MA When: 3rd Friday of every month 7:00 – 8:30 pm

Fairhaven – Location: Unitarian Memorial Church 102 Green St. When: 7pm on the second Sunday and fourth Friday of every month Contact:drumfish@charter.net / drumfish.bravehost.com

Framingham – Location: Ellison Hall, Plymouth Church 87 Edgell Road When: 1st Sunday of each month. 6-9 pm. Contact: http://drummingjohn.tripod.com / drummingjohn@yahoo.com

Gloucester: – Location: YMCA, Gloucester 71 Middle St. Contact: 978-825-9396

Grafton – Location: Grafton Drum Circle When: 2nd Saturday of the month 7pm Contact: susan@graftondrum.com

Leicester – Location: The Federated Church, One Washburn Square When: Second Sunday of every mont: 6:30 to 9:00 pm Contact:Priscilla Olson spidex@earthlink.net

Milford – Location: Drums For One and All Drum Circle UU church, 23 Pine Street When: 1st Thursday of the month 7:00 to 10:00pm Contact: Dave@Drums-ForOneAndAll.com

Newburyport – Location: Yoga Center of Newburyport, 12 Maple St When: 3rd Saturday of each month from 4pm to 6pm Contact: RidimistGS1@aol.com

Northampton – Location: Spirit of the Heart, 47 Market Street When: Sundays4-6pm Contact: (413) 584-3022

MICHIGAN

Bay City –
Location: Unity Church Men's Drumming, MI When: Thursday 6:30pm Contact: 517-652-8169
Location: Mt. Pleasant Mag's Coffee House Main Street When: Tuesday nights Contact: lorifithian@mac.com

Detroit – Location: 18700 Woodward Ave, Close Goldengate Cafe When: Every Wednesday 9PM Contact: 313-366-2247

Flint – Location: 124 W. 1st. Street Flint, When: Second Sunday of the month Contact: (810) 694-3473 / flintlocal432.com / Ken Mathenia kmathenia@gfn.org

International Traverse City – When: Tuesday 8:15pm Contact: 231-276-BEAT / rhythmicadv@hotmail.com

John R. Hazel Park, – Location: Phoenix Cafe Drum Circle When: Every Sunday starting at 7pm Contact: 248-667-8817, PhoenixCafe.org

Lake Orion – Location: Orion Art Center 115 S. Anderson St When: First Sunday of every month 7-9 pm Contact: Sandy Mabery 248-535-6203

Lansing – Location: Magdalena's Tea House 2006 East Michigan Avenue When: first Friday of every month 7 PM Contact: abigailenglish@yahoo.com

Livonia – Location:Unity Drum Circle Unity Church, Fellowship Hall 28660 5 mile rd., MI 48154 When: 1st & 3rd Friday of each month Contact: (734) 421-1760, unityoflivonia.org/index.htm-

Saugatuck/Holland – Location: Shore Acres Park When:second Tuesday of the month Contact: bwyngard@excite.com

Unity Church Bay City When: Thursday 6:30pm Contact: 517-652-8169 Location: Lake Village Portage When:Every Full Moon 8:30pm

MINNESOTA

Duluth – Location: 145 West Winona St., First Unitarian Church of Duluth, MN When: First Friday of every month from 7:00pm until 9:00pm Contact: bholmen@chartermi.net

Minneapolis –

    Location: 2717 Lyndale Ave. S When: Every 3rd Friday of the month 7:00-9:00pm Contact: eyeofhorusinc.com

    Location: First Universalist Church of 3400 Dupont Ave South First Friday of the month 7pm-9:30pm Contact: firstuniv.org/drum/drumhome.html or jaime@drummingthesoulawake.com

    Location: 440 Upton Ave. S., When: every Friday Contact: 612-922-4272

St. Paul – Location: Women's Drum Center 2242 University Ave. W., Studio B-11, Contact: Kari Kjome, Music Director 651-695-1941

Van Cleve Park – When: Every Wednesday in in Minneapolis from 7-10pm Contact: Minneapolis Drummer United Facebook group

MISSISSIPPI

Ocean Springs – Location: Mary C. O'Keefe Cultural Center Ocean Springs When: 1st Saturday of every month Drum Circle facilitator – Jay Twilbeck

MISSOURI

Columbia – Location: Unity Center – Stephens Lake Park When: 6-8pm Thursdays Contact: Email pholmes@coin.org

Kansas City – Location: The Tribal Drum 3603 East 12th St When: Every Monday night at 7 pm Contact: 816-695-3309

Kansas City – Location: 2927 Charlotte St When: Sundays: 3-4pm Contact: James Abbott., MO Phone: 816-561-1811

Riverfront Park Hannibal – Location: Meet every Sunday, @2PM. In Riverfront Park Contact: 2178947061 Email: Seanboy@adams.net

Springfield –

    Location: Oneness Center – 1938 S. Stewart Ave, When: 2nd Saturday of Each Month Contact: Drums4Spirit@mchsi.com or Drums4Spirit@cs.com Website: home.mchsi.com/~drums4spirit/wsb/index.html

    Location: Jordan Valley Park, When:Monday 7pm

St. Louis –

    Location: The Archive – 3213-15 Cherokee Street When: 3rd Thursday of the month 7:30pm – 9:30pm

    Location: St. John's Hospital/O'Reilly Cancer Center Drum Circle (public) When: On the first Wednesday When: Sunday 1pm Contact: 314-644-0235

MONTANA

Missoula –

    Location: Unity Church (Fall-Spring) Jacob's Island (Summer) Contact: 406-543-5810

    Location: changes with seasons When: First Sunday of the month Email: dmr@bresnan.net E-mail: intuitryder@msn.com Contact: 406-495-0774

NEBRASKA

Lincoln – Location: 140 N 8th St (in the Haymarket) When: Third Friday, from 7–9

Omaha – Location: 6113 Maple Street When: 3rd Friday 7 – 9pm

NEVADA

Carson City – Location: 319 N. city When: Held on the last Saturday of every month 7:00pm till sunrise Contact:NV Email: dochaura@yahoo.com

Las Vegas – Location: Redrock Canyon Drum Circle When: We play every Sunday

Tahoe City When: 1st Saturday 7pm Drum Circle w/ Shakerman

NEW HAMPSHIRE

Concord – Location: Universalist Church – 274 Pleasant St., NH When: 1st Friday of every month, 7:00 – 9:00 p.m. Contact: 603-736-4508

NEW JERSEY

Brigantine Beach – Location:"Augie Doggie Drumcircles" in southern New Jersey. Contact: 609-266-0567 or Augie4doggie@hotmail.com (facilitator is featured in *The Healing Power of the Drum*) Call for directions or email Augie2doggie@lycos.com

Brick When: Wednesday Nights 6:00–9:00pm, FREE Contact: thegatheringtree.org, NJ

Brigantine – Location: Southwestern Casa #4 Lagoon Ct. When: 2nd and 4th Thursdays of the month, free 7:30pm–9:00pm, Contact: 609-266-8299

Cape May – When: The third Thursday of every month. Time: 7:00pm-9:00pm Contact: 609-780-7088

Cranford – Location: 11 North Avenue When:meets on the second Saturday of the month at the City Grind CoffeeHouse

Farmingdale – Location: GS Camp Lake Sacajawea When: First Sunday of each month at 7pm

Oceanport – Location: 42 Hiawatha Ave When: First Monday Night of the Month 7:30pm – 9:30pm. Contact: 732-222-8703

Plainsboro – Location: Community Drum Circle Center for Relaxation & Healing, When: First Friday of the month 7:00–8:45pm Contact: 609-750-7432

Red Bank – Location: 52-A Monmouth St. Time: 7:00pm–8:30pm Contact: drummersalley.com/default.htm

West Orange – Location: 158 Southern Blvd, When:1st Sunday 3pm

Wyckoff – Location: 393 Crescent Avenue When: Friday, May 7 (2nd Friday of the month) Time: 7:30 – 9:00 Contact: Renee Fagan 201-891-9100

NEW MEXICO

Albuquerque – Location: 2nd Friday of the month-7 p.m. to 8:30 p.m. Contact: Marshall Henrie

Manzano Mesa Multigenerational Center Street –

Location: 501 Elizabeth SE When: 7:30 PM – 8:45 PM Third Friday of every month

Location: Taylor Ranch Community Center 4900 Kachina St. NW (corner of Kachina & Taylor Ranch Road), NM Contact: 505-897-8620 westsidedrumcircle.com

Santa Fe –
> Location: Tribes Coffeehouse, 139 W. San Francisco When: Last Friday of Month 6:30 pm – 9:00 pm Contact: 505 232-9010
>
> Location: 2639 Agua Fria When: Every Full Moon at 7:00 Contact: 505-501-3300 ninaz@earthlink.net Facilitated by Nina Zelevansky, MA

Women's Healing Drum Circle When: 1st Saturday of the month at 7:00 Facilitated by Nina Zelevansky, MA,

Silver City – Location: Community Built Park, Grant Street When: Every 4 to 6 weeks. Contact: 505 538 0476 Email: 2trees@zianet.com
> Location: HealthRHYTHMS Drum Circle Gila Regional Medical Center When: Thursdays 5:45 to 6:45 Contact: Allee Barr at drummer@gilanet.com

NEW YORK

Amherst – Location: Unitarian Universalist Church of Williamsville Contact: 1st & 3rd Sunday 5pm

Brooklyn – Location: Prospect Park When: Sunday Bi-weekly 12pm Contact: Brian T Carter on FaceBook

Buffalo – When: Tuesday 6:30pm Contact: 716-897-0950 Location: WhiteHouse at Medaille College When: 4th Saturday 9pm Contact: 662-0654

Central Park – Location: 72nd & Central Park West- When: 2nd Saturday of the month 3:30

Central Square – Location: Unitarian Church Rte 49 (near Rte 11) When: second Friday of every month Contact: grunherz63@yahoo.com for details

Freeport – Location: South Nassau Unitarian Universalist Congregation 228 South Ocean When: Thursday nights from 6:00 to 7:30pm Contact: 516-623-1204

Glen Falls – Location: Platt Street Quarry (245 Platt Street) When: 3rd Friday each month Contact: Pete@Earthdrumz.com (518) 636-6500.

Ithaca –
> Location: 409 w. State St. When: 3-4pm Sat. Contact: theuniversalrhythm.webs.com
>
> Location: 111 Chestnut St When: Fall/Winter 5 pm-10pm When: 5pm-10 pm NW Corner Stewart Park, Contact: oneheartcommunitydrummers@yahoo.com or one-heartcommunitydrumming.org
>
> Location: Stewart Park When: Saturdays Ongoing 3 pm

Lilydale –
> Location: Church of the Living Spirit Cleveland Ave, When: 8:00pm
>
> Location: Cleveland Ave between North St and Library Street When: 1st and 3rd Thursday of the month Contact: George 716/410-2369

Liverpool – Location: Liverpool Art Center Drum Circle 101 lake Drive, When: Fridays 7-9pm Contact: artsandhealing.com

Long Island – Location: The Yoga Center 107 East Main St When: First Saturday Drum Circle Contact: 631-893-5445 Contact: mmregan@suffolk.lib.ny.us

Manhattan –
> Location: Fifth Ave. corner of 107 When:Every Saturday from 1– 3pm Contact: Alan: 212 828 1217

Location: 170 E. 116th Street, When: Saturday 4pm Contact: 212-410-2999 Contact: Sandra Fioramonti

Oneonta – Location: Unitarian Universalist Society of Oneonta on 12 Ford St. When: It starts at 8pm. on Friday nights. Contact: bassettentertainment(a)yahoo.com

Oswego – Location: Oswego Tea Company, 157 East 1st St. Oswego NY 13126 When: Meets 2nd Sunday of the month at the John Anderson MSW

Port Jefferson Station – Location: 506 Sara Circle When:(631) 331-3536 myrdin@ optonline.net

Rochester – Location: 34 Elton St When: Sunday 11:30am

Rockville Centre When: 2nd Saturday of the month 7:30pm to 10:30pm Contact: 718-634-2685 – ripnqdd@aol.com

Sayville – Location: 46 Railroad Avenue When: 2nd Sunday of every month 6pm-9pm – $10, Contact: tigerdrum52@optonline.net

Contact: Open Drum Circle of Rochester, NY meetup.com/drumcircle-rochester/ Open to everyone. Please refer to the site for upcoming circles.

Woodstock – Location: Village Green When: Sunday 4pm

NORTH CAROLINA

Asheville –

Location: Movement and Learning Center upstairs at the French Broad Food Co-Op When: Mondays, 7:15-8pm Contact: 828-670-7287

Location: Pritchard Park When: Fridays from 8–11pm Contact: 828-670-7287-drumdance@att.net

Location: Haw Creek area When: Thursdays, 7–9 pm Contact: drumming@wild-bodema.com or Contact: 828-505-1810

Location: Pritchard Park When: Friday night open drum circle at every week.

Brasstown – Location: 1 Folk School Road When: Starts at 7PMl Contact: 828-835-4704 email at kim@kimscreationsonline.com

Charlotte –

Location: BacInTyme Coffee House When: Every other Saturday at in Fort Mill, SC When: Every 2nd and 4th Friday in the NoDa arts district (36th and Davidson) in Charlotte

Location: Mercury Porch (Across from Smelly Cat 514 E. 36th St). When: Sunday Jam at Francis Beatty Park starting at 2p. Meet at the Pavillion or just listen for the drums upon arrival.

Location: 9704 Mallard Creek Road When: 2nd Friday of the month at 7:30 pm. For info, email Susan: jestburns@world.oberlin.edu. or puuc.org/

Location: At Ye Olde Grande Disco Contact: SteveNelson@carolina.rr.com

Coastal Carolina – Contact: Facilitator Ella Noll at hillnoll@aol.com

Concord – Location: Concord Lotus Living Arts Studio Downtown NC When: 1st Sunday of every month Time: Contact: 5:30pm – 7:30pm – Location:

Durham –

Location: 314 NC Hwy 55, Ste 102, NC When: Every 2nd Saturday of each month Contact: 919-484-9090

Location: Eno River Unitarian Universalist Church. When: Fridays. 6:30PM Contact: Yahoo Group = RiverRhythms

Fayetteville – Location: 102 Person St When: Fridays at 8:30pm Contact: 910-321-7383-email lro@carolina.net

Greensboro – Location: 406 State Street, Greensboro, NC. When: twice a month event Contact: eclecticbynature.com Michael Gyurica, a Shamanic Lightworker. Contact: (336) 373-0733 Please call ahead to check dates and to let us know you're coming!

Hillsborough – Contact: wildwomynwisdom.org & also on Facebook search: Contact: wildwomyndrummer@embarqmail.com

Hot Springs – Location: Moonien Arts Studio Contact: 828.622.3787 Contact: Email Adhi at moonien@msn.com

Mt. Airy – Location: Carolina Wellness Center Contact: Marie at 336-789-0370 Contact: marie@ColumbiaReiki.com

Morganton – Location: Courthouse Square When: 5:30-6:30 pm,. Bring a chair. Loaner drums available. Contact: Contact Brenda or Christine at (828) 438-0032 rumoja@hci.net

Raleigh – Heartbeats Drum Circle Location: 2867 Jones Franklin Road When: 4th Sundays 3-4:30pm Contact: website: raleighdrumcircle.org
Location: Lake Johnson Park – 4601 Avent Ferry Rd When: Jam Third Mondays, 7-9pm website: raleighdrumcircle.org

Winston-Salem –
Location: Golden Flower T'ai Chi Center 625 Trade Street When: 2nd, 3rd and 4th Saturdays of each month 8:30 – 10:00 pm Contact:(336) 774-3898
Location: Charlotte Unitarian Universalist Church When: First and third Tuesdays, 7–9pm. Contact: Kathleen Moloney-Tarr at leaders@mindspring.com

OHIO

Akron – Location: Drum Circle Heaven and Earth Gift Shoppe When: Friday 7:30pm Contact: 330-669-2532

Akron/Cleveland area – Location: George's Drum Shop When: Saturdays at 5:30. free. Contact: georgesdrumshop.com

Bellaire – Location: 66166 Kirkwood Heights Rd When: Wednesday night around 8:30. Contact: astrozombierat@aol.com

Cincinnati – Location: Fountain Square When: Fridays from 11:30 – 1:30 pm, 1:00-5:00 pm Contact: jeaunita@bi-okoto.com

Cinti – Location: 2511 Essex Place When: Saturday evenings Contact: 513-221-6112

Cleveland – Location: Behind the Rock and Roll Hall of Fame When: Thursday Sunset – 11pm

Columbus – Location: 2203 North High Street When: Every Sunday 4pm-7pm Contact: stephenwdodge@yahoo.com

Cleveland – Location: MartialArts & Zen center When: First Friday of every month 6-9PM

Location: Winter – Location: Studio 11 2337 W 11th St When: Every Sunday Afternoon 3pm Contact: wally.gunn@yahoo.com

Fairlawn – Location: Stewart's Caring Place When: 1st Monday each month (except holidays) – 6-7 PM Contact: stewartscaringplace.org

Hamilton – Location: Hamilton Zen Center 114 Main Street When: May 7th 7PM to 9pm

Massillon –

Location: West Holistic Health Ctr. 1807 Lincoln Way E., Ohio 44646 When: Third Saturday of each month. Contact: 330-833-3420

Location: Unity Church of Truth – Location: 4016 Wales Ave, Ohio 44646 330-837-3737 (church phone) When: Night before each full moon

Oberlin – Location: The Cindy Nord Center for Renewal 14240 Baird Road When: Third Wednesday of Each Month 6:30 – 8:30pm Contact: 440-965-5551

Oxford – Location: 6385 Contreras Rd. OH When: Every Wednesday Contact: 513-523-8614 Contact: Toni Kellar/ Roots To Rhythm

Strongsville –

Location: Angle House 14217 Mill Hollow Lane When: Last Saturday of each month 5:00pm Contact: 440-846-1789 Led by Rex Bacon

Location: Angel House 14127 Mill Hollow Lane When: Last Saturday of every month Contact: 440-846-1789

Westlake – Location: 23855 Detroit Road When: Every 2nd Friday of the month Contact: 440.835.0400

Youngstown – Contact: bewell-drumon.com / dan@bewell-drumon.com Location: 706 Steel Street When: Sunday from 4

OKLAHOMA

Edmond – Location: 28 E. Main When: Sun 4pm Contact: brennan131@home.com

Tulsa – Location: 3100 E. Overholser Dr. When: Saturday 4pm Contact: 405-495-9357-Email tmossk@aol.com

OREGON

Florence – Location: Florence Unitarian Universalist Fellowship (FUUF) Hall When: Meets every Friday afternoon at 2pm Contact: Krecker at keybythesea@me.com

Newport – Location: Don Davis Park When: Meets on the 1st and 3rd Tuesday of each month 6pm – 8pm

North Bend – Location: 1955 Union Ave When: Monday evenings, 7:00 pm Contact: infocarnival@verizon.net

Portland – When: 7pm Men's Drumming – Wednesdays

Contact: 503-235-6345

When: 2239 E. Burnside, Contact: Cedar Mountain Drums 7:00 – 9:00 p.m

When: Second Wednesday Mixed Drumming [Children, Women, Men]503-235-6345 When: Third Wednesday Women's Drumming at Cedar Mountain Drums 7:00 – 9:00 p.m.

When: 7pm Womanspirit Contact: 503-235-6345

Location: Garden Home Recreation Center When: Thursday 7pm Bamboula Drum & Dance Circle, OR

Location: Psalm Drummers group When: Saturday 3pm

Salem – Location: Salem Riverfront Amphitheatre When: Every Wednesday 7:00 Contact: 503-365-8399

PENNSYLVANIA

Allentown –
   Location: Dave Phillips on Union Boulevard When: First Wednesdays at 6:30pm
   Contact: LVDrumcircle.com
   Location: Unitarian Universalist Church Reading, PA When: 3rd Friday 7pm Contact: 610-374-3730
Bloomsburg – Location: 143 E. Main St When: First Thursday 7pm – 9pm Contact: 570-784-3088
Chambersburg –
   Location: 550 Cleveland Ave When: 1st Sunday of the month Contact: mcchesney@embarqmail.com
   Location: Zion Reformed Church 259 S. Main Street When: 1st Saturday of each month Contact:Bonnie McChesney Contact: mcchesney@embarqmail.com
Dauphin – Location: 1720 Towpath Rd. When: 1st Sunday every month 4- 6pm Contact: 717-921-2599
Erie – Location: Presque Isle State Park When: 35 Peninsula Drive Contact: Every Saturday from noon
Exton – Location: St. Pauls When: First Thursday of the month at 7:30 PM Contact: dtowndrumcircle@verizon.net
Fogelsville – Location: 7725 Main Street When: First Sunday of Every Month 5 to 6:30 PM Contact: To Register call: 610-398-7440 Facilitator: Stephanie Schmoyer
Murrysville – Location: 4326 Sardis Road When: Every 2nd and 4th Sunday Contact: karenlgerard@aol.com
Philadelphia – Location: 1831 Brandywine Street When: Thursdays Contact: billk@animusmusic.com
Pittsburgh – Location: Wishing Tree, 212 S. Broadway When: Third Saturday of each month Contact: Achey at 231-0712 or Ross at 232-2377.
Pottstown – Location: 310 High Street When: First and third Thursdays 6:30pm Contact: WITTA101@AOL.COM
Wilkes-Barre – Location: Unity Church 140 S. Grant St When: 3rd Saturday of the month Contact: 570-824-7722

RHODE ISLAND

Pawtucket – Location: 925 Central Ave. When: First Fridays Drum Circle 6:45-9:15pm
   Contact: 401-723-3900
Wakefield – Location: 315 Main Street When: 1st Friday of every month 7:30 – 9;30 pm Contact: info@allthatmatters.com

SOUTH CAROLINA

Fort Mill – Location: Walter Elisha Park When: 5:30-7:30pm Contact: firesurfer75@hotmail.com
Myrtle Beach – Location: Myrtle Beach State Park When: 6pm Contact: geocities.com/MBdrumcircle

TENNESSEE

Bristol – Location: Downtown Center When: 1st & 3rd Sunday 5 pm Contact:facebook page: facebook.com/bristoldrumcircle

Chattanooga – Location: 231 East Martin Luther King Blvd Coolidge Park When: Sundays 7:30pm Contact: 423-265-2171

Nashville – Location: 1808 Woodmont Blvd

When: Third Saturday of every month Drum Circle 7:30-10:30pm: Contact: info@thelovedrums.com

Sevierville When: 7:00PM Contact: Michael jmbraswell@gmail.com

TEXAS

Austin –

Location: 9603 Dessau Road When: Every second Friday of the month at 7:30 p.m Contact: slatham1@mindspring.com

Location: 600 East 50th Street When: 7-8:30 pm

Location: Zilker Park When: Sunday 3pm Contact: 214-823-DRUM

Location: 3212 So. Congress Ave When: 3rd Monday of each month- 7–9pm

Corpus Christi – Location: Water Street Village When: 3rd Thu Monthly

Dallas –

Location: 1325 E. Levee Street When: 7:30 p.m. to 10 p.m – 1st Friday

Location: Walt Whitman School 9353 Garland Rd When: Thursdays 7pm

Location: 4415 Belmont When: 3rd Friday of the month 8-10pm Contact: Timothy Carmichael at shamanie@aol.com –

Location: 5625 Yale Blvd When: 4th Wednesday

Location: 5625 Yale Blvd When: Wednesday 9pm Contact: 214-823-DRUM

Elgin – Location: The Art of Living Spiritual Center monthly When: Third Saturday of each month. – Gathering opens at 7pm drum jam at 8:30

Fort Worth – Location: Center for Change, Discovery and Support, When: Tuesday 8pm Contact: 817 429-4769

Galveston – Location: Whiskey Blues, 25th St. and Post Office When: Sundays, 9pm Contact: e6980@swbell.net

Garland – Location: 1215 Main Street When: Every 4th Friday 7:30pm Contact: shalin@montagar.com

Location: 1701 S. Fifth When: 3rd Tuesday of every month Contact: Stephanie at mrsdomi@juno.com

Houston –

Location: InstaKarma When: Monday 8pm Contact: 713 528-3545

Location: 4104 Fannin When: 1st Sunday 3pm, TX Contact: Thursday 9:30pm

Location: Markets Square Park When: Tuesday 10 pm-2 am

Location: Natsuoh Coffee Shop When: Tuesday 10pm

Richardson – Location: Pagan Tea Room Pleasant Valley Unitarian Church When: Friday 5:30pm CUUPs

Stephenville – Location: 140 E Long When: Wednesday 7pm

Woodlands – Location: 1370 N. Millbend Dr. When: Every second Saturday. 10AM-Noon Contact: Rebecca Holt 281-288-3778

UTAH

Salt Lake City –

Location: 700 East 1000 S When: Sunday 1pm Contact: weekapaw@hotmail.com
Location: 900 South 600 East Contact: (801) 322-2473-trancelady@rocketmail.com

VERMONT

Middlebury – Location: Bridge School Exchange St. and Rt. 7, VT 05753 Contact: 802-382-8848- joss@justaddfire.com

VIRGINIA

Frederickburg –

Location: 1201 Caroline Street When: 4th Saturday, 12 noon Contact: Kawakib.com/drumming.html
Location: Eyeclopes Studios Downtown – Drum/Dance When: Fridays 7pm Contact: More Information eyeclopes.com/oracle/index.html
Location: Percussion in the Park Hurkamp Park – VA When: Saturday 10am

Leesburg – Location: 41793 Tutt Lane When: 3rd wednesday of every month Contact: 703-771-7755

Martinsville – Location: 301 Starling Ave When: 7pm 2nd and 4th Thursdays of each month

Norfolk – When: Mondays 7-10pm Contact: mysticmoonevents.com Location: 3416 N. Military Highway When: Every Monday 7pm to 10pm Contact: mysticmoonevents.com

Oakton – Location: 2709 Hunter Mill Road When: 3rd Saturday 3-5 pm Contact: jwgill2@msn.com

International Drum Circles

AUSTRALIA

Agnes Water / 1770, deckAdance, The Deck Restaurant – Location: 384 Captain Cook Drive, Town of 1770, When: Every third Sunday of the month, 3pm onwards Contact: Angela email heenan_angela@hotmail.com ph 0749749157

Bagara, Nielson Beach Surf Life Saving Club Courtice Drive When: Monday mornings at 7am, Contact: Lorraine ph 0741547393

Bilarong Reserve, Wakehurst Parkway, Narrabeen – Location: Elanora Scout Hall When: Monthly Contact: Chris – circleofdrums@yahoo.com.au Contact: launch.groups.yahoo.com/group/circleofdrums/

Bli Bli, Finnish Memorial Park – Location: Finland Rd When: 4th Sunday of the month at 1pm, Contact: Rhonda ph 0412720923

Bondi Beach, Sydney, NSW, Australia – Location: Stone Circle, When: on Friday nights nearest a full moon, Oct – April, starting 9pm on the cliffs at Mark's Park in South Bondi, running for past years fire twirlers very welcome! Contact:bleshin@bigpond.net.au for details

Brisbane – Location: Roma Street Parklands When: Thursday 7:00pm – 10:00pm. All Welcome Email: contact@brisdjembe.org

Brisbane North, Bayside Beats, Einbunpin Park, Sandgate, Sunday afternoon 2pm, Contact: John & Peggy, email, johnbonnar@iprimus.com.au ph 0421648096

Brisbane West, Centenary Drum Circle, – Location: Rocks Riverside Park off Counihan Rd, Seventeen Mile Rocks, When: Saturday 12 noon – 2:00pm. Contact: Nahm 0434 261 633 Email: nahmaldai@hotmail.com

Bundaberg Nielson Park – Location: Just south of Nielson Park Beach When: Sundays 4pm onwards Contact: Jason email djembeguru@hotmail.com ph 0438544527

Darlington, Perth, Western Australia Brisbane Central
Location: Roma St Parklands adjacent to Roma St Railway Station When: Thursdays 7pm Contact: Eddie prefers email, ehall-sm@bigpond.net.au ph 0419 500 147
Location: United Church Hall Darlington Rd When: Every Wednesday night at 7.15pm

Gold Coast – Burleigh Beat, Contact: Ken Jacob, email, kenjacob@tpg.com.au ph 07 5533 8960

Hills Community Drumming Circle – Location: Darlington United Church Hall, Darlington Rd in Darlington, When: Meets every Wednesday from 7:15 Contact: simon@hillsdrumming.org.auWeb: hillsdrumming.org.au

Ipswich Drum Circle – Location: From Ipswich in Queensland Australia When: Meets Sundays from 1:30pm Contacts: 54672613 Contact: djcrossing@aapt.net.au or Dave8591@hotmail.com
Drum circles only for Women and on the Full Moon at the moment but more starting in May, my website is jozinasdrum.com.

Labrador Gold Coast Queensland Australia When: Every Sunday from 4:30pm – 8:30pm at Harley park Contact: 0404 703 556 or broadwaterrhythms@y7mail.com

Melbourne: – Location: Coburg Lake Reserve Corner of Murray Road and Lake Grive in Coburg, VIC, 3058 8 Lee Street, East Brunswick When: Time: 6pm – 8ish

Perth When: Every Wednesday night – open to all Contact: www.hillsdrumming.org Facilitated by Simon Faulkner [Facilitator featured in The Healing Power of the Drum]

Stanthorpe Weeroona Park When: 2nd Sunday of each month 10.30am Contact: Gail Paulsen. email: gpaulsen@dodo.com.au

Sunshine Coast, Nomadic Soul Drummers When: Every Monday on Cnr Ocean St and Duporth Ave Maroochydore, When: Every Monday 5pm to 7pm. Beginners and experienced welcome. Contact: Mal, email malcolmsettree@bigpond.com ph 0428 73 00 52

Tascot, Kincumba "Mud Brick" Kiosk, Island View Drive, via Kincumber, When: Thursdays 8pm until 11pm Contact: Tim Green ph 02 4325 5664 email timpat57@hotmail.com

Tenterfield Destination Field When: Good Wednesdays 5.30pm, Contact: Gail Paulsen. email gpaulsen@dodo.com.au

Toowoomba Queens Park from 2:30 every Sunday All welcome Contact: Kim 0438 981356 email watdael2@bigpond.net.au or Jan 0403 546 938

Townsville Gregory Street Ampitheatre on the Strand, When: Full Moons, 5.30pm to 8:00pm, Contact: Alex Salvador, email therhythmconnection@live.com.au ph 0414 803 666

Tuncurry, various – Locations all within 1/2 hours drive When: Fridays 7pm, Contact: Keith Contact: contactkatethompson@yahoo.com.au 0411 523 15

Western Sydney – Location: Alpha Park Hall, Blacktown When: From 7:30pm until 10:30pm When: Each other Friday night from 8th February 2008 Contact: Lawrie on 0414-831-772

Brazil Sao Paulo – Location: Paulo Campos Percussion School When: Saturday 4pm

CANADA

Alberta – Location: 11715E 108 Avenue Edmonton (Centre for Spiritual Living) Time: 7 – 9pm Dates: Mondays – usually twice monthly but check by e-mail for dates Contact: Marilyn mberezowsky@shaw.ca

Alberta Canada – Location:3415b 26 Ave SW When: 2nd & 4th Fri 8pm

Barrie, Ontario – Location: Royal Victoria Hospital, Community Care Centre, Lower Level When: 2nd Tuesday evening of each month 6:30 to 8:00 p.m. 70 Wellington Street West, L4N 1K4 Contact: Anne Marie, (705) 726-7490 Contact: irelandan@rvh.on.ca
Location: 39 High Street When: 4th Wednesday evening of each month 5:30 to 6:45 pm Contact: Kevin Smith, Ph. [705] 726-5033 ext. 404
When: Fridays, 10:00am – noon Location: 175 Bayfield Street Contact: Rachel Strauss earthdrum@hotmail.com

Bracebridge Canada When: Weekly Tuesdays Contact: Mi-Shell Jessen at 1-705-645-4167 Contact: s.tassie@sympatico.ca bearpaw@muskoka.com or Leslee Tassie at 1-705-645-5042

Brampton, Canada – Location: 71 West Dr., Unit 41 Contact: (905) 455-9884 or Toll Free (800) 667-0658 Facilitated by Jeff SalemMonthly, on Sundays-free

British Columbia – Location: Based in 100 Mile House and 108 Mile Ranch in the South Cariboo region of British Columbia, Canada. Contact: www2. bcinternet. net/~newman/drumming/
Location: Mountainview Wellness Centre, South Surrey, 3566 King George Hwy V4P 1P5 Contact: Dr. Connie Wanlin R. Psych. (604) 720-6205 When: Tuesdays 7:30-8:30pm

Calgary, Alberta Contact: dansadrumming.bravehost.com

Dorchester, Ontario When: 1st & 3rd Wednesday of every month – Location: Dorchester Donnybrook Legion (Just off the 401 Hwy. at the intersection of Dorchester Road and Donnybrook Road). Contact: penny@pennywearne.com

Dorset – Location: Dorset Rec Centre – Main Hall When:Saturday September 11th & Saturday October 9th 1 pm – 3 pm Contact: Gillian Thomas ph: 705 766-2323 Gillian@rhythmicbynature.com

Edmonton, Alberta, Canada Contact: drumAdrumDRUM.com

Exeter, Ontario. – Location: Connect Centre in the basement of South Huron Hospital When: Wednesday evenings from 7:00-8:00pm at the Contact: 519-235-4275

Georgina, Canada – Location: SuttonGeorgina Arts Centre 149 High St. When: Wednesday evenings 7-9 Contact: Phil Shaw at phil@shawpercussion.com shawpercussion.com

Kitchener, Ontario, Canada – Location: Victoria Park When: Thursday night from 7-9pm all summer long, from June to September.

Lethbridge Alberta Contact:corestrengths.ca for more information.
Location: Galt Gardens on the corner of 5 St. and 3 Ave. S. When: Every Sat. night (weather permitting). Drum circle begins when the sun goes down.

London, Canada – Location: Christ Anglican Church, 138 Wellington St When: Monthly 7-9pm Contact: Jack Barnes, (519) 641-6566 drumanticks@execulink.com
Location: The Living Centre, 5871 Bells Rd. Contact:(519) 652-9109

Madoc Ontario, Canada When: Every 2nd & 4th Sunday of every month at 6pm Contact: Deborah or Terry at 613-473-1725 – thewildblueyondercabin.com. drumnationfestival.com

Mississauga, Canada – Contact: jimarnold@folkloremusic.com Website: folkloremusic.com

Nelson, B.C. Beacon Hill Park When: On sunny Sundays after lunch Tues 7:15pm – Location: Nelson North Shore Hall Contact: kimmasse@shaw.ca

Newmarket Ontario When: 1st and 3rd Saturday (plus a few more) of every month at "Community Living", When: 460 Oak St., Newmarket, Ontario from 9:30 pm to 1:00 am. Contact: newmarketdrumcircle.com

Pickering, Canada – Location: Pickering Beach, at the bottom of Liverpool Road, on the Beach. Free public parking. – Location: 1895 Clements Road – Location: Unit 155 Pickering. Free public parking. When: Wednesdays, in the summer on the beach, When: Thursdays in the winder at a Pickering studio – Location: 7pm jam, 7:30 – 9:30 is rehearsal Contact: Ron Cross, Orion Drums (orionbiz@bellnet.ca) (905) 427-9514

Sarnia, Ontario, Canada When: Weekly, each Monday evening at 7pm. Contact: 519-332-0310 – 810-982-2498

Sunnyside Beach When it runs: Summer, every Sunday. – Location: Sunnyside Beach. Contact: TBD

Sutton West ON – Location: 5258 Old Homestead Rd. Contact: 905-722-5449 phil@shawpercussion.com – shawpercussion.com

Toronto
When: TBD Contact: dtmike@gmail.com or call 416-236-1099
Location: Gerard and Coxwell, at 79 Hiawatha Ave. Toronto, ON When: Second Tuesday of Each Month. (between Gerrard St and Dundas St, West of Coxwell

Ave) Directions: nuuc.ca/location.htm Contact: William@wmpc.com, (put NUUC drums in subject).

Location: Withrow Park When: Sundays, 3:30pm Contact: 416-465-7006 Email: matthew_rm@hotmail.com

Location: Withrow Park, Logan Av. 1 block South of the Danforth Contact: 416-465-7006 – matthew_rm@hotmail.com

Location: Jewish Community Centre Room 218, Spadina and Bloor When: Monthly, last Monday of the Month, 8:15pm Spring and summer – Christie Pits: fall and winter Contact: Dr. Shari Geller 416-780-1791 Ora Schwartz 647-444-DRUM

When: Every Sunday in Withrow Park from 15.30-18.30 hours (weather permitting)

When: weekly, Saturdays from 8-11pm

Location: 109 Vaughan Rd, upstairs

Location: 2848 Bloor Street West Facilitator: James Freeman When: Thursday evenings, 8:15-9:15 pm

Location: Great Room, Kingsway Conservatory of Music Contact: 416-234-0121 When: kingswayconservatory.ca

Location: Huntington Hills NW Calgary Thusday evening at 7:30 PM When: Thursday evening.

Location: Upper Hastings area, mid-north NSW Coast When: 6.30pm – 8.00pm Beginners drum lesson $15

Location: Jaspers Village Resort, 175 Mt Seaview Rd, Mt Seaview When: 8.00pm onwards Drum Circle When: On the Saturday evening of the Full Moon each month Contact: 6587 7155 or jaspers@harboursat.com.au or website jaspersvillageresort.com.au

Location: 1407 10th Street SW When: Every Thursday night started October 23rd, 2008 at 7:30 PM Contact: beatthestress@telus.net My site is beatthestress.ca

When: weekly on Saturdays starting in Feb 2005, – Location: xing dance Studio, 452 College street. Contact: Michael U, ttt@look.ca

Waterloo, Canada – Location: 25 Regina Street South When: Every other Sunday from 2-4:00 pm Winter/Spring: Jan 30, Feb 13, Feb 27, Mar 13, Mar 27, Apr 10, Apr 24, May 8, May 22 Contact: Sue Shearer at sue_12345@hotmail.com

Waterloo, Canada – Location: University of Waterloo Drum Circle – Location: in the student life centre building on UW campus. When: Every Sunday night from 7:00 – 9:30 pm,

Winnipeg, Canada – Location: North End Womens Centre – 394 Selkirk Avenue Contact: Phone: 1-204-589-7347 Email: crone@wheelweb.com email ttt@look.ca

BRAZIL

Sao Paulo, Brazil – Location: Paulo Campos When: Saturday 4pm

BELGIUM

Djamsession Aalst – Location: Don Bosco School – Location: Meuleschettestraat 9300, Aalst When: Every third Sunday of the month, When: starting at 16.00 hrs Contact: djamsession@pandora.be

De Schakel Djamsession – Location: Roodebeekseweg 270, 1200 Bruxelles When: Every first Friday of the month from 20.00 hours

Drumcircle Turnhout – Location: Draaiboomstraat 6 2300 Turnhout When: Every first Sunday of the month, When: starting at 15.00 hours

BOLIVIA

Cochabamba Bolivia – Location: Plaza Colon When: Every Friday evening/night from 20:00 Contact: davor.pavisic@gmail.com

DENMARK

Location: Nakskov & Maribo Musikskoler When: Every Saturday starting at 20.00 hrs Contact: tubas@image.dk

ECUADOR

Location: Quito Ecuador When: Friday night, new moon Contact: elconsuladodel-ritmo.com

GERMANY

Ratingen near Dusseldorf – Location: In Friedenskirche, Hegelstr., Ratingen OST When: It is now the second Sunday of every month When: Time from 19 – 21 Contact: Facilitated by Wilfried drum-circle-groove.de

Shamanic Drumming Circle Germany – Location: Apu Kuntur Contact: +49-172-8102024 Contact: apu@kondor.de

Contact: never-stop-the-beat.de/

Location: Biblingen Grafenau When: 1st Friday 7pm Contact: trommelkreis.de/

Nordhorn When: last Tuesday of the month, Indoors, starting at 19.00 hrs Contact: anna@drumcafe.de

GREECE

Naxos Greece – Location: Plaka beach Contact: Sanity_is_no_fun@hotmail.com

HONG KONG

Central Hong Kong – Location: Kumi Masunaga Fringe Club When: Tuesday 8pm Contact: drum-jam.com

Location: Cultural Centre PIazza When: Last Sunday 2pm

IRELAND

Belfast, Ireland When: 4pm Drum Circle Menagerie Bar Contact: email: paul@powerhaus.freeserve.co.uk

Location: Menagerie Bar When: Sunday 4pm Drum Circle

Location: Psalm Drummers Circle Downshire Hall When: 1st Monday 8:30pm The Gathering

Cork, Ireland – Location: Kinsale When: Friday eves at 7pm to 9pm.

Dublin Ireland When: Every tuesday and friday @ 7pm. 5 pounds per session. Contact: Phone: 01 4545426 Contact: drumjujujam@hotmail.com

Location: Dublin, Ireland – St Audeons School, When: Tuesday 7:30pm

ISRAEL

Drummer's Beach – Location: Tel-Aviv, Israel Contact: drumbeach.co.il/

ITALY

Bergamo Every month the day changes. Contact: myspace.com/dianatedoldi.

Milan Italy – Location: Percussion Village, Via Anfossi 6. When: Every 2 weeks Friday night, between 7pm and 9pm. Contact: Diana Tedoldi – myspace.com/dianatedoldi

PORTUGAL

Museu do Trajo, Sao Bras, in the Algarve, Portugal. When: Every Monday from 5pm (17.00) to 7pm (19.00) at the Children's drumming is every Saturday from 3pm (15.00) to 4.30pm (16.30) also at the Museu. Cost for the adult group is 5 euros using one of my drums, or 3 euros bring your own. The children's group is free to children of the "Amigos do Museu" (Friends of the Museu) or 3 euros to non-Amigos. I supply the drums for them. URL is tamcandan.no.sapo.pt/

MALAYSIA

Location: Kuala Lumpur, Malaysia When: Sunday 5:30pm, Every Sunday, 6–8pm, Plaza Tugu Negara

MEXICO

Guadalajara, Drumcircle – Location: Bosque Colomos I, Guadalajara When: Every Sunday, starting at 17.30 hours

NETHERLANDS

Bar en Boos Drumcircle, Leiden – Location: Koppenhinksteeg 4, by Kaasmarkt When: First Sunday of the month, When: Indoors, starting at 16.00 hrs Contact: willow_wilg@yahoo.com

Monthly Drum Circle Zeist central Netherlands info – yankadi.cjb.net

Landjuweel, Freeport Ruigoord Annual 3-5 day event, around the full moon of August. The visitors make the festival; participants only please ruigoord@xs4all.nl

WAP-IN Middag, Alkmaar Les Trois Soeurs, Randall Scott Dance Centre, Gedempte Nieuwe Sloot 36, Alkmaar second Sunday of the month, from 13.00–17.00 hours Phillipines

Location: Katribu Drumcircle, Davao City When: Every full Moon Contact: katribu03@hotmail.com

SOUTH AFRICA

Cape Town, South Africa – Location: Lochiel Road, Sunnydale, Kommetjie, Cape Town, South Africa When: Thursdays 6 – 7pm Contact: drumming@naturali-catchi.com

Durban, South Africa – Location: Jacko Jackson Road When: Every Sunday 6:00 – 7:00 Intro Session 7:00 – 10:00 p.m Contact: +27 837044879

Johannesburg, South Africa – Location:Frog & Toad Contact: Muldersdrift – info – frogandtoad.co.za +27836298877 Contact: drumworx@polka.co.za

Durban – Location: BAT Centre When: Tuesday – 7:30pm

Cape Town, South Africa – Location: 32 Glynn St When: Mon, Wed, Fri – 9pm

Scarab Market, Sedgefield – Location: The Dance Studio, Knysna When: Thursday 19h00 20h30 When: Friday 19h00 20h00 Contact:Nidhi 073 060 0008 for more information Contact: drumcafe.com / nidhi@drumcafe.com

Hout Bay, Cape Town, South Africa – Location: Constantia Nek Restaurant When: Sunday 6pm

SWITZERLAND

Richterswil Switzerland Address: Daniel Regg Gartenstrasse Contact: +41 (0)79 737 61 74 Contact: ibis@smile.ch

Trommelkreis Richterswil When: Every third Saturday of the month from 09.30-11.30 hrs Contact: info@rhythmusikus.ch

TAIWAN

Taichung, Taiwan – Location: Dragonfly Jamboree – Location: Taichung Hui-Lai Rd, When: Every Sunday at 14.00 hrs

TURKEY

Istanbul, Turkey When: Monday & Tuesday 7pm Contact: lasestrellas.org/

UNITED ARAB EMIRATES

Dubai Info at dubaidrums.com Phone: 00971-50-659-2874 Facilitator: Julie-Ann Odell

UNITED KINGDOM

London – Location: Venue: Colet House151 Talgarth Road, Barons Court London, W14 9DA When: every 1st Sunday of the month from 6pm to 9pm Contact: londondrumcircle.com

London – Location: St Marks Church, Myddleton Square, London, EC1R 1XX, United Kingdom When: every 3rd Sunday of the month 12:00 – 14:00 Contact: 07944489527 / ntsolak@gmail.com or caravansary.org

Brighton United Kingdom – Location: Preston Park Bowling Pavilion When:every Sunday evening from 5pm – 7pm. Contact: 441273275813 / somesh@drumjam.co.uk

Brighton East Sussex – Location: Unit A1 Scream Music Studios Melbourne street When: Circle Multi-Percussion workshop every Wednesday 7:00pm Contact: 07887560312

London HACKNEY DRUM CIRCLE (LONDON) – Location: St John-at-Hackney church hall (Lower Clapton Road, E5 0PD – opposite Somerfield & Clapton square). When: On the first Sunday of the month (started June 2009) from 12-2pm Contact: HeartOfHackney.com

North Manchester. – Location:St Margaretts Community Centre, St Margaretts Rd, Prestwich When:Weekly in Prestwich every Wednesday evening between 7:30–9:30

Plymouth – Location: Elburton village Hall UK When: every Wednesday 6–7pm

London – Location:R.I.S.C. Conference Hall, Rear entrance to the Global Café When:First Sunday Every Month, 2-4 PM Contact:rhythmzone.co.uk or, FaceBook: facebook.com/group.php?gid=22384805069

Surrey – Location: UK Drum Circle Guildford and Raynes Park When: Thursday evenings

Contact: julie@drumheadslive.com website: drumheadslive.com 01483 894741

Rochdale – Location: St Andrew's Church, Smith Street When: Last Saturday of every month. 2.00 – 4.00pm Contact: Pandemonium on 01706 521731 or pandemonium at rochdaleonline.org

West Yorkshire – Location: Rhythmbridge Monthly Community Drum Circle Square Chapel Halifax When: Saturdays 11am till 1pm Contact: rhythmbridge.com or call Paul 01422845748

Somerset – Location: Wincanton Drum Workshop,The Balsam Project Balsam Center Wincanton, England When: Every Thursday 7–9pm Contact:Ryan Tucker on 01963 824204

Plymouth – Location: Estover Community College, The Barn Kits Hill Crescent, Barne Barton When: every tuesday night from 7.00 to 9.30 Contact: 01803 864 538 / drumcircles@drumcrazy.co.uk

West Midlands – Location: Psalm Drummers West Midlands Top Church High Street, Dudley When: 1st Tuesday starting at 20.00 hrs Contact: timcazeve@yahoo.com or chip.bailey@psalmdrummers.org

Hampshire – Location: Soaring Eagle Circle of Drums, Basingstoke, England When: Tuesday

Middlesex – Location: Harrow Drum Circle Bernay's Memorial Hall Stanmore, UK When: Wednesday 7:45pm

Wiltshire – Location: BeatRoots Church Hall Wroughton Swindon, UK When: Wednesday 7pm Contact: madondrums@hotmail.com

Liverpool – Location: Bluecoat Arts Centre When: last Saturday

Leeds – Location: Horsforth Drum Circle Horsforth Music Centre Horsforth School Horsforth, UK When: Saturday 9am

Liverpool – Location: Bluecoat Arts Centre When: Last Saturday

Middlesex – Location: Harrow Drum Circle Bernay's Memorial Hall Stanmore When: last Wednesday 7:45pm

Wiltshire – Location: BeatRoots Church Hall Wroughton Swindon When: Wednesdays 7pm

Somerset – Location: Wincanton Drum Workshop EnglandBalsam Centre When: Thursdays weekly Contact: 01963 824204 / nikki.tucker@tiscali.co.uk

Leeds – Location: Kirkstall Community Drum Circle, Paxton Horticultural Society Hall When: First two Wednesdays each month then Tuesdays for the remaining weeks 7pm

Middlesex – Location: Park Avenue Disability Resource Centre [PADRC] 65c Park Avenue – Bush Hill Park When: 2nd and 4th monday of Every Month 7.30 to 10.00 Contact: 44 020 8 360 1195 / Steve Ball – Facilitator

Hertfordshire – Location: House of Life Drum Circle, 31 North Street – Bishops Stortford – CM23 2LD When: 1st & 3rd monday of any month 8–10pm Contact: Half Moon Acoustic Club Email: info@acousticclub.co.uk- Steve Ball – Facilitator

Bideford – Location: Tapely Drumcircle, Instow When: Every Sunday, starting at 20.00 hrs Contact: eurozulu@btopenworld.com

Liverpool Mana Bozho Drumcircle, Bluecoats Arts Centre, School Lane When: last Saturday of the Month, starting at 14.00 hrs

References

Bittman, Barry MD, Berk LS, Felten DL, Westengard J, Simonton OD, Pappas J, Nine-houser M (2001) "Composite Effects of Group Drumming Music Therapy on Modulation of Neuroendocrine-Immune Parameters in Normal Subjects", *Alternative Ther Health Med* 2001: 7:38-47

Bittman, Barry MD, Karl T. Bruhn, Christine Stevens, MSW, MT-BC, James Westengard, Paul O. Umbach, MA (2003) "Recreational Music-Making: A Cost-Effective Group Interdisciplinary Strategy for Reducing Burnout and Improving Mood States in Long-Term Care Workers", *Advances in Mind-Body Medicine* Fall/ Winter 2003, Vol. 19 No. 3/4

Bittman, Barry MD, Lee Berk, Mark Shannon, Muhammad Sharaf, Jim Westengard, Karl Guegler, David Ruff, (2005) "Recreational Music-Making Modulates the Human Stress Response: a Preliminary Individualized Gene Expression Strategy," *Med Sci Monit* 2005; 11(2):BR31-40 ICID: 14140

Bittman, B., Dickson, L., Coddington, K. (2009) "Creative Musical Expression as a Catalyst for Quality-of-life Improvement in Inner-city Adolescents Placed in a Court-referred Residential Treatment Program." *Advances in Mind-Body Medicine.*

Blacking, J., *How Musical is Man?* 1973, Washington: University of Washington Press.

Blacking, J., *Music, Culture and Experience: Selected Papers of John Blacking,* ed. R. Byron. 1995, Chicago: University of Chicago Press.

Blanck, G. & Blanck, R., *Ego Psychology II: Psychoanalytic Developmental Psychology.* New York: Columbia Univ. Press, 1977.

Blanck, G. & Blanck, R. *Ego Psychology II: Psychoanalytic Developmental Psychology.* New York: Columbia University Press, 1979.

Burt, J. W. (1995). "Distant Thunder: Drumming with Vietnam Veterans." *Music Therapy Perspectives,* 13, 110-112.

Clynes, M., & Walker, J. (1982). *Neurobiologic Functions of Rhythm, Time and Pulse in Music.* In M. Clynes (Ed.), *Music, Mind, and Brain: The Neuropsychology of Music.* New York, London: Plenum Press.

Cross, I., "Music, Cognition, Culture and Evolution." *Annals of the New York Academy of Sciences,* 2001(930): p. 28-42.

Cross, I., *Music and Meaning, Ambiguity and Evolution, in Musical Communication,* D. Miell, R. Macdonald, and D. Hargreaves, Editors. 2005, Oxford University Press. p. 27-43.

Cross, I., "Music, Mind, and Evolution." *Psychology of Music,* 2001. 29(1): p. 95-102.

Faulkner, Simon C., "An Evaluation of the Music Therapy Intervention 'DRUMBEAT' with Alienated Youth in the Wheatbelt of Wesern Australia," *Holyoake Institute for Drug & Alcohol Addiction Resolutions,* Western Australia

Fenicle, O. *The Psychoanalytic Theory of Neurosis.* New York: Norton, 1945

Freud, A. *The Ego and the Mechanisms of Defense.* New York: International Univ. Press, 1946

Gedo, J. *Advances in Clinical Psychoanalysis*. New York: International Univ. Press, 1980.

Gordon, H.W. (1978). *Left Hemisphere Dominance for the Rhythmic Elements in Dichotically Presented Melodies*. Cortex, 14, 58-70.

Greenson, R, *The Technique and Practice of Psychoanalysis*. New York: International Univ. Press, 1967.

Hallam, S., I. Cross, and M.H. Thaut, "Where Now?," *The Oxford Handbook of Music Psychology*, S. Hallam, I. Cross, and M.H. Thaut, Editors. 2009, Oxford University Press. p. 561-567.

Hartman, H. *Ego Psychology and the Problem of Adaption*. New York: International Univ. Press, 1958

Hull, A. (1998) *Drum Circle Spirit: Facilitating Human Potential through Rhythm* White Cliffs Media: Reno: NV.

Hull, A (2006) *Drum Circle Facilitation: Building Community Through Rhythm Village Music Circles*, Santa Cruz, CA

Hull, A. (1994). *Guide to Endrummingment* [booklet accompanying video]. Brattleboro, Vermont: Interworld Music.

Hart, M.(1990). *Drumming at the Edge of Magic*. San Francisco: Harper.

Jung, C.G. *The Undiscovered Self*. New York: Mentor, 1957.

Kernberg, O. *Object Relations Theory and Clinical Psychoanalysis*. New York: Aronson, 1976.

Kohut, H. *The Analysis of the Self*. New York. International Univ. Press, 1971.

Luce, G. G. (1971). *Biological Rhythms in Human and Animal Physiology*. New York: Dover.

Mahler, M. *On Human Symbiosis and the Vicissitudes of Individuation*. New York: International Univ. Press, 1968

Malloch, S. and C. Trevarthen, eds. *Communicative Musicality: Exploring the Basis of Human Companionship*. 2009, Oxford University Press: Oxford.

May, R. (1985). *My Quest for Beauty*. Dallas: Saybrook.

Meyers, C. (1993). *The Drum-Dance-Song Ensemble: Women's Performance in Biblical Israel*. In. K. Marshall (Ed.), *Rediscovering the Muses: Women's Musical Traditions*, (pp. 49-67). Boston: Northeastern University Press.

McNeill, W. H. (1995). *Keeping Together In Time: Dance and Drill In Human History*. Cambridge: Harvard University Press.

O'Boyle, M. W., & Sanford, M. (1988). *Hemispheric Asymmetry in the Matching of Melodies to Rhythm Sequences Tapped in the Right and Left Palms*. Cortex, 24, 211-221.

Perls, Frederick S., *Gestalt Therapy Verbatim*. Lafayette: Rea People Press, 1969, p.99. Frederick S. Perls, *Gestalt Therapy Verbatim*. Lafayette: Rea People Press, 1969, pp. 67, 100 Perls, F. *Gestalt Therapy Verbatim*. New York: Bantam, 1971.

Piaget, J. *The Essential Piaget*. Gruber & Voneche (Eds.). New York: Basic Books, 1977

Slotoroff, C. (1994). "Drumming Technique for Assertiveness and Anger Management in The Short-Term Psychiatric Setting for Adult and Adolescent Survivors of Trauma." *Music Therapy Perspectives*, 12, 111-116.

Wachi, Masatada, Masahiro Koyama, Masanori Utsuyama, Barry Bittman, Masanobu Kitagawa, Katsuiku Hirokawa (2007) "Recreational Music-Making Modulates Natural Killer Cell Activity, Cytokines, and Mood States in Corporate Employees" 2007 *Medical Science Monitor* 2007; 13(2):CR57-70 ICID: 473761

Wilber, K. *Integral Psychology*. Boston: Shambala, 2000

Wilber, K, *The Spectrum of Consciousness*. Wheaton, Ill.: Quest, 1977 Wilber, K.; J. Engler; and D.P. Brown. *Transformations of Consciousness: Conventional and Contemplative Perspectives on Development*. Boston: Shambala. 1986. Wilber, K. *Integral Psychology: Consciousness, Spirit, Psychology, Therapy*. Boston: Shambala, 2000

Winkelman, Michael. "Complementary Therapy for Addiction: 'Drumming Out Drugs'" *American Journal of Public Health*; April 2003 Vol. 93 No. 4

Winnicott, D. *Collected Papers*. New York: Basic Books 1958.

Index

ADHD, 79

Alice Springs Prison, 81

Alzheimers, 98

Arthur Hull, 9, 15, 17, 30, 33, 36, 40, 63, 66, 97, 103, 107, 132, 141–2, 145, 147–50, 187

Augie "Doggie" Peltonen, 107–8, 142

Babatunde Olatunji, 9–10, 17, 40, 134

Bacharach Rehabilitation Hospital, 108

Barry Bernstein, 10, 17

Barry Bittman, MD, 10, 18, 28, 66–7, 71, 185

Barry Wakefield, 66, 82

BASHOOOWEE!, 56

Beat for Peace, 45

Becker House, 110–18

Bill Lewis, 20, 144

Bill Matney, MT-BC, 66, 85, 147

Billy Cobham, 5-6, 9

Bob Bloom, 9, 17, 87, 138, 156

Body Beat, 37, 147, 149

Body Beat™ cards, 37

Bonnie D. Harr, 69, 141

Cameron Tummel, 9, 50, 143

Capoeira, 27

Carl Jung, 54, 116

Cherokee Indians, 22

Christine Stevens, 9, 17, 28, 37, 40, 42, 138, 143, 147–9, 183

Dave Holland, 9, 3, 85–86, 140, 147–8, 150

Developmental Community Music, 66, 84

Dr. Barry Bittman, 10, 18, 66–7, 71

Dr. Herbert Bensen, 29

Dr. Michael Winkelman, 130

Drum Circle Facilitator's Guild, 107, 190

Drum Circle Facilitators Guild, 9, 38, 77, 135, 150, 189

Drum Circle Magazine, 40, 42, 134, 146

Drum Circle Spirit, 17, 36, 40, 141, 147, 184

Drumagination, 63, 66, 85, 147

DRUMBEAT, 9, 11, 66, 77–83, 144

Drumming Away Stress, 140

DrumsForCures, 45, 47, 48, 143, 146

drumSTRONG, 40, 45–9, 158, 164

Frank Shaffer, 76

Group Grooves, 31

Guinness World Records, 48

gyil, 25

Hazel Honeyman-Smith, 83–4

Healing Power of the Drum, 15–8, 66, 77, 132, 146, 150, 154, 156, 166, 174

Healing Power of the Drum Training Program, 66

Healing Power of the Drum Workshop, 85

HealthRHYTHMS, 10, 28, 66–72, 76–77, 139–42 148, 167

HealthRHYTHMS Adolescent Protocol, 67

Hippy Hill, 41–3

Holyoake, 77, 82, 144, 146, 183

Huron people, 23

Indigenous tribes, 19

Intentional Rhythms, 53, 54

Jana Broder, 9, 40, 42, 96, 139

Jane Bentley, 9, 59

Japanese Peace Drum Circle, 28

Jim Anderson, 9, 52, 128, 138
Jim Greiner, 9, 21, 28, 30–1, 54, 58, 140, 148–9, 153–4
Jim Oshinsky, 142, 147
John Fitzgerald, 10, 60, 77, 140
John Scalici, 9, 91, 126, 143, 151
John Yost, 143–5, 149
Jonathan Murray, 9, 10, 86, 101, 103, 142, 145
Kalani, 66, 84–5, 138, 147
Kaoru Sasaki, 9, 99
Kurdistan Save the Children, 42–3, 45
Life Rhythms, 21–2, 29, 54, 58, 154
Lobi/Brifo, 24, 26
lucid dreaming, 20
Lulu Leathley, 9, 87, 97, 144
Mad Dogg Athletics, 27
Malaysia, 19, 20, 144, 178
Margaret Sowry, 9, 67, 71, 72
Moe Jerant, 9, 68
Music Therapy Drumming, 66, 85, 147
Nagoya Japan Peace Drum Circle, 28
Nathan Brenowitz, 9, 100, 138
Nellie Hill, 9, 10, 38, 141
Nichiren Buddhism, 26
North Central Bronx Hospital, 113-4
Online Stress Management Training Program, 86
Orenda, 23
Othaday, 129, 142
Paralounge Drum Gathering, 133
Parkinson's Disease, 83, 104–5
Partial Hospitalization Program, 113–4
Patricia Hatfield, 9, 93, 110, 141
Randy Brody, 9, 98, 139, 156
Remo, 10, 28, 38, 60, 66, 77, 97, 129, 139, 149, 150

Remo Belli, 10
REMO Inc, 44
Remo Inc., 28, 67
Remo Paddle drums, 37
Rhythm Planet Workshop, 66, 86
Rhythmical Alchemy Playshop, 66
Rip Peterson, 17
Robert Lawrence Friedman, 15, 85–6, 149, 189
Say & Play, 29, 55
scat, 27
Scat cards, 27, 28, 37, 149
schizophrenia, 113–4, 118, 125
Schizophrenia, 113
Scott L. Swimmer, 143,
Scott Swimmer, 9, 40, 45–6, 146, 150
Senoi Tribe, 19–20
Shannon Ratigan, 9, 18, 88, 147, 150–1
Simon Faulkner, 9, 66, 77–8, 144, 174
Steve Durbin, 9, 95, 139, 144
Tamanrasset, 28
The Brain Trauma Center, 100–1
The Mozart Effect, 111
Therapeutic Drumming Foundation, 66, 83–4
Through the Eyes of a Child, 57
Tony Scarpa, 7, 9, 113, 135, 138
Tuareg, 29
Ute Nation, 23
Valerie Naranjo, 9, 23
Village Music Playshops, 66
Wellbriety, 22–3
White Bison, 23
World Burn Congress, 105
Youth Villages, 77

Robert Lawrence Friedman, M.A.

Robert Lawrence Friedman is the president of Stress Solutions, Inc. and Drumming Events. He provides workshops and seminars focusing on leadership development, teambuilding and stress management throughout the United States, Europe and Asia.

He is the author of "The Healing Power of the Drum – A Psychotherapist Explores the Healing Power of Rhythm," "How to Relax in 60 Seconds or Less" and his latest book, "The Healing Power of the Drum – A Journey of Rhythm and Stories." Healthy Learning, Inc. has produced fifteen of Mr. Friedman's workshops and seminars on DVD. Mr. Friedman was the Director of the Stress Management Corporate Training certification program for Queens College of CUNY, the first program of its kind in the United States

He has appeared on national and international television programs, including the Discovery Health Channel program, "Class of '75". He has also appeared on "The Morning Show on Today" (NBC), "Fox News", and "The Alive and Wellness Show" (CNBC), along with Fuji and Sankei television in Japan.

Robert has been interviewed by Cosmopolitan Magazine, Drum Magazine, New York Newsday, Self Magazine, and The Washington Times on his views of using drums as a vehicle for positive change. Robert was the columnist for the "Healing Rhythms" column in Drum! Magazine and is currently the "Stresswise" columnist in Healthwise Magazine. He is a Co-Chairman on the Health and Wellness Committee of the Percussive Arts Society and an Advisor of the Drum Circle Facilitators Guild.

He has offered his presentations to such corporations and hospitals as Accenture Corporation, American Express, BBDO International, Chase Manhattan Bank, Cornell Medical Center, Comedy Central, First Boston Corporation, Forbes, HBO, Hyatt Hotels, Inc., Hoffman-LaRoche, Pitney Bowes, Schering Plough Corporation, Saatchi & Saatchi, Saint Barnabas Health Care System, Standard & Poors, Viacom and Xerox Corporation, among many others.

He has designed a cutting-edge software programs, "Relaxation On-Demand" and "Confidence On-Demand" for individuals seeking immediate

Robert Lawrence Friedman

relief in areas of stress and empowerment. He recently launched MyPersonalOasis.com, a website dedicated to teaching individuals how to de- stress, feel empowered and take better care of themselves using conventional and alternative approaches.

Mr. Friedman is a professional member of the National Speaker's Association and the American Counseling Association.He is on the Advisory Board of the Drum Circle Facilitator's Guild, and Chairman of the Drumming and Wellness Committee for the Percussive Arts Society.

Additional information on Robert's rhythm-based and stress management products can be found at www.stress-solutions.com, www.drumming-event.com and http://shop.stress-solutions.com